Joseph Baldwin

Elementary Psychology and Education

ISBN/EAN: 9783743344358

Manufactured in Europe, USA, Canada, Australia, Japa

Cover: Foto ©ninafisch / pixelio.de

Manufactured and distributed by brebook publishing software (www.brebook.com)

Joseph Baldwin

Elementary Psychology and Education

Joseph Baldwin

Elementary Psychology and Education

ELEMENTARY PEDAGOGICS.—BALDWIN.

ELEMENTARY PSYCHOLOGY AND EDUCATION. VOLUME I. (VOLUME VI., *Int. Ed. Ser.*)
- I.—Attention, Instinct, Sensation.
- II.—The Perceptive Powers.
- III.—The Representative Powers.
- IV.—The Thought-Powers.
- V.—The Emotions.
- VI.—The Will-Powers.

THE ART OF SCHOOL MANAGEMENT. VOLUME II.
- I.—Educational Instrumentalities.
- II.—School Organization.
- III.—School Government.
- IV.—Courses of Study and Programmes.
- V.—Study and Teaching.
- VI.—Class Management.
- VII.—Examinations, Records, and Graduation.
- VIII.—Professional Education.
- IX.—System and Progress in Education.
- X.—Graded Schools.

APPLIED PSYCHOLOGY AND TEACHING. VOLUME III. (In preparation.)
- I.—Education of the Perceptive Powers.
- II.—Education of the Representative Powers.
- III.—Education of the Thought-Powers.
- IV.—Education of the Emotions.
- V.—Education of the Will-Powers.
- VI.—Art of Teaching.

EDITOR'S PREFACE.

It is often said that the teacher needs to know psychology because it is his business to educate the mind. "He ought to understand the nature of the being that he is trying to unfold and perfect."

This position seems so obvious that all assent to it, and yet it must be admitted that teachers, as a class, are not specially devoted to the study of psychology. It is true, however, that they are constantly occupied with a critical observation of the mind in a few of its aspects; for this is necessary in order to manage a school successfully. The teacher must observe the pupil's grasp of the topic of his lesson. He must interpret the pupil's conduct by such knowledge as he can attain of his disposition and the spirit of his intentions. He must assign lessons of a length suited to the mental capacities which he knows his pupils to possess; he must grade them in classes according to his knowledge of those capacities. He must arrange a course of study in accordance with the laws of mental development.

If the teacher knows nothing of psychology as a science he must copy in detail the methods of others, and rely on his general knowledge of human nature derived from experience. Like all uneducated workmen he may succeed, after a sort, by following tradition, unaided by science; but he will not develop beyond a narrow degree of perfection in details. He will have no insight into the general relations of his work. He can not safely deviate from routine, nor venture to criticise his own work or the work of others. If he has learned good models he may pass for a good teacher; if he has learned bad ones he is unable to perceive their defects. Possessing no scientific knowledge of the mind, he can not lift himself above the details of his art to the principles which govern them, and become himself an original source of directive energy.

Some knowledge of the mind every successful teacher must have, although in so many cases it is unsystematic and consequently unscientific. Ordinary experience differs from science through its lack of completeness and consistency. It is fragmentary and disconnected. Science compensates the inequalities of individual experience by re-enforcing it with the aggregate of all other experience.

Psychology aims to inventory the facts of mind and to arrange them systematically, so that each fact may help to explain all other facts, and in its turn be explained by all.

It is confessed that psychology has hitherto borne the reputation of being the dryest and least interesting of all the sciences. This is partly due to the circumstance that an inventory of facts of consciousness contains only what is already familiar to us in the fragmentary form of experience. It seems a waste of time to go over and collect with so much painstaking what is already known. Other sciences collect fresh and interesting facts. Psychology by introspection seems to the beginner to be a sterile occupation, dealing with what is trite and stale. But this is not found to be so by the adept.

Introspection begins with this dull process of inventorying the already familiar facts of mind, but it forthwith proceeds to the second and higher process of reflecting on the general form of our mental processes. It then begins to enter a field of generalization entirely unknown to ordinary consciousness and full of astonishing results. By reflecting on the forms of mental activity we come, for the first time, to see the real nature of mind. We begin to discern those most important of all fruits of human knowledge—the truths that sit supreme as directive powers on the throne of life—the truths of God, Freedom, and Immortality.

But we are met here by an objection. We are reminded that there are two hostile schools of psychology. There is one founded upon physiology which attempts to explain mind as a function of the body. It condemns introspection, and teaches that the soul has no subsistence apart from the body. All individuality is corporeal. The other school, founded on introspection, contends that true individuality is not corporeal by any possibility. The corporeal is moved by external forces, and is divisible, changeable, and perishable, while self-active energy which is the substance of mind is incorporeal and the owner of all individuality. It denies, moreover, that any really psychical facts may be discovered by external observation—by taste, smell, touch, hearing, or seeing.

Here we must take notice of the broad distinction that exists between external and internal observation. There are two distinct and strongly-marked attitudes of mind. The first is directed outward to the facts in space, and may be called objective perception or sense-perception. Its characteristic is found in the circumstance that it always sees things as related to environments: To it all things are dependent and relative.

The other attitude of mind is directed within, and beholds the self-activities of the mind itself. Self-activity is essentially different from relative and dependent being, because it does not receive its determinations from its environment, but originates them itself, in the form of feelings, volitions, and thoughts. All objects of introspection belong to one of these three classes, and every possible feeling, idea, or volition, is a determination of an activity which is, so to speak, polarized into subject and object. Each feeling, idea, or volition, is the product of an energy which is both subject and object. It is said to be self-determined. While external observation sees its object as separated into thing and environment, or effect and cause, internal observation sees its object as a unity containing both effect and cause in one. It is what Spinoza called *causa sui*. This is true individuality—called by Aristotle "entelechy," and by Leibnitz the "Monad."

Be this as it may, all must concede that no form of external experience applies or can apply to internal experience; our apparatus for observing material objects can not perceive feelings or thoughts. This being so, it is evident that physiological psychology can make no progress whatever without introspection. It is limited to noting the relation of concomitance and succession between two orders of observation—the objects of the one being movements and changes of organic matter, and the objects of the other being feelings, ideas, and volitions. The progress of this science will be marked by a continually approximating accuracy in locating and defining physiological functions.

There has been recognized from the first an interconnection between mind and the body. Decapitation has always been recognized as a means of disconnecting the mind from the body. Alcohol, tobacco, coffee, opium, and many other drugs have been used since prehistoric times for their supposed mental effects—effects negative rather than positive, as they dull the action of the nerves of sensation, or diminish the mental control over the nerves of motion, and thereby allay the pain of weariness, or the worry that arises from a vivid consciousness of the body and the outer world. Physiology is engaged in determining more precisely the location of these effects and their extent. Although it will not discover how the corporeal becomes mental, or how the external becomes internal, for the reason that objective experience can never perceive thoughts and feelings; yet it will yield rich results in all departments wherein the mind uses the body as an instrument to gain knowledge, or to execute its volitions. Insanity, idiocy, the use and abuse of the five organs of sense, all that relates to the proper care of the body; the influence of age, sex, climate, race; the phenomena of sleep, dreams, somnambulism, catalepsy; whatever relates to these and the like important topics, will receive elucidation. The negative conditions of mental unfolding will be defined. But that which is an original energy can not be explained by its environment, because it is independent. Nor is it strictly speaking correlated to the body, although it uses it in sense-perception and in volition as an instrument of communication with the outer world.

This work of Professor Baldwin is intended by its author expressly for elementary classes. It seeks to aid them, by many happy devices, in making an inventory of the mental processes and in arranging the items methodically. It aims to familiarize those commencing the study with the technical nomenclature and useful discriminations used by writers of our day in treating this theme. Above all, it expects to teach the pupil how to attain the second order of observation; how to pass from the attitude of mind, which observes external things, to that attitude of mind which observes internal activities. To make this transition is to acquire a most important power of thought. To think things and environments is to think the phenomenal, the transient, and variable; to think self-activity is to think the noumenal, the true individuality, and what is divine in human nature.

Although the author has purposely omitted from this work the subtle and profound discussions which arise in advanced psychology, he has done it in the interest of the beginners for whom the book is made. The author is well assured that, once drawn into the study of mind and well disciplined in the habit of internal observation, it is only a matter of time with the pupil when he shall arrive at all the precious arcana of psychology.

W. T. HARRIS.

CONCORD, *August*, 1887.

AUTHOR'S PREFACE.

SUBJECT-LESSONS, or mind-lessons, are as necessary as object-lessons. Object-lessons give a direct knowledge of the matter-world, while subject-lessons give a direct knowledge of the mind-world. A knowledge of self is more important than a knowledge of things.

Youth is the time for subject-lessons. A youth who can learn algebra and physiology and rhetoric is ready for Elementary Psychology. The third year of the high-school course and the second year of the normal-school course are considered pre-eminently fitting periods for subject-lessons.

A subject-lesson text-book is needed. Our literature is rich in psychologies adapted to colleges and to senior classes in our normal schools, but is destitute of a text-book suitable for our high-schools and for the lower classes in our normal schools. The want of such a text-book is widely felt. The author has given the best years of his life to the effort to prepare such a text-book, and thus meet this want. Each lesson here submitted has been given scores of times to large classes, with highly satisfactory results. While it is true that subject-lessons, like object-lessons, must be largely oral, yet a suitable text-book is deemed indispensable.

An Elementary Psychology deals with the plain

facts of mind. The advanced student wishes to know what Locke and Reid thought, what Kant and Hamilton taught, and what McCosh and Wundt said; but the discussion of these conflicting views, which constitutes so large a part of our text-books on psychology, only confuses and discourages beginners. An incomparably better plan, it is thought, is to lead the learner to look into his own mind, to analyze his own mental acts, to discover for himself the capabilities of the soul. The subject-lessons are thus made the counterpart of object-lessons. The author believes that the time has come when we can make our text-books for beginners in mental science just as we make our elementary arithmetics and chemistries, without reference to the history of the science or the peculiar views of authors.

A simple and exhaustive nomenclature is a desideratum in mental science. The time has come, it is believed, to reject the pedantic and misleading terms of a crude and antiquated psychology. Fortunately, few unfamiliar terms are now necessary. Every one has some knowledge of mind. However illiterate, each man has his own crude psychology. So far as correct, the language of the people is best. By using the language of literature and life, Sully, Hopkins, Porter, McCosh, and others have done much to popularize mental science. It seems fitting in an elementary work to still further popularize the subject.

The constant effort has been to present each point with sunlight clearness. Short sentences, in plain Anglo-Saxon, is the rule. Object-lessons, bold type, outlines, study-hints, examples to work out, original analyses, original definitions, original applications, and helpful illustrations are called into constant requisition. Mental science, it is claimed, may be as fully illustrated as physical science. The student is taught to observe and analyze the operations of his own mind; to look within and describe what he sees going on. Thus he becomes an observer, an original investigator. He brings to the study of the soul the same methods that Agassiz applied with such wonderful effect to the study of the natural sciences. When this is done the student is interested, and the study of Psychology becomes as easy and fascinating as that of Botany or Zoölogy.

Leading the learner to build on his own experience is the fundamental idea in this work. He is led to observe the workings of his own mind, to analyze his own mental acts, and to compare the recorded or observed mental acts of others with his own. Thus he is enabled to make definitions, to discover laws, and to apply principles.

The facts of mind are our common heritage. The ways of presenting these facts are individual. It gives the author special pleasure to acknowledge his indebtedness to the many excellent works on mental science and education. Wherever possible, acknowledgment is made in the body of the work; but, in numerous cases, this has been impracticable. For a third of a century the matter of the volume has been presented in lectures to normal classes and normal institutes. The endeavor to completely adapt the matter and the method to the wants of beginners, has led to many changes in the language, so that authors, even in direct quotations, must not be held strictly responsible for the form in which their thoughts here appear.

Applied Psychology and teaching. The original purpose was to combine Elementary and Applied Psychology, but it is now thought best to present Applied Psychology in a separate volume. Two reasons led to this change: 1. The combined volume would have been inconveniently large. Brief outlines are excellent for reviews, but are useless for beginners. 2. Many students will wish to study Elementary Psychology who will not care to study Applied Psychology. Then, in normal schools, Elementary Psychology is studied during the second year, while Applied Psychology is not taken up before the third or fourth years. Besides, it became evident that the latter subject could be treated far more satisfactorily in a separate volume.

The best, rather than the original, has been the aim. Each true workman builds on the achievements of the race, and merely adds his mite. A science is the product of innumerable minds. The plan of these lessons, however, may be claimed as in some degree original; in fact, a new departure, both in plan and execution, was found to be a necessity in order to adapt psychology to the wants of beginners.

Subject-lessons prepare the student for advanced work. As object-lessons are needful to prepare the learner to study natural science, so subject-lessons are necessary to prepare the student to understand advanced psychologies, and to read with profit advanced educational works. As an introductory work, this volume is submitted. The author earnestly hopes that these lessons will prove a real help to many teachers, and an inspiration to many young people.

CONTENTS.

PART I.
INTRODUCTORY LESSONS.

CHAPTER	PAGE
I.—Attention	4
II.—Instinct	15
III.—Important Terms examined	25
IV.—The Sensorium	35
V.—Sensation	44

PART II.
THE PERCEPTIVE POWERS.

VI.—Sense-Perception, or Sense-Intuition	59
VII.—Conscious Perception, or Self-Consciousness	71
VIII.—Noumenal Perception, or Noumenal Intuition	85
IX.—Perceptive Knowing—General View	100

PART III.
THE REPRESENTATIVE POWERS.

X.—Memory	108
XI.—Phantasy	124
XII.—Imagination	133
XIII.—Representation—General View	146

PART IV.

THE THOUGHT POWERS.

CHAPTER	PAGE
XIV.—Conception	155
XV.—Judgment	171
XVI.—Reason	180
XVII.—Thought-Knowing—General View	195

PART V.

THE FEELINGS.

XVIII.—The Instincts	15, 206
XIX.—The Physical Feelings—The Appetites	44, 207
XX.—The Emotions—Egoistic Emotions	215
XXI.—The Emotions—Altruistic Emotions	222
XXII.—The Emotions—Truth Emotions	231
XXIII.—The Emotions—Æsthetic Emotions	234
XXIV.—The Emotions—Ethical Emotions	240
XXV.—The Emotions—General View	252

PART VI.

THE WILL-POWERS.

XXVI.—Attention	264
XXVII.—Action	266
XXVIII.—Choice	273
XXIX.—The Will-Powers—General View	285

SUGGESTIONS TO THE PRIVATE STUDENT.

MANY young people, teachers of common schools and others, greatly desire to study the mind, but are compelled to struggle upward without the aid of the living teacher. Each line of this work was written in view of helping this large and deserving class. These hints, though given directly to teachers, apply equally to others.

1. *Look within.* What object-lessons are to children, subject-lessons are to you. Observe the workings of your own mind, and verify each statement by your own experience.

2. *Study the child.* You have the key, for the child knows, feels, and wills, just as you do. Put yourself in its place. Study intently child-effort. These subject-object lessons will be invaluable to you as well as to your pupils.

3. *Hasten leisurely.* You can well afford to devote a week to each chapter. Gradually the wonders of the soul-world will open to you. Select some interested friend with whom you can talk the lesson over.

4. *Work out your own definitions and illustrations.* This is essential. Build on your own experience. Work out everything for yourself, just as you do in arithmetic and algebra.

5. *Write the letters.* Select an appreciative friend who will respond. Try to make each subject clear to this friend. Above all, tell just how the subject looks to you. Writing these letters will greatly benefit you.

6. *You will work in the light.* You are painfully aware that you are now liable to blunder at every step because you are ignorant of child-mind and of the laws of child-growth. As you advance, all will become clear, and you will begin to feel the inspiration of the artist. To rightly direct the development of an immortal soul is the grandest of all work.

TEACHING ELEMENTARY PSYCHOLOGY.

The experienced teacher needs no suggestions, but a page from the book of experience may assist one who teaches psychology for the first time:

1. *Oral lessons.* I have found it necessary to give one or more oral lessons on each subject to prepare the student to study the lesson in the book. Then, the text needs to be supplemented by much oral work. Illustrate from students' daily work.

2. *Clearness.* It is marvelous how crude and confused are the psychological and educational notions of most of the persons we meet. But our stupid methods of teaching this subject are largely to blame. Here and everywhere we must build on personal experience, and manage to have the student grasp fully the elementary facts of mind. The suggestions to the private student may benefit all students.

3. *Reviews.* Each lesson should in some way involve all the previous lessons. No other branch requires such constant reiteration and review. All possible combinations of the facts of mind must be woven into the warp and woof of the learner's mental economy.

4. *Troublesome questions.* Psychology touches and to some extent underlies all other departments of knowledge. Questions involving philosophy and theology and sociology can not be ignored. I have found it best to frankly answer these questions as best I could, avoiding alike all semblance of either dogmatism or mysticism. But no time or energy must be wasted in discussing these questions. Young people will understand that such discussions belong in the advanced work.

5. *Short lessons.* The student enters a new field of inquiry. The terms, as well as the ideas, are new. Then the learner has to learn the new art of introspection. Usually it will be best to give about three pages for a lesson. The work can thus be completed in twenty weeks. I have not been able to secure satisfactory results in a shorter period. Short book-lessons and long oral lessons is the true policy.

6. *Reference books.* A few choice volumes are indispensable.

PART I.

INTRODUCTORY LESSONS.

CHAPTER I.—Attention.
      II.—Instinct.
      III.—Important Terms Examined.
      IV.—The Sensorium.
      V.—Sensation.

WAYS OF STUDYING MIND.

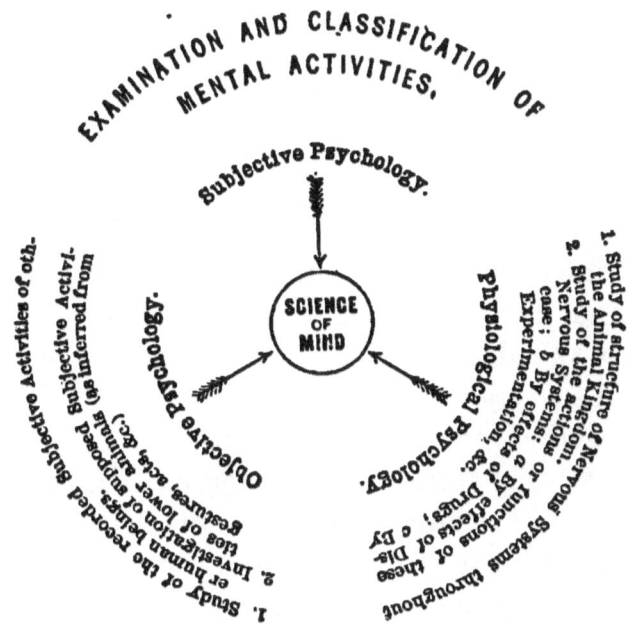

The true psychology gathers up from every source the established facts of mind. The old, or metaphysical psychology, inclined to ignore the body; the new, or physiological psychology, inclines to ignore the soul; the true psychology finds in the brain and nerves the bridge between mind and matter. The theories and metaphysical speculations of both the old and the new psychology disappear; but all the established facts of mind reappear in the true psychology.

FIRST PART.

INTRODUCTORY LESSONS.

MIND-STUDY AND EDUCATION.

By this is meant becoming acquainted with ourselves and developing our powers. Self-knowledge is the most valuable. "Know thyself" is the key to wisdom and success.

Our earlier years are largely devoted to the mastery of the material world. The study of Nature interests and educates the child, but does not satisfy the youth. He begins to realize that the mind-world is even more wonderful than the matter-world. What am I? What can I do? How can I make the most of myself? These questions now obtrude themselves, and must be answered. "Elementary Psychology and Education" will seek answers to these questions, or, rather, will try to lead you to find out the answers for yourself.

In your study of physical science you began with physical phenomena and worked up to physical laws. Each step forward was based on your own experience. You thus gained the keys to the accumulated experience of the race. To you physical science has become an open book. You can now read with delight the works of the great scientists.

In your study of mental science you will begin with mental phenomena and work up to mental laws. Here, too, each step will be based on your own experience. You will thus gain the keys to the treasured wisdom of the race. Mental science will become to you an open book, and you will be able to commune with the great thinkers of all ages.

As attention is the condition of knowledge, it is fitting that you should begin the study of mind with the examination of this capability.

CHAPTER I.

ATTENTION.

The art of learning, as well as the art of teaching, is based on the power of attention. Few problems are too difficult for the student who can *concentrate* upon them all his energies. Right study and true teaching develop the power and the habit of complete attention.

Analysis of Acts of Attention.—Attention! Examine these crystals. You tell me that each is a cube, that some have beveled corners, and that the mineral is lead. Now examine *these*. You turn away from the lead crystals, and fix your mind on these new forms. You tell me that each is a hexagon, and that the mineral is graphite. You find that you can direct your own efforts. You can place your mind on one object, can examine it for a time, and can turn to something else. The capability of self thus to direct his efforts is called Attention.

Office of Attention.—The special work of a capability of the mind is called its office; as, the office of memory is recalling. Self-direction, or concentration, is the office of attention. Your analysis gives you three forms of attention :

1. *Self, as attention, concentrates his efforts.* Examine the word *attend* (*ad*, to; *tendo*, I stretch). You get the idea of turning to something and fixing all your energies upon it. You throw your powers of body and mind into the work. As the burning-glass concentrates all the rays of the sun upon a single point, so you concentrate all your powers upon the matter in hand.

2. *Self, as attention, prolongs his efforts.* The problem can not be solved in a moment. You bend all your energies to its mastery; you drive out other thoughts; you refuse to be interrupted; you hold yourself to the work. After hours of mighty effort, you exclaim, "I have found it!" This is study. Dreamers do not learn. Truth opens her doors to those only who knock hard and long.

3. *Self, as attention, changes his efforts.* Frequent change is a physical necessity. Great mental efforts exhaust the portion of the brain most used. After two hours devoted to mathematics, and a rest of twenty minutes, you turn with fresh vigor to natural science. Versatility is as necessary as concentration.

Were the mind a ship, Attention would be the captain; were the mind an army, Attention would be the general; were the mind a school, Attention would be the teacher. In figures such as these the comparison must be limited to the capability of self to concentrate, prolong, and change his efforts. Attention is one species of self-direction. Self-direction includes much more than attention.

Characteristics of Attention. — Attention is distinguished from other mental powers by two marked characteristics:

1. *Attention is the power to concentrate effort.* Take away this power and the soul would merely drift, and life would be one long revery. Man would be an idle dreamer. Attention is our ability to concentrate our efforts. We thus gain mastery.

2. *Attention accompanies all mental activity.* Like memory and consciousness, attention in some degree is present in all knowing and feeling and willing. It enters as an essential element into all effective mental operations. There can be no distinct thinking, no vivid feeling, no deliberate action, without attention. It energizes and quickens mental effort.

Attention defined. — You are now prepared to define attention:

1. *Attention is the capability to concentrate, prolong, and change effort.* Mind is both self-acting and self-directing. Thinking is self-activity; but I also direct my thoughts. Attention is clearly a power of self-direction.

2. *Original.* Write a brief definition embodying your own conception of attention. The definitions given are suggestive. Your definition must be worked out and polished, then treasured in memory.

Various Definitions. — 1. PORTER: Attention is our power to concentrate effort. 2. SULLY: Attention is the power of active self-direction. 3. BASCOM: Attention is our capability to direct and handle our faculties. 4. ROSENKRANZ: Attention is the power to adjust self to the object. 5. TRUMBULL: Attention is the energetic application of the mind to any object. 6. SCHUYLER: Attention is the concentration of the thoughts upon a given phenomenon.

"Attention is self-activity. It is the will acting on the intellect. Attention selects one special field and refuses to be diverted from it. It neglects all else, and returns again and again to the object of special attention. Attention isolates one object from others, and concentrates effort upon it to the exclusion of all other objects. Isaac Newton ascribed his superiority to other men in intellectual power simply to his greater power of attention." *

Kinds of Attention.—I give attention to the rose. I observe its color, its odor, and its structure. I find that I can direct my energies to the mastery of the outer world. We may call this *Outer Attention.*

1. *Outer attention* is self attending to external things. Outer attention looks to the world of sense. When the teacher says " Attention !" she usually means " Listen " or "Look." Objective attention, external attention, and outer attention, are synonymous and simply mean *self* attending to the external world. As the outer world is called the objective world, the self-direction of the mind to outer things is called *Objective Attention.*

2. *Inner attention* is self attending to what is going on within. I concentrate my powers upon a problem, upon a composition, upon a desire, upon a choice. This is inner attention. We mean by inner attention, self attending to the inner world. As the inner world is called the subjective world, inner attention is called *Subjective Attention.*

3. *Objective and subjective attention.* We fix our minds upon the rainbow. We observe the primary and secondary colors. This is objective attention. Now we study the relations of colors, the

* Dr. W. T. Harris.

laws of combinations, etc. We fix our minds upon our acquisitions and try to discover relations. Self attends to his own products and processes. This is subjective attention.

Physiology of Attention.—The brain and nerves are the physical organism in connection with which the soul works. Instinctively man and brute turn the sense-organ toward the object, the sound, the odor. Prolonged attention exhausts the physical organism. It is physically impossible for children to give close attention for a long period. As the years advance, attention may be prolonged more and more.

Attracted and Purposed Attention.—A loud sound, a brilliant object, or a strong odor excites the sensor organs and attracts attention. Brute attention is chiefly of this nature. The teacher finds it necessary to *attract* the attention of her young pupils. She finds that new objects, sudden changes, and striking movements *arrest* attention. But the child soon develops the power of purposed attention. Attracted attention is merely the sensuous arrest of attention. Sensor affections occasion attention.

Reflex and voluntary attention. Reflex action is destitute of will-power. Attention means power of self-direction. Clearly, the expressions, reflex attention and involuntary attention, are unmeaning and misleading.

Growth of Attention.—The idiot is incapable of self-direction. Because he can not attend, he can not learn. The attracted attention which he seems to give is not concentrated mental effort. Brutes can give a degree of attention, and hence can learn some things. The child begins to notice attractive objects. This is the germ of voluntary attention. We can not fix the period when

ATTENTION.

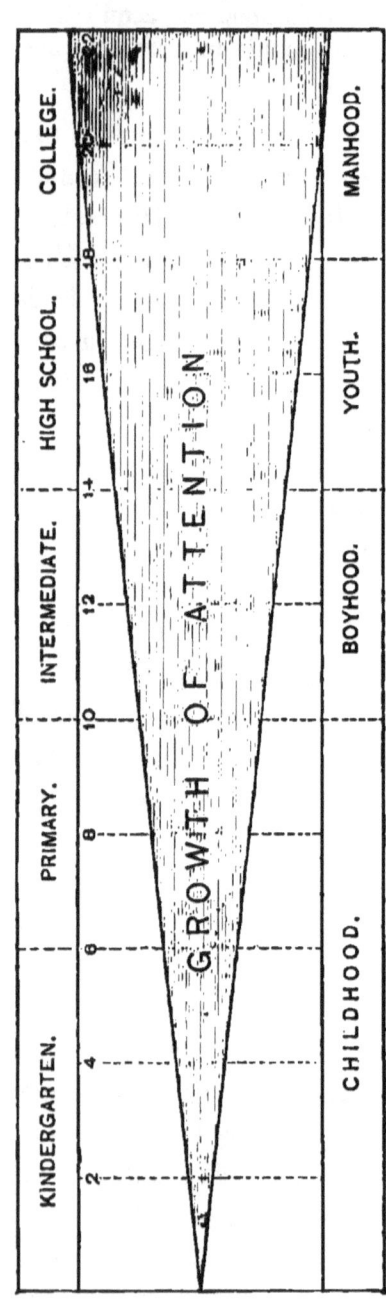

the infant begins to attend. When a few weeks old, it recognizes its nurse. When a few months old, it recognizes many objects, but can hardly be said to attend before the fifth or sixth month. The child learns slowly because he attends feebly and but for a very short time. The boy can learn more rapidly, as he can attend more closely and for a longer time. The well-trained youth can throw his energies into his work for several hours, and hence can do much more than the boy. The educated man can do vastly more than the youth because he can concentrate his entire energies for many hours. At twenty, attention is fully active, but may grow more and more vigorous up to the meridian of life.

These familiar facts indicate the slow but gradual growth of attention, as well as its relation to achievement.

Education of Attention.* —Teaching is the art of promoting human growth. The mother lays the foundation on which the teacher builds. She supplies her little Kindergarten with attractive objects. In a thousand ingenious ways she manages to draw and hold the attention of her budding loved ones. The teacher continues the same line of work. She will spare no effort to win the interested attention of her young pupils. Each exercise will be so conducted as to develop the power and the habit of attention.

Well-directed effort in concentrating the mind upon the work in hand develops the power of attention. You try to give your entire attention for a short time daily to some subject. In a few months you find that you can attend more closely and for a longer time. When you can attend completely, your power of attention is educated.

Attention and Learning. —The drill will not penetrate the granite unless kept to the work hour after hour. The mind will not penetrate the secrets of science unless held long and vigorously to the work in hand. Agassiz insisted on a radical reform in all our systems of education. His students came to him so deficient in the power of penetrating observation that they could not learn science until educated to observe. This great naturalist considered the development of attention as paramount in education. Dickens considered his power of attention the secret of all his achievements. Hard work fosters genius; but only well-directed and persistent effort counts. The sun's rays burn only when concentrated. Self achieves mastery only when he hurls all

---

* See "Applied Psychology"; also, Sully's "Psychology."

his forces upon one point. "Scatter-brained" roughly characterizes the large class of half-idiots who can not learn because they can not give close and continued attention. Who has sinned—these stupid pupils, or their more stupid teachers?

Attention and Retention.—Good memory means close and continued attention. You become intensely interested in your history lesson; you bend all your powers to its mastery. You close your eyes and think it over. You fix your mind on the facts in their relations. You in this way deeply impress the lesson upon your memory, and you will be able to recall it readily. When there is slight attention, as in revery or half-study, the slight impressions speedily fade away. *Attending is work.* Lazy persons have poor memories because they are too indolent to give attention. As a rule, interested attention and good memory go together.

Attention and Power.*—No element of personal power is greater or more potent than specialization. No man can be so much of a man, in any one direction, as when he is a whole man in that direction. He who can concentrate his whole being, all his energies and all his capabilities, for the compassing of the one thing on which his mind is fixed for the time being, is obviously more potent in behalf of that object of his endeavor than would be possible were his energies divided, and were only a portion of himself given up to that for which he is striving. And this power of concentration it is, that makes the man of pre-eminent practical efficiency in any and every sphere of human endeavor—

* Trumbull.

material, mental, and spiritual—from the lowest plane to the highest.

Educational Laws.—The great truths relating to human growth and development are called educational laws or principles. Thus early you have discovered some of these fundamental truths. Farther on these laws will be examined and applied.

1. *Self-effort educates.* The soul is self-acting. Spontaneously we put forth effort. All development comes from self-effort.

2. *Strenuous effort, well directed, educates.* This is the condition of all improvement. Directed endeavor develops power.

3. *Attention energizes mental effort.* It gives vividness and vigor. The inattentive mind drifts but does not achieve.

4. *Achievement is in the ratio of concentration.* Effective effort is concentrated effort. The narrower the field of attention the greater is the penetrating power of the mind. "One thing at a time"; "Concentrate all your energies"; "Give your entire attention"; "Do with all your might"; are some of the excellent rules deduced from this law.

5. *Pleasure sustains attention.* Gentle pleasure, present and prospective, fixes and holds attention. Painful study repels and dissipates energy; pleasurable study attracts and sustains attention.

SUGGESTIVE STUDY-HINTS.

What do you do when you give attention? Write an analysis of an act of attention. What do you mean by the office of a faculty? What is the office of the heart in the physical organism? Of the memory in the mental economy? What single word expresses the office of attention? Give the etymology of attention. Give two examples of concentration. Give an example of prolonged attention. Give two examples of change of effort.

How do you distinguish attention from memory? Give two characteristics of attention. Give examples.

Give the author's definition of attention; give yours; give Porter's.

Give the distinction between outer attention and inner attention. Illustrate. Give your reasons for using also the terms objective attention and subjective attention. Give five examples of each.

Why should prolonged attention not be required of children? Why does forced attention fail to benefit the pupil?

Why can not an idiot learn? Why can the boy learn more than the child? Tell what you know about the growth of attention. What do you mean by growth?

What is teaching? Describe the work of the mother and of the primary teacher.

Why did Agassiz find it so difficult to teach science to his students? What do you mean by "scatter-brained"? What did Dickens consider the secret of his success? Is inattention the fault of the pupil or of the teacher?

Why have inattentive people poor memories? What do you remember best? What do you do when you give attention? Why can you readily recall the things to which you give great attention? How can you cultivate your power of attention?

Letter.*—I venture to ask you to write a letter to some friend, telling what you know about attention. Give your own thoughts in your own way. Nothing

---

* In a long experience I have secured the most satisfactory results by having each pupil write a letter to some interested friend, giving his notions about the faculty discussed. As far as possible I have these letters read in class and criticised.

will help you more. You may be called upon to read the letter. Send with your letter to your friend a topical outline showing your analysis of this chapter.

Topical Analysis of Chapter I.—Attention.

I. Acts of Attention analyzed.
Objective Attention.   Subjective Attention.

II. Office of Attention.
Concentration of effort.   Change of effort.
Prolongation of effort.

III. Characteristics of Attention.
Power of self-concentration.
Active self-direction energizes all mental action.

IV. Attention defined.
Author's definition.   Sundry definitions.
Original definition.

V. Kinds of Attention.
Objective and Subjective.   Attracted and Purposed.

VI. Physiology of Attention.
Physical limits of Attention.
Vigorous health and Attention.
Rest and Attention.

VII. Growth of Attention.
Attention in childhood.   Attention in youth.
Attention in boyhood.   Attention in manhood.

VIII. Education of Attention.
Teaching and Attention.   Attention and Retention.
Attention and Learning.   Attention and Power.

IX. Educational Laws.
Self-effort educates.
Strenuous effort, well directed, educates.
Attention energizes mental effort.
Achievement is in the ratio of concentration.
Pleasure sustains attention.

CHAPTER II.

INSTINCT.

BY this is meant the capability of animals to do blindly the best for themselves. A mind is capable of knowing, feeling, and willing. What a mind can do is called a mental power. The simplest of the mental powers are the *guiding* impulses, called instincts. It is deemed best to begin the study of mental phenomena with the lowest and least complex manifestation of mind.

Instinctive Acts analyzed.—We are wonderfully familiar with brute-life. The cat, the dog, the bird, and the horse are our intimate companions. From infancy to age, brute-life interests us. Even Solomon and Aristotle intently studied animal life. We see brutes doing blindly what man, with ages of experience, can scarcely do. The bee builds a perfect cell without having studied mathematics, and compounds delicious honey without having studied chemistry. Birds migrate thousands of miles by land and sea without chart or compass. The animal, without knowing why, does what is best for itself. The blind feelings which lead animals to act for their best interests are called instincts. Observe the sitting hen: at regular intervals she turns her eggs. Why? It took a thousand years for man to answer this question. The hen, without knowing why, does the right thing. The blind impulse which moves the hen to thus act is termed instinct.

Office of Instinct.—Each organ of the body and each capability of the mind has a specific purpose, called its office. The office of the stomach is digestion. The office of attention is self-direction. The office of instinct is to move and guide animals to wise ends, where it is impossible that intellect should act.

1. *Instincts tend to the physical well-being of the individual.* Spontaneously the young animal seeks its proper food. Without knowing why, squirrels and bees lay up stores for the future. Without a knowledge of geography or climate, birds and beasts migrate with the season. Inborn feelings move and guide the animal to its own good.

2. *Instincts tend to the well-being of the race.* The salmon leaves the sea and ascends the river to spawn safely in shallow water. The bird conceals her nest. Even lions and eagles mate. Strong impulses move animals to act so as to preserve the race. These blind impulses are termed instincts.

3. *Instincts move brutes to fulfill the purposes of their creation.* Its instincts move the silk-worm to spin its cocoon. The bee is moved to sip sweets from every flower. Its instincts move the coral to build islands. Marvelous chapter, this, in the book of Nature!

Characteristics of Instinct.—The peculiarities that distinguish one endowment from others are called its characteristics. How may we know instinct?

1. *Instincts are blind but guiding impulses.* Bees and ants organize republics, build cities, and lay up stores. Without knowing the principles of government or architecture or political economy, they wisely adapt means to ends. Blind feelings, implanted by Infinite Wisdom, guide as well as move them. Instincts are the only *guiding* impulses.

2. *Instinct is a perfect guide.* An instinct is innate and perfect from the first. Intellect hesitates and blunders; instinct advances to its end with mechanical certainty. Intellect improves; instinct is practically stationary.

3. *Instinct is conscious activity.* The bird is aware of its nest-building impulses. However dim in the lower orders of animals, consciousness may be safely inferred wherever instinct is manifested. Instincts, therefore, are now classed as mental; wherever we find instinct we find mind. The plant has life, but not mind. The brute has life and mind, but not self-conscious personality.

4. *Instinct is limited to physical activity.* Instincts are mental impulses leading to physical acts and physical ends. The mother-impulse in the bird to care for her young is mental; the act of securing food and feeding her birdlings is physical. All instincts seem connected with the perpetuation of organic life.

To speak of moral instincts or religious instincts is clearly incorrect. Intellect guides beings capable of moral acts.

Instinct defined.—Instinct is feeling. Like all feelings, instinct is blind; but, unlike all other feelings, instinct guides. Instincts are blind feelings implanted by Infinite Wisdom to move and guide animals where intellect can not act.

1. *Instinct is blind impulse guiding to wise ends.* Instincts are blind impulses to adapt means to ends without knowing why. Without either knowledge or experience, the young bee constructs a perfect cell. Instincts are blind feelings moving and guiding to wise ends.

2. *Original.* Write a definition containing your view of instinct. What does instinct mean to you?

3. **Various Definitions.**—1. WHITE: Instincts are impulses which prompt and direct appropriate action in the absence of intelligence. 2. ROMANES: Instincts are adaptive impulses. 3. HOPKINS: Instinct is regulative impulse. 4. HAMILTON: Instinct is a blind tendency to intelligent ends. 5. VON HARTMANN: An instinctive act is one conformed to an end of which the actor is not conscious.

Reflex Action and Instinct.—The clock marks time, but its organism and action are wholly mechanical. The sensitive-plant responds to the touch, but its organism and action are wholly vegetable. The animal perspires and respires, but the organism and action are wholly vital. The order of the various forces is: mechanical forces, chemical forces, vital forces. Reflex action is a vital force. Like the sensitive-plant, the lower nerve-centers respond to stimuli and cause motion. Where the stimuli lie within the body, reflex action is called automatic action.

1. *Reflex action is unconscious action.* Bound up in the animal are forces which regulate nutrition, circulation, respiration, and non-voluntary motion. But mind is wanting in such acts. These actions are intrusted to ganglia and nerves and tissues which respond to stimuli. *Reflex action is devoid of will-power and is wholly physical.* Animals of the lowest orders are little more than reflex machines—they are nearly destitute of instinct as well as of intellect.

2. *Instinctive action is conscious action.* Reflex action is the highest physical force; instinct is the lowest mental energy. The action of the new-born infant in sucking is reflex action; but the act of the young

animal in seeking food is instinctive action. Instinct moves the spider to spin her web to capture her prey; but the act of spinning is reflex. Below instinct, no indication of mind appears. To some degree the animal seems to be aware of its instinctive acts, but is utterly unconscious of its reflex acts. Here we may venture to draw the line between the physical and the mental. Reflex action and all the lower forces are wholly physical. Instinctive action appears to be spontaneous as well as conscious action, and hence belongs to the realm of mind.

Instinct and Intellect.—Instinct is blind impulse which directs animal action in a way beneficial to the individual and the race. Intellect adapts means to ends and guides the feelings. Brutes and men are endowed with intellect as well as with instinct. Intellect enables its possessor to find out and act from knowledge; instinct moves the possessor to adapt means to ends without knowing why. Instinct guides the migrating bird; intellect guides the mariner. Instinct guides the bee in constructing a cell; but intellect guides the engineer in constructing a bridge.

1. *As intellect increases, instinct decreases.* Mollusks and still lower forms of animal life exhibit instinct and even infinitesimal intellect. But they are little more than creatures of reflex action. In fact, many orders are scarcely more than automatons. The bee, the ant, and the spider seem most gifted with instinct. They also exhibit some intellect. In birds, beavers, dogs, and elephants we find instinct decreasing and intellect increasing.

2. *As instinct increases, intellect decreases.* The

elephant, the horse, and the dog manifest considerable intellect, but much less instinct than spiders, bees, and ants. As we go down the scale we find instinct increases just as intellect decreases.

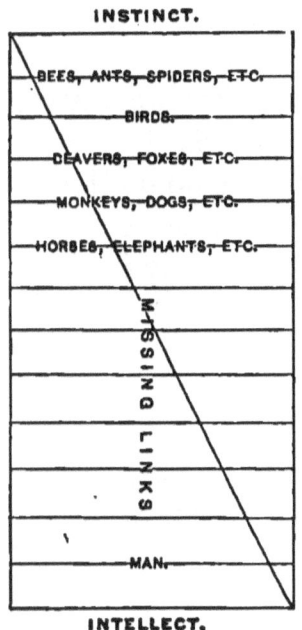

3. *Man stands alone.* Intellect vastly predominates in man; instinct in brutes. The gap here between the lowest man and the highest brute is immense. There appear to be many missing links.

In the accompanying diagram the relations of instinct and intellect are roughly indicated.

Man was created in the rational and moral image of God. Physically, he is separated, by a great gap, from all the animals nearest to him; and, even if we admit the doctrine, as yet unproved, of the derivation of one species from another, in the case of the lower animals, we are unable to supply the "missing links" which would be required to connect man with any group of inferior animals. Mentally, the gap between man and the brute is practically infinite. Those who deny this must adopt one of two alternatives. Either they must refuse to admit the evidence in man of any nature higher than that of brutes—a conclusion which common sense, as well as mental science, must always refuse to admit—or they must attempt to bridge over the "chasm," as it has been called, which separates the instinctive nature of the animal from the rational and moral nature of man—an effort confessedly futile.*

The Instincts.—Instinct is a simple mental energy, as gravity is a simple physical force. It is ever the

---

* Principal Sir J. William Dawson, C. M. G., LL. D., F.R.S., President of the British Association.

same blind impulse moving to wise ends, and nothing more. But the instincts—the promptings of the instinctive energy—are numerous. These may be classed as strictly brute instincts, as instincts common to brute and man, and as strictly human instincts.

1. *The brute instincts.* The honey-making instinct of the bee, the web-weaving instinct of the spider, the nest-building instinct of the bird, the dam-building instinct of the beaver, the migratory instinct of many animals, are familiar examples of strictly brute instincts. The list of this class of instincts may be extended without limit. Are these specific brute instincts endowments or developments?

2. *Instincts common to brute and man.* These also are numerous. Sex-instincts, mother-instincts, danger-instincts, food-instincts, etc., are common to brute and man.

3. *Human instincts.* Instinct in man, as in the brute, is ever the same blind feeling, guiding actions to beneficial ends. In the domain of instinct, the brute stands vastly higher than man. The human infant is the most helpless and dependent of all young animals. It takes long years for us to learn to do intellectually what the brute does instinctively. Man is poor in instincts. Crying, smiling, frowning, etc., appear very early in infancy, and are strictly human instincts. The student is left here to find out other human instincts.

Origin of the Instincts.—Few questions now engage more thought. The following conclusions are believed to be safe:

1. *Each instinct is an original endowment.* Instincts are innate. Evolution modifies but does not

create. All organic forces, all vital forces, all mental energies, are inborn endowments. Instinct uniformly tends to wise ends; but the wisdom is back of the law, back of the energy. The brute, without knowing why, adapts means to ends. This blind impulse to wise action is implanted by Creative Wisdom.

2. *Instincts are transmitted.* However far back, the instinct-germ, in some degree, is regarded as an endowment. That instincts may be greatly modified, and that modified instincts may be transmitted, is now science. The pigeon is endowed with the homing instinct, but centuries of training were necessary to give us the carrier-pigeon. The pointer-dog is one of many good illustrations. The striking modifications in the instincts of domesticated animals is the most familiar proof. While it is an established law of heredity that like tends to produce like, we know that environment works striking modifications. Man trains animals on the line of native instincts. This is the only improvement of which brutes are capable. But no amount of training or change of environment can produce a honey-making quadruped; something can not be evolved from nothing. Given instinct-germs as endowments, and the laws of heredity and evolution may account for all modifications of instincts and all phases of instinctive action.

References.—For fuller accounts of instinct the reader is referred to "Instinct in Brute and Man," Chadbourne; "Mental Evolution in Animals," Romanes; "Mind in the Lower Animals," Lindsay.

INSTINCT.

SUGGESTIVE STUDY-HINTS.

Review.—Give the three offices of attention. Give *your* definition of attention. What distinction do you make between outer attention and inner attention? Why is it so difficult to teach inattentive pupils? Why can the youth do more than the child? Etc., etc.

Give an example of instinct that you have observed. Why does the hen turn her eggs? Analyze the nest-building instinct of the bird, and the dam-building instinct of the beaver.

Give a distinction between the office of attention and the office of instinct. What do you mean by the office of a faculty? Give the three special offices of instinct. Illustrate each by cases you have observed.

What do you understand by the characteristics of a faculty? Give the four characteristics of instinct. Give examples.

Give your definition of instinct. Why do you prefer it to the other definitions?

What do you mean by reflex action? by automatic action? Give distinctions between gravity and reflex action; reflex action and instinct. Give examples of each. What do you understand by unconscious action? by conscious action? by self-conscious action?

How do instinct and intellect differ? Give five examples. Explain the diagram showing the relations of instinct and intellect. Why does man stand alone?

Name the three classes of instincts. Give five strictly brute instincts; five common to man and brute; five strictly human.

Give the distinction between an endowment and an evolution. Is the honey-making instinct an endowment, or the hereditary experience of the race? May instincts be modified by experience? Illustrate by domesticated animals. Are modified instincts transmitted? Like tends to reproduce like, is the great law of heredity: does this law extend to mind?

Letter.—You may now write a letter to your friend, telling him what you know about instinct. Try your best to make clear to him the nature of this wonderful endowment. Above all, give him your own thoughts and your own illustrations in your own way. Writing such a letter will lead you to study instinct with the greatest care. Inclose with your letter *your* analysis of this chapter.

Topical Analysis of Chapter II.—Instinct.

I. Analysis of Instinctive Acts.
    Beaver building his dam.   Hen turning her eggs.

II. Office of Instinct.
    Individual good.   Cosmic good.
    Race good.

III. Characteristics of Instinct.
    Guiding impulses.   Conscious activity.
    Limited to physical activity.   Unerring guide.

IV. Definitions of Instinct.
    Author's definition.   Various definitions.
    Original definition.

V. Reflex Action and Instinct.
    Reflex action—physical.   Instinct—mental.

VI. Instinct and Intellect.
    Instinct decreases as Intellect increases.
    Intellect decreases as Instinct increases.
    Instinct predominates in the brute.
    Intellect predominates in man.

VII. Classes of Instincts.
    Strictly brute Instincts.   Strictly human Instincts.
    Common Instincts.

VIII. Origin of Instincts.
    Not organized habits.
    Not inherited experiences.
    Instincts are endowments.
    Instinct is modified by experience and natural selection.
    Modified Instincts are transmitted.

CHAPTER III.

IMPORTANT TERMS EXAMINED.

Science, in our times, must be presented in the language of the people. But new ideas need to be embodied in new terms. In your study of the matter-world, you have found it necessary to learn new terms to express your new acquisitions. As you explore the mind-world, you will at every step discover ideas new to you. For their expression some unfamiliar terms must be used. Easy and familiar terms, when they express the ideas exactly, are the best; but precision must be secured, though at the cost of thoughtful research. The effort will be to lead you to form clear-cut ideas, and to give, in your own words, clear-cut definitions. When quarried and polished, you will treasure *your* definitions. You will find them more precious than diamonds.

In order that you may begin to build on the rock, you will find it best at the outset to master a few leading terms. In each case, work up to the idea before attempting a definition. A good dictionary is indispensable. Study the etymology and history of the word. Notice its uses. Endeavor to grasp its full meaning. Write in your own language a brief definition. Apply the definition by giving your own explanation and illustration. Consider as suggestive these brief hints. As in mathematics, work out everything for yourself. Mastery characterizes each successful educational step. Only weaklings cower and turn back in the face of difficulties. Strenuous and persistent effort educates.

I. **Phenomena.**— $\begin{cases} \text{Physical Phenomena,} \\ \text{Mental Phenomena.} \end{cases}$

The word phenomenon means an appearance, and the plural, phenomena, appearances. The rose appears red, sweet-smelling, soft. I appear to myself cheerful, thankful, hopeful. Whatever appears to us is termed phenomena.

1. **Physical Phenomena.**—The apple appears white, soft, and delicious. The cube appears to have length, breadth, and thickness. Gold appears yellow, heavy, and malleable. All appearances coming to us through the senses are termed physical phenomena. *Whatever of matter appears is called physical phenomena.*

2. **Mental Phenomena.**—I *perceive* the beautiful lily. I *remember* the cheering song. I *discern* that the sum of the three angles of a triangle is equal to two right angles. I *grieve* over the loved and lost. I determine to study psychology. I perceive myself remembering, thinking, feeling, and choosing. I am aware of my various mental acts; they appear to me, and hence are termed mental phenomena, or psychical phenomena. *Whatever of mind appears is called mental phenomena.*

II. **Noumena.***— $\begin{cases} \text{Substances,} \begin{cases} \text{Matter.} \\ \text{Mind.} \end{cases} \\ \text{and} \\ \text{Necessary Relations.} \begin{cases} \text{Time,} \\ \text{Space,} \\ \text{Causation,} \\ \text{etc.} \end{cases} \end{cases}$

---

* See "Noumenal-Perception," chap. viii.

We mean by noumena the enduring realities which underlie and make possible phenomena. Noumena condition phenomena. We class as noumena substances and necessary relations. Appearances are phenomena; the realities of which we affirm phenomena, or which make phenomena possible, are noumena.

1. **Substances.**—The enduring entities which underlie phenomena are called substances. As there are two kinds of phenomena, so there are two substances.

(1.) *Matter.* Glass is brittle, hard, transparent. These properties of glass are termed physical phenomena. The material substance of which we affirm brittle, hard, transparent, is called matter. In the matter-world we find extension, weight, impenetrability. Matter is the enduring noumenon of which we assert extension, weight, impenetrability. *The noumenon, or reality of which we assert physical phenomena, is called matter.*

(2.) *Mind.* You remember the multiplication-table. You write essays. You hate lying. You choose truth. Whatever it is that does these things is called a mind, a spirit, a soul. The enduring self, the Ego, the noumenon that thinks, is called a mind. I am, therefore I think. *The self of which we assert mental phenomena is called a mind.*

2. **Necessary Relations.**—That substances and phenomena *may* be, time and space and causation *must* be. As these and such like relations are necessary and enduring realities, they are classed as noumena.

III. **Energies.**—
{ Physical Energies, or Forces.
{ Soul-Energies.
{ Divine Energies.

We try to understand the dynamics of the universe. We learn to call the energies which produce changes, causes. "Force, energy, and cause are not identical or equivalent, though they are synonymous. Force is used to signify an energy that requires another energy outside of it to incite it to action, and still another to guide it. But the energies of the soul are self-incited and self-directed. Self-related force is not thought of when we speak of force, and hence force is a bad term to express soul-energies."

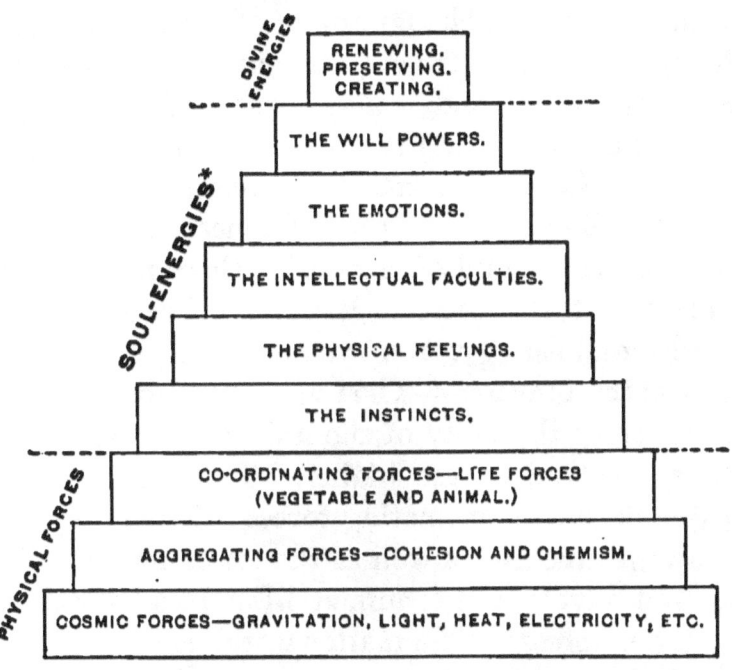

PYRAMID OF ENERGIES.

It is extremely difficult to arrange the soul-energies from the standpoint of cause. Self acts spontaneously. Strictly, no mental act is caused. Sensor excitations occasion sensations, sensations occasion perception, ideas occasion emotions, emotions occasion choice, choice occasions action; but the series is of conditions and not causes. Each rational mental act is self-caused. Then the marvelous interaction of knowing, feeling, and willing makes the task doubly difficult. Feelings not illuminated by intellect are blind and brutal. Intellect not moved by feeling and directed by will is effortless and aimless. Choice not guided by intellect is irrational. At best the arrangement of our mental powers must be in the order of dependence; and of this each one judges for himself and varies the arrangement accordingly.

1. Physical Forces.—Bound up in matter are the stupendous energies which cause perpetual change. We dwell amid whispering breezes, rippling brooks, heaving oceans, and revolving worlds. *The energies which cause physical changes are called physical forces.*

2. Soul-Energies.—Minds are endowed with the marvelous energies which change infant Newtons into philosophers, and savage tribes into enlightened nations. A mind is self-acting and is a self-cause. Soul-energies are self-incited and self-directed. *The energies which cause mental changes are called soul-energies.*

3. Divine Energies.—Herbert Spencer, in his final summary, says: "Amid all mysteries, there remains one absolute certainty: we are ever in the presence of the Infinite and Eternal Energy, from whom all things proceed."

Unity of the Universe.—The pyramid of energies may help us to grasp the unity of the universe. Each lower energy is involved in the higher. The plant-unit involves cosmic and co-ordinating forces. The brute-unit involves vegetable life as well as the lower forces. The human unit involves the animal life-forces as well as all the lower forces. The matter-world is a unit. All the physical forces work in harmony and give us the reign of law. So, too, the mind-world is a unit. All the mental energies work in harmony and give us men and women, society, government.

In our times it is not difficult to complete the pyramid by adding Divine Energies. We thus reach absolute unity. All substances, all forces, all laws are but expressions of the Infinite Will. The Divine includes all and unites all. The universe is a unit.

IV. **Laws.**—$\begin{cases} \text{Physical Laws.} \\ \text{Mental Laws.} \\ \text{Moral Laws.} \end{cases}$

The whole distance through which a body falls in a given time is equal to the space passed through during the first second multiplied by the square of the time. This is a uniform way in which the force of gravity acts, and is called a law of falling bodies. That well-directed effort promotes growth, is called a law of human development. *A uniform way in which an energy acts is called a law.*

1. **Physical Laws.**—We speak of the reign of law in the matter-world. We mean that the physical forces act in certain fixed ways. We observe the fall of the apple. We find that all material bodies attract each other in proportion to the mass and inversely as the square of the distance. We have discovered a law of gravity, or a uniform way in which the force of gravity acts. Law reigns in the matter-world. *The modes or ways in which physical forces uniformly act are called physical laws.*

2. **Mental Laws.**—We notice that some incident enables us to recall long-forgotten events. We find that present ideas tend to suggest past ideas. We have discovered a law, or a uniform way in which the memory acts. Law reigns in the mind-world. *The uniform ways in which the mind acts are termed mental laws.*

V. Sciences.—$\begin{cases} \text{Physical Sciences,} \\ \text{Mental Sciences,} \\ \quad\text{etc.} \end{cases}$

Science is more than classified knowledge. Take botany: the central idea is plant-life; the field of research is plant-phenomena. We group around the central idea the laws of plant-phenomena. Under these laws we arrange principles, facts, illustrations, applications. We thus build up the science of botany. *The systematic arrangement of the laws of phenomena is called science.*

1. **Physical Sciences.**—The sciences that treat of physical phenomena are called the physical sciences. Take zoölogy: the central idea is animal life; the phenomena of animal life is the field of inquiry. Around the central idea we group the laws of animal phenomena. Under these laws we arrange principles, facts, illustrations, applications. We have created the science of zoölogy. *The systematic arrangement of the laws of physical phenomena in a special field of research is called a physical science.*

2. **Mental Sciences.**—The sciences that treat of mental phenomena are called mental sciences. A mental science is the systematic arrangement of the laws of mental phenomena in a special field of inquiry. Take psychology. Here mental phenomena is the field. The central idea is mind. We discover the mental powers and their modes of action. We arrange around the central idea the laws of mental phenomena. Under the laws we group principles, facts, illustrations, applications. We thus form the science of psychology. *The systematic classification of the laws of mental phenom-*

ena is called psychology. Take education. The central idea is human development. The field is the phenomena of human growth and human culture. Around the central idea are grouped systematically the laws of growth and development. Under the laws are grouped the principles, the facts, the illustrations, and the applications. Thus the science of education is created. *The systematic arrangement of the laws of the phenomena of mental growth and mental development is called the science of education.*

VI. **Terms designating Self.**—
{ A Mind.
A Soul.
A Spirit.
An Ego.
A Self. }

We know and feel and will. The self that thinks, loves, and chooses is called a mind. *Mental philosophy is a science of the mind.* As a human mind is embodied, it is called a soul. *Psychology* (*psyche*, the soul; *logos*, science) *is a science of the soul.* Psychical means pertaining to the soul. As the mind is a spirit entity capable of knowing, feeling, and willing, it is also called the spirit. A mind is sometimes called a spiritual organism.

"Is mind an *organism?* If it were, could it possibly be immortal? What is the true definition of organism? The body is an organism, but the mind is something above organism. In an organism there are unity and variety of functions—this is probably the reason for calling mind an organism. But life and mind are distinct; a plant *lives* but does not possess *mind.* Mind includes all that life includes, and much more. In an organism *each part is the means of realizing every other part,* and it is likewise *the end for which every other part exists.* Each part is both means and end for every other part. But mind is *whole* in each part. It is an indivisible unit in knowing, in willing, and in feeling."

Mind, soul, and spirit are now used in literature and science as synonyms. Occasionally we find mind still used in the sense of intellect. Soul was formerly used to designate animal life and instincts. Spirit is sometimes used vaguely to designate something, no one knows what, different from mind. But these distinctions are now practically obsolete.

To the scholar as to the millions, the self that knows, feels, and wills, is the mind, the soul, the spirit.

SUGGESTIVE STUDY-HINTS.

Review.—Give a distinction between attention and instinct. Give the office of attention; of instinct. Give the characteristics of attention and also of instinct. State the relation between instinct and intellect, etc.

Why are some hard words necessary? How do you work out definitions? Give the etymology and meaning of phenomena. Write a definition of physical phenomena; mental phenomena. Illustrate each.

Why is the unfamiliar word *noumena* used? Have we any familiar word that expresses the idea? Write a definition of substance; of matter; of mind. Give a distinction between phenomena and noumena; between mind and matter. Are you sure you grasp the distinction?

Give the synonyms of energy. Write a definition of energy in which all occur. Write a definition of physical force; of soul-energy. What relation do you discover between the lower and the higher energies? Is the universe a unit?

Write a definition of laws; of physical laws; of mental laws. Give a distinction between an energy and a law. What do you mean by laws of phenomena?

Why is mere classified knowledge not science? Write a definition of science; of physical science; of psychology; of education.

Give the etymology and meaning of psychology, psychological, psychologist, and psychical.

Define mind; soul; spirit; ego; self. What do you mean by a *causa-sui?* Show that a mind is not an organism. Give distinctions sometimes made between mind, soul, and spirit. Are these terms now generally used as synonyms?

Topical Analysis of Chapter III.—Important Terms Examined.

I. **Phenomena.**
    1. Physical Phenomena.   2. Mental Phenomena.

II. **Noumena.**
    1. Substances.
        Matter.   Mind.
    2. Necessary Relations.
        1. Space Relations.   3. Cause Relations,
        2. Time Relations.   etc., etc.

III. **Energies.**
    1. Physical Energies, or Forces.
    2. Soul-Energies.
    3. Divine Energies.

IV. **Laws.**
    1. Physical Laws.   3. Moral Laws.
    2. Mental Laws.   4. Etc., etc.

V. **Sciences.**
    1. Physical Sciences.
        1. Botany.   2. Zoölogy.
    2. Mental Sciences.
        1. Psychology.   2. Education.
    3. Etc., etc.

VI. **A Noumenon endowed with Soul-Energies is called—**
    1. A Mind.   4. A Self.
    2. A Soul.   5. An Ego.
    3. A Spirit.

CHAPTER IV.

THE SENSORIUM.

We see the landscape, hear the song of birds, smell the rose, taste the orange, touch the paper, press the hand of friendship. Vibrations caused by light and sound and odor and flavor and contact excite the organism. The mind feels the excitation. These feelings are called sensations. The part of the organism thus excited is called the sensorium. The sensorium is here used to include sensor ganglia, sensor nerves, and sensor organs. You have diligently studied the body, the organism in which we live and work. You will now re-examine the brain and nerves from the stand-point of mind. Here you find the bridge that connects mind and matter.

A Nerve-Cell *is a microscopic clot of granulated gray matter.* Each cell is inclosed and has one or more connections. The cell-substance is granular and extremely mobile. An excitant, as odor-waves or light-waves, causes molecular changes in the cell- 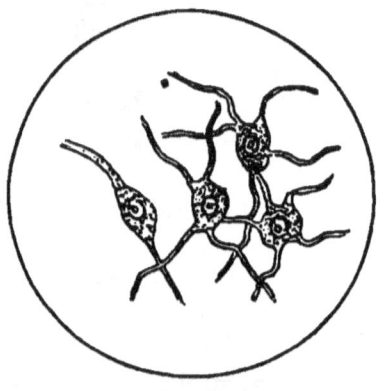 substance. The conscious feeling of the excitation of sensor nerve-cells is known as sensation. In a human brain there are estimated to be more than a billion of these nerve-cells.*

* By permission the above cut is taken from Tracy's "Physiology."

A Ganglion *is a group of nerve-cells connected by nerve-fibers.* Ganglia have nerve-connections with other ganglia. The gray matter of the brain is organized into ganglionic groups. "The mind uses the gray matter in some unknown way to affect the body, or to

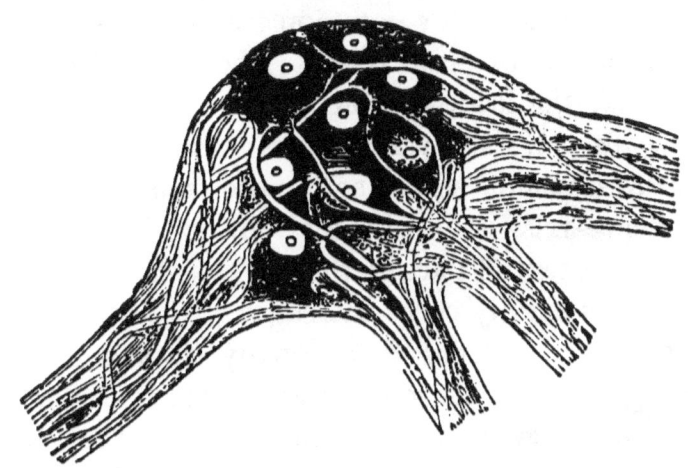

gain impressions through the body." Draw a group of nerve-cells; connect the cells as you do the cells of a battery; inclose by a membrane; make nerve-connections with similar groups. You will have a rude picture of a ganglion, as in the above cut.* Reflex sensor ganglia are found in the roots of the spinal nerves and throughout the sympathetic system.

A Nerve *is a white connecting cord through which nerve-currents pass.* These nerve-fibers permeate the system and form the white matter of the brain, the spinal cord, etc.

1. *Structure.* A nerve consists of three parts: (1.) The external sheath, a transparent membrane; (2.) The

---

* Taken by permission from Bastian's " Brain the Organ of Mind."

medullary sheath, a white, fatty substance, isolating and protecting the nerve-axis; (3.) A thin thread of gray matter called the axis. The axis is composed of minute fibrils. Illustrate with a common lead-pencil—the paint representing the external sheath; the wood, the medullary sheath; the lead, the nerve-axis.

2. *Office.* Nerves transmit vibrations. Their sole office is to transmit sensor and motor molecular waves. As the nerve-axis conducts the vibrations, it may be considered the essential part of the nerve. Like telegraph-wires, nerves simply carry messages.

3. *Classes.* Nerves that convey impressions from sensor organs to sensor ganglia are called sensor nerves; as, the optic nerves are the sensor nerves that convey impressions from the eyes to the optic ganglia. Nerves that convey motor impulses from motor ganglia to motor organs are called motor nerves.

The following classification of the cerebro-spinal nerves, by Dr. S. S. Laws, is simple and complete:

Cerebro-Spinal Nerves.—

SENSORY NERVES IN PAIRS:	MOTOR NERVES IN PAIRS:
1. *Cranial.*—1. Olfactory.	1. *Cranial.*—1. Oculomotorius.
2. Optic.	2. Patheticus.
3. Trifacial.	3. Small root of V.
4. Gustatory.	4. Abducens.
5. Auditory.	5. Facial.
6. Glossopharyngeal.	6. Spinal accessory.
7. Pneumogastric.	7. Hypoglossal.
2. *Spinal.*—31 pairs of posterior roots.	2. *Spinal.*—31 pairs of anterior roots.
38 pairs of sensory nerves.	38 pairs of motor nerves.

4. *Nerve-fibers are continuous.* Sensor nerves extend without break from sensor organs to sensor ganglia. Motor nerves are continuous from motor ganglia to motor organs. Let silk threads represent sensor nerves and cotton threads motor nerves. Trace these threads through all their windings. You will find each continuous. Nerves do not divide or unite.

Nerve - Currents. — Touch a warm surface. The stimulus in some unknown way starts nerve-currents which move through tactile nerves to tactile ganglia. You feel the dangerous warmth. You will the withdrawal of your hand, and thus start currents in the motor ganglia. The motor currents move through motor nerves to muscles. The muscles contract and thus withdraw your hand. The nature of the change produced in nerve-fiber by stimulus is quite unknown. How matter affects mind or mind matter must be classed with the many unsolved problems of science. But science now claims to have demonstrated that (1) sensor nerve-currents move at the rate of 140 to 150 feet per second, and motor nerve-currents about 100 feet per second. (2) Stimuli excite vibratory nerve-currents. A wave of molecular movement passes through the nerve. These nerve-currents are the only media of communication between the mind and the outer world. (3) Sensation takes place only in the sensor ganglia found in the gray matter of the cerebrum.

A Sensor Organ is a *vital mechanism capable of receiving and transmitting sensor vibrations.* Each sensor organ is connected by sensor nerves with its sensor ganglia in the surface of the brain. Take, for example, the optic apparatus:

Objective World — { Eyes } + { Optic Nerves } + { Optic Ganglia } — Mind.

Striking the retina of the eye, light-vibrations in some unknown way excite sensor vibrations, which move in molecular waves through the optic nerves to the optic ganglia. The nerve-currents agitate the optic ganglia, and the mind feels and interprets the vibratory signals —sees the rising sun. The ear does not change sound-waves into sensor waves, but in the ear sound-waves excite sensor waves.

A Special Sense *receives extra organic messages.* The world of color and form comes to us through the eye; the world of sound through the ear; the world of odor through the nose; the world of flavor through the mouth; the world of touch through the skin. As each of these senses opens to us a special world, they are called the five special senses.

A General Sense *transmits organic sensations.* Conditions of the organs of the body come to us through the general senses. Sensations of indigestion are messages from the stomach. Toothache is a message from a nerve. Pain and comfort, hunger and satisfaction, temperature, and so forth, are some of the messages received through the fifteen general senses.

The Brain.—Organism reaches its climax in the human brain. A human brain, it is estimated, embraces not less than one billion nerve-cells, nor less than five billion nerve-fibers. To produce an imperfect brain-map has required ages of toil. Much remains for other ages to discover. The brain and its connections must continue to be the most absorbing field of scientific research. The brain includes the lower, middle, and higher nerve-centers. The cuts on pages 40, 42, and 46 give different views of the brain.

The lower nerve-centers are the medulla oblongata and the cerebellum. Like the spinal cord, these are reflex and distributing centers. Some claim that the cerebellum is a relay-battery to enforce nerve-currents. Others claim that it is connected with the co-ordination of movements. The following cut represents a perpendicular section of the brain on the median line.*

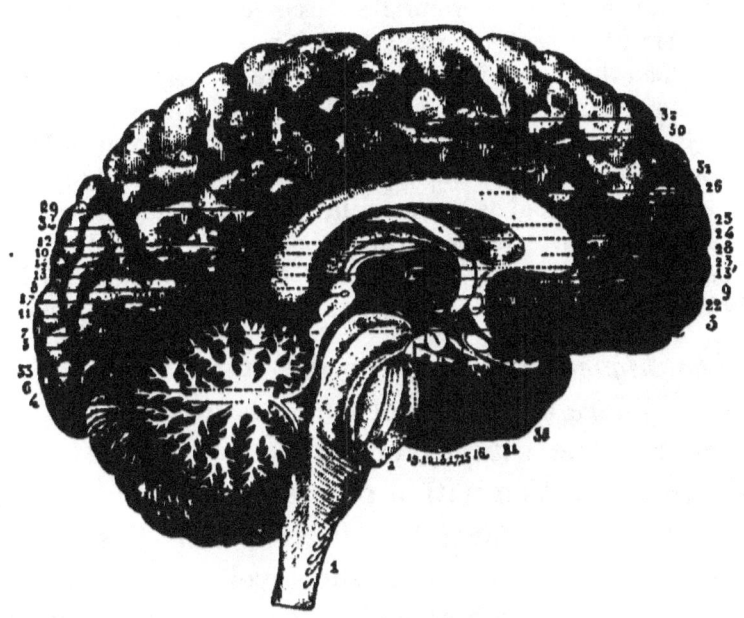

The middle nerve-centers are the pons Varolii, the cerebral peduncles, the corpora quadrigemina, the optic thalami, the corpora striata, etc. These ganglia are geographically central, and, as all messages between the outer and inner worlds seem to pass through these cen-

* The above cut is taken by permission from Bastian, p. 452.

ters, they may be considered telegraphic headquarters. Who can tell what changes take place in these mysterious centers? Destroy these centers, and you render sensation as well as voluntary action impossible. Sever the nerve-connections between the tubercula quadrigemina and the cerebrum, and vision is wholly reflex. The animal is utterly unconscious of seeing.

Remarks.—The spinal cord, the lower nerve-centers, and the middle nerve-centers, with their nerve-connections, make a wonderful organism for reflex action; but it is only a machine. When stimulus falls upon the appropriate sensor surface, a wave of molecular movement is sent up the attached sensor nerves to a nerve-center, which thereupon issues another wave of molecular movement down a motor nerve to the group of muscles over whose action it presides. When the muscles receive this wave of nervous influence, they contract. This kind of response to stimuli is purely mechanical, or non-mental, and is termed reflex action. Thus far we fail to find mind. Remove the cerebrum: the animal may still show reflex action, but all traces of mind will have disappeared. All activity below the cerebrum is unconscious activity, is non-mental.*

The higher nerve-centers are the cerebral hemispheres. Here is the border-land where mind and matter meet. The soul is embodied; it dwells in and works in connection with a physical organism. In man the cerebrum is so large that it completely fills the arch of the skull as far down as the level of the eyebrows. The two hemispheres of which it consists meet face to face in the middle line of the skull, which runs from the top of the nose backward. The cerebrum is composed of two conspicuously distinct parts, called respectively the gray matter and the white matter. The gray matter is external, enveloping the white matter

* Holbrook.

like a skull-cap, and is composed of a vast number of nerve-cells connected together by nerve-fibers, and forming many ganglia.

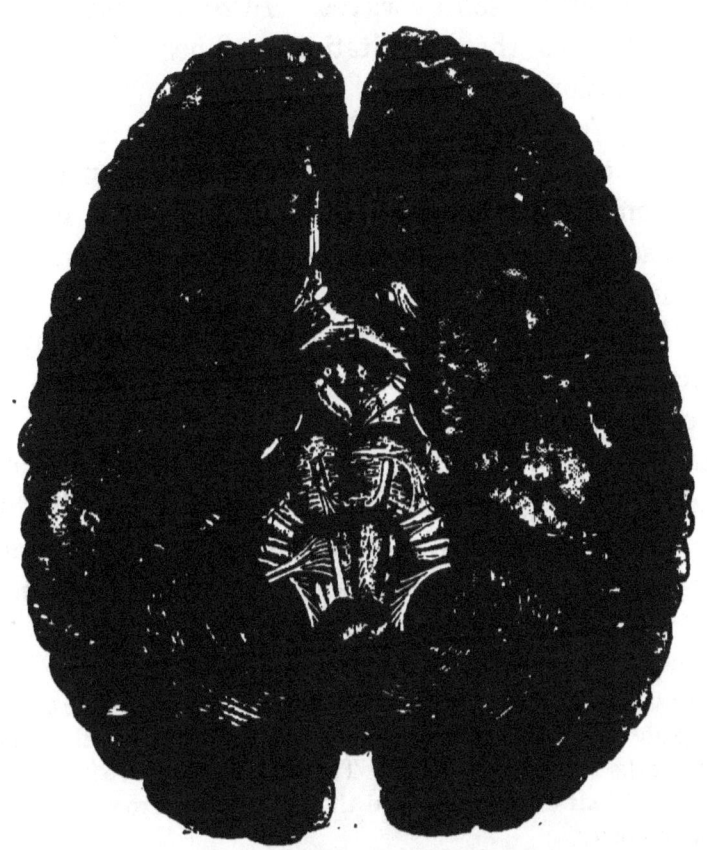

Under surface of the brain, showing the great complexity of its structure. At the lower part of the cut is the cerebellum.*

The Cerebral Ganglia.—The locations of some of the ganglia are known, but the construction of a reliable cerebral map is the work of the future. A classification of cerebral ganglia with reference to office is all that

* Taken by permission from "Anatomy, Physiology, and Hygiene," Tracy, Fig. 58, p. 195.

is here attempted. Such a classification is considered sufficient both for psychological and educational purposes:

1. *The sensor ganglia* are the portions of the cerebrum agitated by sensor waves. In some unknown way the mind feels these excitations. These feelings are called sensations.

2. *The intellective ganglia* are the portions of the cerebrum connected with knowing; as, when we perceive, remember, think. In some unknown way the mind uses these ganglia in perceiving, remembering, and reasoning.

3. *The emotive ganglia* are the portions of the cerebrum called into activity in feeling; as when we love or rejoice.

4. *The motor ganglia* are the portions of the cerebrum excited by volition. A mind is a creative first cause, and originates motion. Self, as will, starts motor nerve-currents—in some unknown way excites motor ganglia and thus originates motion.

Remarks.—1. *The cerebral hemispheres are duplicates.* Each is complete in itself. In case one is paralyzed, the soul in all its powers works through the other. The right hemisphere is connected with the left half of the body, and the left hemisphere with the right half of the body.

2. *The cerebral ganglia are interconnected* by nerve-fibers so as to form an organic unit. Each ganglion supplements all other ganglia. Thus may be seen the unity and harmony of the brain and local brain-centers.

3. *Specific mental activities occur in connection with specific ganglionic areas.* Thus, just behind the forehead, on either side, we find the language ganglia. Injure these, and we are unable to express ideas in words. The location of the special sensor ganglia by Ferrier and others seems to be now accepted.

4. *The cerebrum dominates.* Orders issued from headquarters

take precedence. Reflex action becomes the servant of volition. Walking is ordinarily reflex action; but, when we meet obstructions, action becomes intelligent and voluntary. Mental life is connected with the action of the higher nerve-centers. Only when the cerebrum is called to take part is there any distinct mental accompaniment. The cerebrum thus stands in relation to the lower centers somewhat as the head of an office stands in relation to his subordinates. The mechanical routine of the office is carried on by them. He is called on to interfere only when some unusual action has to be carried out, and *reflection and decision* are needed. Moreover, just as the principal of an office is able to hand over work to his subordinates when it ceases to be unusual, and becomes methodized and reduced to rule, so we find that the brain, or certain portions of it, are able to withdraw from actions when they have grown thoroughly familiar.

5. *Cerebration is merely brain-action in knowing, feeling, and willing.* The mind perceives, thinks, acts; but it works in connection with the ganglia. The brain produces no thoughts. Unconscious cerebration means unconscious mental activity. The cerebral ganglia are merely the instruments of mind.

6. Ganglia performing different offices may be near together, as in the spinal cord; while ganglia performing similar offices may be far apart. The difficulty of constructing a cerebral map is apparent.

7. We do not understand the precise nature of the relation of the body and the soul. In some unknown way the mind uses the gray matter of the brain to affect the body, or to gain impressions through the body.

CHAPTER V.

SENSATION.

By this is meant the capability to feel sensor excitation, as in seeing, hearing, and smelling.

Luminous bodies cause vibrations of luminiferous ether. Light-waves strike against the retina of the eye, causing sensor waves; these sensor nerve-currents, in molecular waves, flash through the optic nerves, passing through the optic thalamus, and the tubercula quadrigemina to the optic ganglia. The sensor light-waves excite, agitate, or affect the optic ganglia of the cerebrum. The mind feels the agitation and is aware of the feeling. This conscious feeling of sensor excitation is called sensation.

Reflex Sensor Action.—The mind in sensation is conscious of feeling the excitation. Sensor currents sent back from reflex centers are not felt—do not occasion sensation. Even agitations of the cerebral sensor ganglia do not necessarily occasion sensations. The clock struck ten, but I did not hear it, because I was absorbed in my work.

> "What sees is mind,
> What hears is mind;
> The ear and eye
> Are deaf and blind."

SENSORIUM AND MOTORIUM.

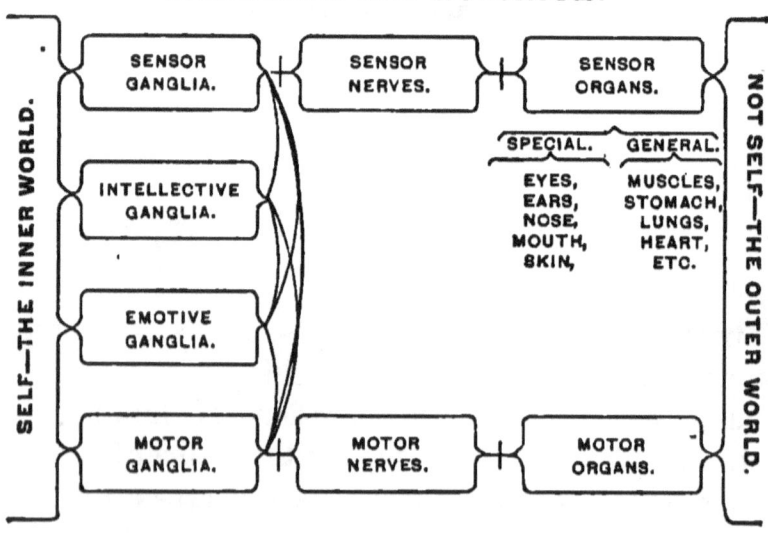

46 ELEMENTARY PSYCHOLOGY AND EDUCATION.

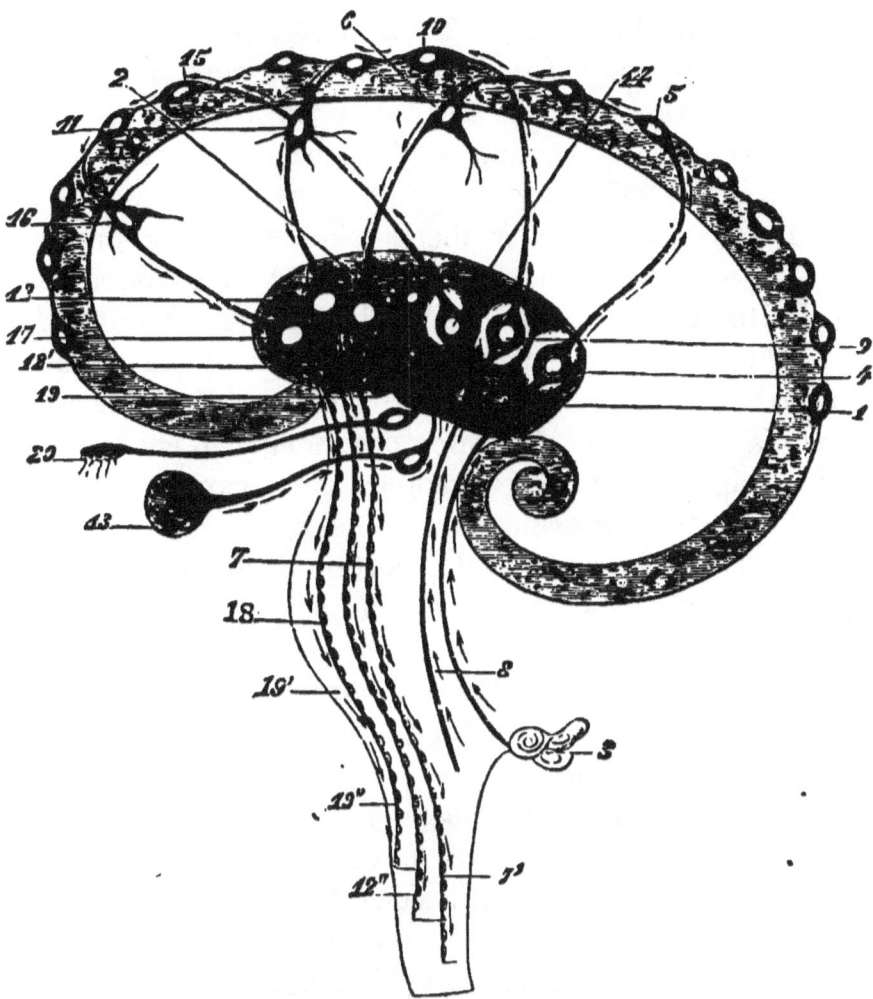

Diagram of the sensori-motor processes of cerebral activity. 1, *optic thalamus* with its centers and ganglionic cells. 2, *corpus striatum*. 3, course of the propagation of acoustic impressions: these arrive in the corresponding center (4), are radiated toward the *sensorium* (5), and reflected at 6 and 6' to the large cells of the *corpus striatum*, and thence at 7 and 7' toward the motor regions of the spinal axis. 8, course of tactile impressions: these are concentrated (at 9) in the corresponding center, radiated thence into the plexuses of the *sensorium* (10), reflected to the large cortical cells (11), and thence propagated to the large cells of the *corpus striatum*, and finally to the different segments of the spinal axis. 13, course of optic impressions: these are concentrated (at 14) in their corresponding center, then radiated toward the *sensorium* (at 15); they are reflected toward the large cells of the *corpus striatum*, and afterward propagated to the different segments of the spinal axis.—(Luys, "The Brain and its Functions," p. 61. Inserted by permission.)

The Sensorium and the Motorium.—Self reigns in the cerebral ganglia. Here he receives messages and issues his mandates. Mind is the inner world, is self. All else, even the sensorium and motorium, is the outer world, is the not-self.

1. *The sensorium* is the portion of the nervous organism which conditions sensation, and in common use is limited to the cerebral hemispheres. It is here used, for the sake of brevity, to include the sensor organs, special and general, the sensor nerves, and the sensor ganglia. As sense-perception occurs only in connection with the cerebral sensor ganglia, these ganglia strictly constitute the sensorium.

2. *The motorium* is the portion of the nervous organism through which self sends messages to the outer world. It includes the motor ganglia, the motor nerves, and the motor organs or muscles. As voluntary motion begins in the motor ganglia, these strictly constitute the motorium.

3. *Intellective and emotive ganglia* are inserted to give completeness of outline. These are the cerebral ganglia, in connection with which knowing and feeling occur. It is important to note the nerve-connections between the various ganglia. Though composed of a billion nerve-cells and five billion nerve-fibers, the brain is an organic unit. Marvellous structure! Truly our bodies are fearfully and wonderfully made!

Cerebral Action—Sensor Motor.—The thoughtful student will linger over this inside view of brain-activity in sensation and volition.

Place on the board the diagram on page 45 and the cut on page 46. Let each student trace sensor stimuli through each sensor line

48 ELEMENTARY PSYCHOLOGY AND EDUCATION.

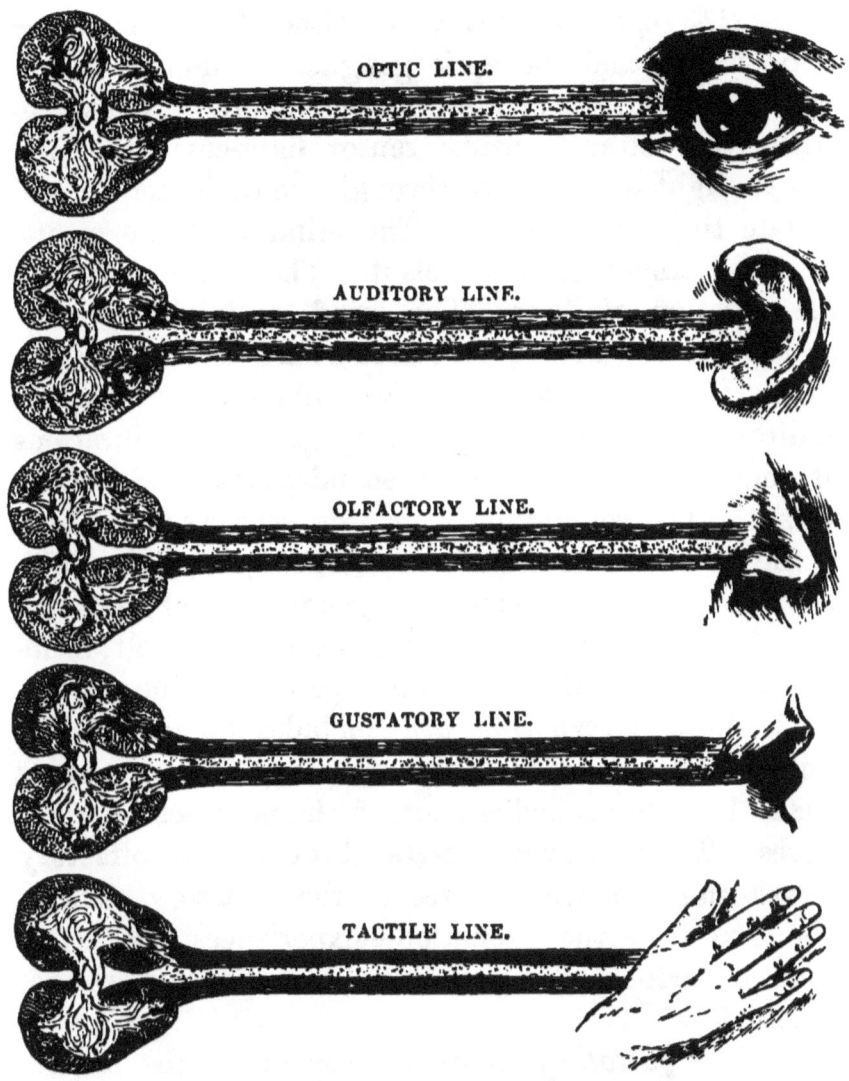

to the mind; also trace motor stimuli through the motor apparatus to the outer world. Here patient work will reward effort.

The Five Special Sensor Lines convey impressions from the outer world to the inner world. They are called special, because each line opens up to us a new world. Each sensor line is called a sensor apparatus.

1. *The optic apparatus* consists of the eyes, the optic nerves, and the optic ganglia. Luminous bodies produce vibrations in luminiferous ether. Light-waves strike the retina, causing sensor light-currents. Molecular light-waves move through the optic nerves and agitate the optic ganglia. The mind feels the excitation, and knows that it feels it. The soul experiences the sensation of light. The mind, as intellect, interprets these sensations; perceives colors, forms, sizes.

2. *The auditory apparatus* embraces the ears, the auditory nerves, and the auditory ganglia. Vibrations of sonorous bodies produce sound-waves. The clock strikes. The sound-vibrations start sensor sound-waves in the ear. The sensor waves vibrate through the auditory nerves and in the auditory ganglia. Self, as sensation, feels the excitation—hears the strokes; self, as intellect, interprets the sensations—perceives nine o'clock.

3. *The olfactory apparatus* includes the nose, the olfactory nerves, and the olfactory ganglia. Odor-waves caused by odorous bodies start, in the nose, sensor odor-waves. These waves vibrate through the olfactory nerves, and produce changes in the olfactory ganglia. The soul feels the excitation—experiences the sensations of odor; interprets the sensations—perceives sweet odors.

4. *The gustatory apparatus* consists of the mouth, the gustatory nerves, and the gustatory ganglia. Contact of the gustatory organs with articles possessing flavor excites gustatory nerve-currents. These currents pass in molecular waves through the gustatory nerves and affect the gustatory ganglia. The conscious affection of the gustatory ganglia is the sensation called taste. Self, as

intellect, interprets these sensations—perceives sugar as sweet and grapes as delicious.

5. *The tactile apparatus* includes the skin, the tactile nerves, and the tactile ganglia. I touch the paper; the contact starts tactile waves which vibrate through the tactile nerves and in the tactile ganglia. The soul is conscious of the excitation—experiences tactile sensations. The soul interprets the sensations—perceives the paper as smooth.

General Sensor Lines.—The fifteen general sensor lines carry messages from the organs and tissues of the body. The excitant is within the body. For illustration we may take the

Muscular line. The muscular apparatus embraces muscles, muscular nerves, and muscular ganglia. Besides their contractile office, muscles seem to be sensitive to pressure or straining. The nerves which convey from the muscles to the muscular ganglia the sensor waves of pressure are called muscular nerves. We feel sensations of pressure or weight. It is still questioned whether the muscular should be classed as a special or a general sense. The student is left to study out and diagram the general sensor lines.

Comparative Psychology.—You have taken a lively interest in the study of comparative anatomy and physiology. I trust that you will feel a still deeper interest in comparing human and brute mind. We have no sense which we do not find in some brute; and the senses of brutes, so far as we can judge, are affected in the same way as ours are, by the same objects. They may have some of the senses more acute than ours are, but they differ from ours only in degree, as the senses of men differ in strength and delicacy. Acuteness of sensation is a characteristic of the lower animals. So far as we know, no brute has a sense that differs from ours in kind. If we judge, as we do in every other case, it must be plain to every observer that brutes have the same kind of enjoyment and suffering, through the senses, that men have. To heat and cold, hunger and thirst, food and poison, sickness, pain, and death they have the same bodily relations in kind that we have.*

Education of the Senses.—"The senses are all capable of being educated. Our tastes may become more delicate, and may keep us from using deleterious food. The sense of smell may be cultivated, and add to our enjoyments; and odors, especially by means of flowers, may be provided to gratify it. Hearing may be improved and made more sensitive and accurate. Music is a source of pleasure, which may be enhanced until it becomes elysian. Feeling may be made very delicate in its perceptions, and capable of distinguishing very nice differences of objects. The senses of pressure and of weight may be so trained as to give us very accurate measurements. But the eye is the most intellectual of all our sense-organs, enabling us at a glance to take in the vast and the minute, the near and the distant.

"All these should be cultivated by training in the family and at school. Children should be taught from their earliest years to use their senses intelligently and habitually. They should be encouraged to observe carefully the objects around them, and taught to describe and report them correctly. It has been said that there are more false facts than false theories, and this arises from persons not being trained to notice facts accurately, neither adding to them nor taking from them, nor gilding them by the fancy, nor detracting from them to serve an end. Pictures and models are used very extensively in modern education, and serve a good purpose, as they call in the senses to minister to the intellect. But the things themselves are vastly more instructive than any representation can be. So children should be taught to use their senses, especially their ears

* "See Instinct in Animals and Men," Chadbourne.

and their eyes, in observing the objects around them, and the events that occur, and storing them up for future reflection. Plants and animals and stars, men and women and children, fall under our eyes at all times, and their nature, shapes, and actings should be diligently scanned for practical use and for scientific attainment." *

Physiological Psychology. — Carpenter's "Mental Physiology," Wundt's "Physiological Psychology," and Ribot's "Empirical Psychology" are remarkable works. The latter gives an account of German investigation in this field. These researches have, for the psychologist, an intense interest. They throw light upon the conscious acts of the mind. They demonstrate the infinite importance of hygienic living. Even their failures are invaluable. The true psychology gathers up the facts of mind established by all schools of investigators.

The investigations of physiologists have thrown much light on the manner in which material objects affect the different sense-organs, and also on the excitation and action of the sensorium, and especially of the brain; but they necessarily stop with sensorial phenomena. It is impossible to cross the line that divides the physical and the psychical, and explain physiologically the action of the soul.†

Body and Mind.‡—"A human being consists of two clearly distinguishable parts—body and mind, or soul. The body has its distinctive capacities and powers, and so has the soul. To the body belong weight and extension; to the soul, the powers of knowing, feeling, and willing. To the question, What is the soul in its essence? we may return the question, What is the body in its essence? The one question is as easy of solution as the other. The human mind is forced to assume a substance to which belong the known properties, or powers, of matter. In like manner it is compelled to assume a substance, or being, in which exist the powers of the soul. If, then, the question be returned, What is the soul? we answer, It is the part of man that has the powers of knowing, feeling, and willing."

* McCosh. † White. ‡ Larkin Dunton.

SUGGESTIVE STUDY-HINTS.

Review.—Give distinctions between phenomena and noumena; force and law; instinct and intellect. Define science, education, psychology, mind. Etc., etc.

Draw and describe a nerve-cell; a ganglion; a nerve. Give the office of nerves; of sensor nerves; of motor nerves; of afferent nerves; of efferent nerves. Show that nerve-fibers are continuous; compare to telegraph-wires. Explain the meaning of nerve-currents.

Give the meaning of sense-organs; of terminal organs. Show the office of sense-organs. Give the distinction between the special and the general senses.

Give the estimated number of nerve-cells and nerve-fibers in a human brain. Name the lower nerve-centers of the brain; the central nerve-centers; the higher nerve-centers.

Define sensorium; what does it include? Define motorium; what does it include? Give the office of sensor ganglia; of intellective ganglia; of emotive ganglia; of motor ganglia.

Place on the board a diagram of the sensorium and motorium, and also the cuts on pages 46 and 48. Trace impressions from the outer to the inner world through each of the special sensor lines.

Describe, give office of, and illustrate the workings of the optic apparatus; of the auditory apparatus; of the olfactory apparatus; of the gustatory apparatus; of the tactile apparatus; of the muscular apparatus. Give examples.

Define sensation. Do agitations of the sensorium of which you are not conscious produce sensation? What is it that hears and sees? What is reflex action? automatic action?

Why should we spare no effort to keep our bodies in the best possible condition? Why is it criminal to violate hygienic laws?

What is meant by comparative psychology? How do brute and human sensations differ?

Letter.—Tell your friend some things you know about the sensorium and sensation. Dwell upon the wonders of the organism in connection with which mind works. Explain in detail and fully how messages pass between the outer and the inner world. Inclose *your* outline of these chapters.

Topical Analysis of Chapters IV and V.—Sensation.

I. **Nerve-Cells.**
   Nerve-fluid.
   Nerve-force.

I. **Ganglia.**
   Reflex ganglia.
   Motor ganglia.
   Sensor ganglia.

III. **Nerves.**
   Structure.
   Classification.
   Office.
   Nerve-currents.

V. **Sense-Organs.**
   Special.
   General.

V. **The Brain.**
   Lower nerve-centers.
   Higher nerve-centers.
   Middle nerve-centers.

VI. **Cerebral Ganglia.**
   Sensor ganglia.
   Emotive ganglia.
   Intellective ganglia.
   Motor ganglia.

VII. **Definitions.**
   Sensorium.
   Sensation.
   Motorium.

VIII. **Reflex Sensor Action.**
   Automatic action.
   Reflex action.

IX. **Sensorium and Motorium.**
   Explain sensation.
   Explain motion.

X. **Special Sensor Lines.**
   Optic apparatus.
   Gustatory apparatus.
   Auditory apparatus.
   Tactile apparatus.
   Olfactory apparatus.

XI. **General Sensor Lines.**
   Muscular line.
   Thirst-line.
   Hunger-line.
   Digestive line.
   Etc., etc.

XII. **Comparative Psychology.**

XIII. **Hygiene and Education of the Senses.**

PART II.

THE PERCEPTIVE POWERS.

CHAPTER VI.—Sense-Perception, or Sense-Intuition.
       VII.—Conscious Perception, or Self-Consciousness.
       VIII.—Noumenal Perception, or Noumenal Intuition.
       IX.—Presentation—General View.

SECOND PART.

PERCEPTIVE-KNOWING—THE PERCEPTIVE POWERS.

SOUL-ENERGIES.

Before beginning the study of your capabilities in detail, it is important that you take a general view of your powers. To aid you in this, the soul-energies are here represented by a tree. "Like all graphic devices, it represents the facts only *approximately*." It is earnestly hoped, however, that this device will help you to gain true conceptions of the human soul.

Soul-Energies.
 Knowing.
  Perceptive knowing.
   1. Sense-perception.   3. Noumenal perception.
   2. Conscious perception.
  Representative knowing.
   4. Memory.   5. Phantasy.   6. Imagination.
  Thought-knowing.
   7. Conception. 8. Judgment. 9. Reason.
 Feeling.
  Instincts.
   Strictly brute instincts.   Strictly human instincts.
   Instincts common to brute and man.
  Physical feelings.
   Appetites.   General senses.   Special senses.
  Emotions.
   Egoistic emotions.   Cosmic emotions.
   Altruistic emotions.
 Willing.
   Attention.   Action.   Choice.

The one soul is capable of acting in different ways. These distinct soul-energies are called capabilities, or powers, or faculties. Self is an indivisible unit in knowing, in feeling, and in willing. A faculty is simply a method in which the mind can act. With the tree on the opposite page in view, you may examine carefully the outline of soul-energies.

Keep constantly in mind the central fact that the mind is one and acts as a unit. Each capability supplements all other capabilities. "The soul feels while it knows, and determines while it feels." As you study your individual powers you will recur often to this connected outline, and thus learn to view each of your energies in its relations to your other powers. You will learn to think of a mental power as merely one of your capabilities.

The Perceptive Powers.—By these we mean our powers to know immediately. We know at once that ice is cold, that we are glad, that things exist and occupy space. We do not need to reason up to these ideas. We are endowed with capabilities to know some things directly. Our powers of direct insight are known by the following

Names.— { The Perceptive Powers.
The Presentative Powers.
The Intuitive Powers.
The Simple Cognitive Powers.

We behold immediately material things having qualities. We perceive the mountain as lofty and snow-capped. We perceive ourselves recalling and reasoning. Our capabilities to *make present,* or to know immediately, are called our *presentative powers.* As we know directly, or intuitively, we call these faculties our *intuitive powers*. As perceptive knowing is the simplest form of knowing, we term these capabilities the *simple cognitive powers*. *Cognize*, to know, *cognition*, the act of knowing, and *cognitive*, the power to know, are valuable terms in mental science.

The Perceptive Powers are— { Sense-Perception, or Sense-Intuition. Conscious Perception, or Consciousness. Noumenal-Perception, or Noumenal-Intuition.

That he may explore the matter-world, man is endowed with *sense-perception*. That he may gain self-knowledge, he is endowed with *conscious-perception*. That he may cognize the world of necessary realities and thus build on the rock, he is endowed with *noumenal-perception*.

CHAPTER VI.

SENSE-PERCEPTION.

By this is meant the power to perceive directly material objects. Self as sense-perception stands face to face with physical phenomena. I know at once this tree as large, green, cone-bearing. This capability is designated by the following

Names.— { Sense-Perception, or Objective-Perception. Outer-Perception, or External-Perception. Sense-Intuition, or Perception.

Each term embodies the same idea—self endowed with the capability to know immediately the outer world. *Sense-perception*, the power to gain knowledge through the senses, is most expressive, and is now universally used. For brevity, perception is often used, but is indefinite.

Sensation is the power to feel consciously sensor excitations. You speak. Sound-waves vibrate through the air, in my ears, through my auditory nerves, in my auditory ganglia. I feel the excitation; I hear you speak. I interpret the sensations; your words are to me signs of ideas. Self, as sense-perception, interprets sensations—converts sensations into ideas.

Sensation is the basis of all knowing. Without sensations there can be no sense-perceptions. Without particular notions there can be no general notions. In order that sense-perceptions may be, sensations must be. It is a curious fact that all our knowing begins with blind feelings. Out of these blind feelings we make our sense-ideas. Sense-perception includes sensation.

Acts of Sense-Perception analyzed.—Notice carefully yourself perceiving. What do you do when you perceive? What are the steps in acts of sense-perception? What are the products? Take this object. You press it; it is soft. You touch it; it is smooth. You smell it; it is fragrant. You drop it; the sound is slight. You see it; it is white. You interpret these sensations, and cognize the object as a rose. In this way you may profitably examine many acts of perception. You find in an act of sense-perception four distinct elements: sensation, recalling, perceiving, and self-perceiving.

1. *Sensations* are the stuff out of which sense-ideas are made. The blind see no colors; the deaf hear no sounds. The blind gain no percepts of color; the deaf gain no percepts of sound.

2. *Recalling* other experiences, you refer your sensations, immediate and revived, to the object. You perceive the fragrant white rose.

3. *Perceiving.* Fusing the sensations, immediate and recalled, you form an idea of the object. You interpret your sensations, and make out of them the notion, this soft, fragrant white rose. This is sense-perceiving.

4. *Self-perceiving.* You are aware that you perceive the rose. You stand face to face with material objects. You know directly self perceiving material things.

From your analysis of many acts of sense-perception you discover the

Office of Sense-Perception.—The soul is a unit, but is capable of acting in many ways. The distinct ways in which the soul can act are called soul-energies, mental powers, mental faculties, or mental capabilities. *Office* is used to designate the special work of a mental power in the mental economy. Self, as attention, concentrates effort; concentration is the office of attention. Self, as memory, recalls; recollection is the office of memory. Self, as sense-perception, interprets sensations, or converts sensations into ideas; interpreting sensations is the office of sense-perception. The mind, as sense-perception, forms sense-ideas, or gains a direct knowledge of material objects. From your analysis of acts of sense-perception you discover the

Characteristics of Sense-Perception.—This power of self is distinguished from all his other capabilities by marked peculiarities:

1. *Self, as sense-perception, knows intuitively physical phenomena.* I know the board is black because I

see it black. I know the sugar is sweet because I taste it sweet. So with all sense-knowing. I look directly on material phenomena. The soul, as sense-perception, stands face to face with the outer world. I know immediately objects as extended and resisting. I do not need to prove to myself that the rose smells sweet; I know it intuitively. I know the wall is here, for I see it extended, and feel it resisting my efforts to pass through.

2. *The mind, as sense-perception, is limited to physical phenomena.* A being endowed merely with sense-perception would forever remain ignorant of self. Self, as sense-perception, knows physical phenomena, and nothing more.

3. *The mind, as sense-perception, gains only concrete individual notions of material objects.* Beings not endowed with other powers are incapable of forming class-notions. The brute perceives individual trees, but is incapable of thinking the many trees into one class.

Definitions of Sense-Perception.—Self, as sense-perception, explores the outer world. Physical phenomena come to us vibrating in our sensoriums. The soul is aware of its sensor excitations, and assimilates its sensations, immediate and revived, into notions called sense-ideas. The capability to convert sensations into ideas is termed sense-perception.

1. *Sense-perception is the power to know immediately material objects.* Strictly, sense-perception is the power to know immediately physical phenomena. But sensations are signs of material things. The mind, as sense-perception, translates these signs into notions of things. These concrete individual notions of material

things are termed sense-ideas. Self stands face to face with the material world—hence knows immediately, knows intuitively material objects as having properties. We see the tall tree, not the abstract phenomena, tall. We perceive noumena as well as phenomena. We gain a knowledge of things, not of mere abstract impressions.

2. *Original.* Write your definition of sense-perception. What does it mean to you? Remember that what others have thought will prove beneficial to you only as it leads you to better and clearer thinking.

3. Various Definitions.—1. SULLY: Sense-perception is the power to integrate sense-impressions, immediate and revived, into percepts. 2. PORTER: Sense-perception is the power to gain a knowledge of material objects through the sensorium. 3. MAHAN: Sense-perception is the faculty to apprehend the qualities of material substances. 4. McCOSH: Sense-perception is the power to gain a knowledge of things affecting us, external to ourselves and extended. 5. WHITE: Sense-perception is the power to know directly present and material objects.

Some writers seem to teach that self as sense-perception knows directly the noumena as well as phenomena. To me it is clear that self as noumenal-intuition perceives substance underlying phenomena, while self as sense-intuition perceives physical phenomena and nothing more.

Sense-Percepts.—The ideas we gain through the senses are called sense-ideas, or sense-percepts. A sense-percept is a product of sense-perception. I see, hear, touch, smell, and taste this orange. The idea, *this orange,* is a sense-percept. *Sense-percepts are our ideas of material things.*

1. *Sense-percepts are concrete notions.* Concrete ideas are ideas of things with qualities. The notion, red, is abstract; but the notion, *this red rose,* is a concrete idea—is a sense-percept.

2. *Sense-percepts are particular notions.* Fruit is a general notion, but *this green apple* is a particular notion—is a sense-percept. Sensations, immediate and remembered, are the materials of which sense-percepts are made. Sense-percepts are our concrete individual notions of material things.

3. *Re-percepts are remembered percepts.* You observe the ocean-steamer. The idea thus made present is a sense-percept. When you recall this idea and thus make it present again, it is called a *re-percept.*

Remark.—Some critical thinkers limit the use of sense-percept to the product of a single sense, and call our ideas of objects sense-concepts, or individual concepts. But Sully, McCosh, Porter, and others, term our concrete ideas of external objects sense-percepts. Percept is used in this sense in literature and life. A concept is always a class-notion, but a percept is a notion of an individual thing.

Direct and Indirect Sense-Percepts.—I see, and hear, and feel, and smell, and taste this red, dull-sounding, mellow, fragrant, sweet apple. I thus gain a *direct* sense-percept. Ideas gained directly from sensations, immediate and revived, are direct sense-percepts. They are also called original sense-percepts. But my idea of the distance across the river involves judgment and experience, as well as sensation, and is an indirect sense-percept. I hear sounds in a distant room which I know are caused by a piano. The blind *substitute* touch and hearing for sight. We learn by experience to know the presence of musk by the peculiar odor. By experience we learn to locate the sense of smell in the nose. Ideas thus gained indirectly from sensations are *indirect sense-percepts.*

Organism and Products of Sense-perception.—This diagram is not claimed to be either perfect or exhaustive, but is designed to suggest lines of inquiry. What knowledge do we gain directly through each sense? What indirectly? What excitants affect each sensor apparatus? etc. The student is referred to recent physiologies for descriptions and details. Please re-read Chapters IV and V in connection with this diagram.

SENSES.	APPARATUS.	MEDIUMS.	EXCITANTS.	DIRECT PRODUCTS.	INDIRECT PRODUCTS.	SUBSTITUTES.
Seeing.	Optic.	Light—ether.	Light-waves.	Color, Shape, Size, etc.	Figure, Size, Solidity, Distance, etc.	Feeling, Hearing, Tasting, etc.
Hearing.	Auditory.	Air, etc.	Sound-waves.	Sound.	Direction, Distance, Source, etc.	Seeing, Feeling, etc.
Feeling.	Tactile.	Contact.	Tactile-waves.	Figure, Texture, Solidity, etc.	Size, Distance, Hardness, Space, etc.	Seeing, Hearing, etc.
Smelling.	Olfactory.	Air, etc.	Odor-waves.	Odor.	Source, Direction, Distance, etc.	Tasting, Seeing, etc.
Tasting.	Gustatory.	Contact.	Flavor-waves.	Flavor.	Source.	Smelling, Seeing.
Pressing.	Muscular.	Pressure.	Pressure-waves.	Movement, Strain, etc.	Weight, Solidity.	Seeing, Feeling.
Etc.						

Growth of Sense-Perception.—As matter is endowed with the force of gravity, so mind is endowed with the power of sense-perception. Infants, idiots, and even the lowest orders of animals give indications of possessing rudimentary sense-perception. Your observation satisfies you that sense-perceiving is one of your first mental activities. Until awakened by sensations, the soul in all its embryonic powers seems dormant. Is it? Who can tell? Life is the deepest of all mysteries. The beginnings of soul-activity are shrouded from mortal view. One fact is now unquestioned: an infant is endowed with capabilities, but not with ideas. All ideas are acquired. In early infancy the babe begins to take notice. Slowly the child gains the power to form ideas out of sensations. These imperfect early notions grow more and more distinct, and the little one learns to use words as the signs of ideas. We usually find children under two years of age actively exploring the material world. But sense-perception does not seem to reach its greatest activity much before the fourteenth year. Between the ninth and fourteenth years this power seems to reach its full vigor. In boyhood and girlhood the sense-world fills the cup of joy to the brim. After that, sense-perception is kept vigorous by well-directed activity, but ceases to be the end of effort. It now becomes a means to higher ends.

Education of Sense-Perception.* —That we may master the outer world, we are endowed with sense-perception. The infant makes feeble efforts; the child becomes more and more capable; the boy masters in a good degree objective nature; the youth seeks to mas-

* See "Education of Sense-Perception," "Applied Psychology."

ter and classify physical phenomena, and thus becomes familiar with physical sciences. Development expresses the change from the feeble infant to the masterly youth. Further on, this topic is discussed from the stand-point of the teacher. Here we examine it briefly from the stand-point of the student.

1. *Hygienic conditions.** Mental achievement depends on the condition of the brain. Nothing is more certain. High success is impossible to individuals or to races having inferior brains. Physical elevation underlies mental elevation. Perfect health gives perfect sensations. Perfect sensations condition perfect sense-percepts. Perfect sense-percepts are the basis of clear and vigorous thinking and efficient acting. Obedience to hygienic laws is therefore imperative. Brain-culture underlies mind-culture.

2. *Objective basis.* All knowing begins with perceiving material objects. Words are signs of ideas already in the mind. "Blue" is empty sound to the blind boy; the idea "blue" is not in his mind. Attempts to understand words and definitions without ideas are about as successful as attempts to build railroads on clouds. Only through the senses do we get elementary ideas of the world around us. Words, spoken and written and remembered, represent these ideas. A firm foundation of sense-knowledge must underlie all mental achievement. Grasping this truth, modern education strives to build on the rock of sense-experience.

3. *Objective teaching.*† "An appeal to children's own observation is now rightly resorted to as much as possible in every branch

---

* See Baldwin's "Art of School Management," p. 63.
† Sully, "Outlines of Psychology."

of instruction. The teaching of natural science sets out with the object-lesson, which in its simplest form is a mere exercise of the pupils' observing powers in noting the properties of a thing. Whatever the difficulties of the object-lesson, nobody really doubts that a large amount of valuable knowledge about simple substances, as chalk and coal, natural forms, as those of plants and animals, as well as art-products, can be given to a number of children in this way. This first-hand knowledge of things through personal inspection is worth far more than any second-hand account of them by description. While the senses may thus be appealed to in almost any branch of instruction, they are far more concerned in some departments than in others. It is now generally admitted that the careful and thorough study of one or more of the natural sciences supplies the most efficient means of educating sense-perception."

Comparative Psychology.—The life of the brute is distinctly one of sensation. Acuteness of sensation characterizes the brute, but in the proportion that their sensations are strong are their perceptions weak. Mr. Darwin says, "Sensations brutes have, but never ideas." Brutes lack language because they have nothing to say. The sense-impressions of the brute are associated and recalled; but can we properly call these impressions and *re*-impressions ideas? Does the brute so discriminate and assimilate as to gain clear-cut sense-percepts? We can not so think. The brute perceives, but its percepts are something lower than ideas.

SUGGESTIVE STUDY-HINTS.

Review.—In the mental economy, what is the office of attention? of instinct? of sensation? Give the distinction between sensorium and motorium. Define soul, psychology. Etc.

Give the meaning of sense-perception. What other names are applied to this faculty? Give the meaning of each name. Why is sense-perception preferred?

Give the meaning of sensation. Draw a picture of the auditory apparatus and explain auditory sensation. Are sensations the basis of all knowing?

Analyze two of your acts of sense-perception, giving the four facts you discover. Why are these called elements of sense-perception?

Define faculty. Are power, capability, and faculty synonyms? What is the office of sense-perception? How do sensation and sense-perception differ? What do you call your ideas gained through sense-perception?

Name the three characteristics of sense-perception. What do you mean by characteristics? by intuitive? by concrete?

State and explain the author's definition of sense-perception; your definition; Sully's definition; McCosh's definition.

What do you mean by sense-percepts? Illustrate. Give and explain the two peculiarities of a sense-percept. Out of what do you make sense-percepts? Turn to diagram and cuts on pages 45, 46, 48, and show how we gain optic percepts, auditory percepts, and tactile percepts.

Give the distinction between a direct and an indirect sense-percept. What is understood by substitution? Place the diagram on the board and explain the mechanism and products of sense-perception.

Trace the growth of sense-perception. What does development express? Give hygienic conditions of sense-development. Tell about the objective basis. What does Sully say about objective teaching?

Which of the senses seem to involve all the others?

Which of the senses are active in the dark?

Do our senses, or our perceptions, give us complete ideas of things?

Are our senses reliable? State your arguments, *pro* or *con*.

Does the child generally apply one or more senses to an object?

Does he exercise the faculty of perception before coming to school?

Letter.—You may now give your friend your ideas about sense-perception. Try hard to make each point clear to him. Present the plain facts, as you understand them, and illustrate from your own experience.

Topical Analysis of Chapter VI.—Sense-Perception.

I. **Names.**
   Sense-perception and sense-intuition.
   Outer-perception and external-perception.
   Objective-perception and perception.

II. **Elements of Sense-perceiving.**
   Sensations.   Perceiving.
   Recalled experiences.   Self-perceiving.

III. **Office of Sense-perception.**
   To ideate sensations.

IV. **Characteristics.**
   Acts intuitively.   Limited to material objects.
   Gains concrete ideas.

V. **Definitions.**
   Author's definition.   Various definitions.
   Original definition.

VI. **Kinds of Sense-percepts.**
   Direct sense-percepts.   Substituted sense-percepts.
   Indirect sense-percepts.

VII. **Education of Sense-perception.**
   Stages of growth.   Objective basis.
   Hygienic conditions.   Objective teaching.

VIII. **Laws of Sense-perception Growth.**
   A good brain conditions the growth of sense-perception.
   Well-directed effort in acquiring sense-knowledge develops sense-perception.
   Objective work educates sense-perception.

IX. **Comparative Psychology.**
   Brutes perceive.   Brutes do not have ideas.

CHAPTER VII.

CONSCIOUS-PERCEPTION, OR SELF-CONSCIOUSNESS.

By this is meant the power to perceive self-acting. We live in a wonder-world. Beneath us, around us, above us, are the earth and the heavens with their varied tenantry. From this outer world come to us, vibrating through the sensor lines, marvelous messages. Light flashes along the optic line, and I behold a world of color, form, and beauty. Sound-waves vibrate through the auditory line, and I live in a world of speech and song. Flavor and odor-waves come to me, and I live in a world of grateful food and sweet odors. Touch moves his magic wand, and I am gratified by balmy breezes. Endowed with sense-perception, I stand face to face with the outer world.

We perceive also an inner world, and find it likewise infinitely wonderful. This new world is called the world of mind. Self imagines, sympathizes, wills. The soul perceives itself perceiving, reasoning, choosing. The capability to perceive self acting is called conscious-perception. Endowed with this power, I stand face to face with the inner world. This power is designated by various

Names.— { Conscious-Perception.
Conscious-Intuition.
Self-Consciousness.
Consciousness.
Inner-Perception.
Subjective-Perception.
Ap-Perception, or Internal Vision.

Inner-perception and outer-perception, subjective-perception and objective-perception, are significant and corresponding terms. As all perceiving is intuitive, we call the power of immediate insight into the mind-world conscious-intuition, just as we call the power of direct insight into the matter-world sense-intuition. Consciousness and self-consciousness, however, are the commonly accepted names of this faculty.

Acts of Self-Consciousness analyzed.—We look within and see self at work. I perceive myself observing the evening star. I perceive myself grieving over the loved and lost. I perceive myself resolving to work more systematically. The perceiving of self as beholding, grieving, resolving, is an act of self-consciousness. In such acts we discover the elements of an act of consciousness.

1. *Mental phenomena.* Mind is self-acting and always acting. As mental acts appear—are perceived by the soul—they are called mental phenomena. The expression, mental phenomena, includes all knowing, feeling, and willing of which the soul is conscious. Where there are no mental acts, there can be no consciousness.

2. *Self-consciousness.* There never can be an appearance unless some *thing* appears. Intuitively we perceive substance underlying phenomena. You taste the sweet apple, not abstract sweetness. You see the beautiful picture, not abstract beauty. You perceive intuitively physical substance having physical powers or properties. So you perceive yourself thinking; you do not perceive abstract thought. You perceive yourself rejoicing, not abstract joy. Intuitively you perceive self exerting mental power. As you perceive yourself acting, you are self-conscious.

3. *Conscious-percepts.* As ideas gained through the senses are called sense-percepts, so ideas gained through consciousness are called conscious-percepts. Through consciousness, directly or indirectly, self gains its elementary knowledge of the inner world. A being not endowed with consciousness would have no inner world. By analyzing your own conscious acts, you will gain an insight into the mind-world. Of what are you conscious? What is it that is conscious? What are the products of consciousness? How do you know the distinction between sensation and perception? between desire and will?

Office of Consciousness.—Mind is self-acting. A faculty is a mode of self-activity, and is merely a power or capability of the mind. The office of a faculty is its function in the mental economy. Function, office, work, are synonymous terms. Self as consciousness perceives himself acting; internal vision is the office of consciousness. The work of this faculty will be better understood by a more minute examination:

1. *Self, as consciousness, intuitively knows his own acts as his.* I know, I feel, I will, and I know that these are my acts. As outer-perception, self knows immediately the outer world. As inner-perception, self knows immediately the inner world.

2. *Self, as consciousness, perceives himself knowing, feeling, willing.* We behold ourselves choosing, enjoying, thinking. We gaze directly upon self acting. Consciousness opens to us the inner world.

3. *Self, as consciousness, unitizes his experiences.* Inner-perception performs an office in our mental economy similar to that of the connective tissue in our

physical economy. The one gives unity to our bodies, the other to our mental acts.* The experiences of a long and eventful life are woven into one marvelous web. Consciousness gives unity to mental activity and mental achievement.

Characteristics of Consciousness.—The soul is endowed with the capacity to perceive itself remembering, repining, resolving. What peculiar features mark this marvelous power? How do we distinguish self-consciousness from other mental capabilities?

1. *Self, as consciousness, beholds himself acting.* Like sense-knowing, conscious-knowing is intuitive. We have direct insight into the workings of our own minds. Consciousness is the mind's eye, or, as Wundt terms it, internal vision.

2. *Certainty characterizes conscious-knowing.* I *know* that I feel disappointed. I know that I intended to tell the truth. I know that I see the setting sun. I can not be mistaken. The testimony of consciousness is final. *I know* ends controversy. Consciousness is infallible.

3. *Consciousness attends all our distinct mental acts.* In this particular, consciousness resembles attention and memory, but differs from all the other faculties. Whenever a thought, a feeling, or a purpose stirs a soul, consciousness is there. Waking or sleeping, self seems to be ever acting and ever conscious. Inner-perception, it is certain, accompanies all distinct mental acts. An act that does not occur in the field of consciousness is not a distinct mental act.

* Hopkins.

What shall we call the operations that seem to be constantly going on in the secret laboratory of the mind? Is it true that the soul in its secret chambers prepares material for its conscious acts? Does the conscious spring from the unconscious? Is it possible for science to explore the hidden springs of mental life?

4. *I am conscious of actual and present mental acts only.* I am conscious that I now remember my mother's advice, I am conscious of my present determination to study geology next year; but I am not conscious of past or future experiences, or of ideas not now in my mind. We are conscious of our representations and determinations; they are present mental acts. I am conscious of actual and present mental acts only.

Self-Consciousness defined.—The soul perceives itself acting. We intuitively behold the inner world. We know ourselves knowing, feeling, and willing. We are endowed with the power of direct insight into the mind-world:

1. *Self-consciousness is the capability to perceive self acting.* Consciousness is being aware of mental activity. In psychology, *consciousness* is commonly used in the same sense as *self-consciousness*. Self-consciousness is being aware of self acting; the brute is not self-conscious.

2. *Original.* Embody your notion of self-consciousness. What does consciousness mean to you? Have you earnestly watched the workings of your own mind? Are your notions of self-consciousness clear? Unless you see for yourself, books and teachers will not avail.

3. **Various Definitions.**—McCosh: Self-consciousness is the power to know self in his present state as acting and being acted on. Hamilton: Self-consciousness is the power by which we apprehend the phenomena of the inner world. Porter: Consciousness is the power by which the soul knows its own acts and states. Schuyler:

Consciousness is the capability of knowing our psychical acts and states. MAHAN: Consciousness is the faculty by which we perceive the operations and states of the mind itself. WHITE: Consciousness is the power of the soul to know self acting. WUNDT: Consciousness, or inner vision, is the capability that unites all psychical activity.

Conscious-Percepts.—We gain our elementary ideas immediately; hence we call these ideas intuitions, or percepts. Self, as sense-perception, gains sense-percepts; self, as conscious-perception, gains conscious-percepts. As sense-perception, we know directly the properties of matter; as conscious-perception, we know directly self acting.

1. *Conscious-percepts are concrete notions of mental acts.* I *was* conscious of seeing Mount Washington. I *am* conscious of remembering that I saw Mount Washington. In this case I perceive self remembering, not abstract memory. I gain the concrete notion, this memory, which I term a conscious-percept.

2. *Conscious-percepts are individual notions of mental acts.* I am conscious of this feeling, not of feeling in general; of this judgment, not of judgment in general. I am conscious of self performing a single act. The individual idea thus gained is a conscious-percept. I feel hopeful; the idea, this hoping, is a conscious-percept. I choose peace; the idea, this choosing, is a conscious-percept. I judge that man is mortal; the idea, this judging, is a conscious-percept. This list may be extended without limit.

3. *A conscious-percept is a concrete notion of an individual mental act.* Take away sense-perception, and the outer world would be a blank. Take away self-consciousness, and even the existence of an inner

world would be unknown. Our simple cognitions of ourselves knowing, feeling, and willing, are conscious-percepts. Such knowledge is called self-knowledge.

Attention, Consciousness, Memory.—I attend, am conscious, and remember. Self, as attention, concentrates his efforts upon the theorem; self, as thought, discerns that three points not in the same straight line determine a circle; self, as memory, distinctly recalls the theorem; and self, as consciousness, perceives himself doing these things. I am fully conscious when I give complete attention, and I then remember distinctly. When I give little attention, I am dimly conscious, and I remember indistinctly. Where there is no attention, there can be no consciousness. Where there is no consciousness, there can be no recollection. You are absorbed in your work; the clock strikes. As you were not conscious of hearing it strike, you can not remember hearing it strike. Because attention, consciousness, and memory are thus interdependent, some writers confound these faculties. But it would be as reasonable, in my judgment, to confound the digestive, circulatory, and respiratory organs of the body. No soul-energies are more distinct. Self, as attention, concentrates his efforts; self, as consciousness, perceives self acting; self, as memory, recalls his past experiences.

Growth of Self-Consciousness.—The child-world is the outer world. Outer-perception, the power to master the outer world, is now most active. Object-lessons intensely interest the little ones. The child is dimly conscious. The little one attends feebly, and hence consciousness and memory are indistinct. As the child learns to attend more closely, consciousness and memory increase in distinctness. How early children begin to be conscious we do not know. During the third year the child begins to use intelligently *I, me, my*. Before the fifth year few children give conclusive indications of clear self-consciousness. But boys and girls are very positive as to objective knowing. John sees the horse black, and he knows that the horse is black because he sees him black. In youth, self-consciousness becomes fully active.

Education of Consciousness.* —As consciousness enters into all our knowing, feeling, and willing, it develops incidentally as our other powers develop. The growth of consciousness, up to fourteen, is promoted chiefly by incidental effort. Up to this age the outer world, for the most part, absorbs attention and effort. The inner world is still a mystic realm. But the youth begins to feel a longing to explore the mind-world. Now is the time for direct and systematic culture of consciousness. We do not find it easy at first to examine mental phenomena. In fact, we meet with difficulties at every step; but, through patient effort, we learn to conquer.

1. *We tread the inner courts alone.* Hundreds may observe the eclipse of the sun. The mistakes of some may be corrected by the keener scrutiny of others. Not so in the soul-world. I alone perceive my mental acts. I need to repeat the act many times, to guard against erroneous inferences.

2. *We are conscious of mental phenomena but for an instant.* Physical phenomena stay with us, and we can conquer the material world at our leisure. Mental phenomena linger but an instant. To avoid mistakes

---

* See "Education of Consciousness," "Applied Psychology and Teaching."

we must repeat the act, and recall in memory the phenomena.

3. *Young persons feel like strangers when they enter the inner world.* Their young lives have been spent in the world of sense. Few have ever lingered for an hour in soul-land. When they enter, everything seems new, and their inferences are liable to be far from the truth: "I never was so happy!" You are conscious of feeling happy, but the inference may be false. Often and often you may have felt happier. You will constantly mix inference and consciousness. Consciousness, but not inference, is infallible. By inspecting mental phenomena with the same care that you have inspected physical phenomena, you will develop your power of inner-vision.

Comparative Psychology.—All beings endowed with intelligence are endowed with some degree of consciousness. The degree of consciousness increases as intelligence increases. But no brute gives evidence of distinct self-consciousness. The horse, in some degree, is conscious of knowing, feeling, and acting; but not of self as acting. No brute can say, "I am, I think, I choose." Only rational beings are self-conscious persons.

Clear Consciousness, Obscure Consciousness, and Non-Consciousness.—Your consciousness may be clear as the sunlight, or it may grow dimmer and dimmer until it is lost in the darkness of unconsciousness. You look without. You see clearly the lofty pine; you see more or less distinctly the trees near it; but more distant trees fade into obscurity. You look within. You are clearly conscious of your deep sorrow. Your grief stands out in the field of consciousness like the lofty pine in the forest. Flitting hopes and fears and desires appear like shadows, and fade into unconsciousness.

1. *Clear self-consciousness.* Everything appears in the light. The soul perceives itself thinking, grieving, determining. The mind intuitively knows itself acting. This is self-consciousness. In this sense it is used in psychology and literature as well as in common life. This is consciousness as you define it, human-consciousness, self-consciousness.

2. *Sub-consciousness is obscure consciousness.* It is by some termed semi-consciousness. However designated, indistinct consciousness is implied. The orator is conscious only of the thought he is uttering, but back in the misty chamber of sub-consciousness are many thoughts struggling into consciousness. Webster tells us that, when he was preparing his reply to Hayne, burning thoughts like clusters of stars crowded for utterance. This shadowy region may be called the antechamber of consciousness. But, even in this mystic chamber, the soul seems to dimly perceive itself working.

3. *Unconsciousness is utter blankness.* Imagine self absolutely dormant—no knowing, no feeling, no willing; this is unconsciousness. *Non-consciousness* means that phenomena do not appear to the conscious soul. I am non-conscious of your thoughts or feelings or purposes, or of my own mental operations that are supposed to occur in the hidden laboratory of thought.

Unconscious Cerebration.—"Nothing could be more grossly unscientific than the famous remark of Cabanis, that the brain secretes thought as the liver secretes bile. It is not even correct to say that thought goes on in the brain. What goes on in the brain is an amazingly complex series of molecular movements, with which thought and feeling are in some unknown way correlated, not as effects or as causes, but as concomitants. By no possibility can thought and feeling be in any sense the products of matter. Unconscious cerebration is a fiction of a false theory."* Self may do work of which he is dimly conscious, but that a material brain reaches conclusions and makes rational choices is simply inconceivable. That the mind is self-acting in all its powers is a stupendous fact. That it is ever consciously active in some degree, I do not doubt; but is the soul distinctly conscious of all its workings? No one thinks so. Does the mind carry on lines of work of which it is itself unconscious? Let Dr. McCosh answer:

Unconscious Mental Action.—"It was an opinion entertained by Leibnitz, and held by many since his time, that we are unconscious of many of our mental operations. They point to acts of mind which have left effects behind them, but of which we have not the dimmest recollection. We are sure that we must have issued a great many volitions in passing from one place to another, but after they are over we can not recollect one of them. The question arises, How are we to account for such a phenomenon? I believe it can all be explained by the ordinary laws of mind, without our calling in such an anomalous principle as unconscious mental action. I hold that we were conscious of the acts at the time, but that they were not retained, as there was nothing to fix them in the memory."

Here is sunlight clearness. Here is the granite. Some profound thinkers, however, take a widely different view. Wundt is easily the master-mind among physiological psychologists. His views in brief will interest even beginners. No one needs to wander off and lose himself in the imaginary mystic chambers of the unconscious. You can afford to leave to daring speculators the exploration of the mysterious realms of the unconscious, the hidden springs of mental life, and the unknown laboratories of the soul. In the following paragraph, Wundt's ap-perception is McCosh's self-consciousness and our conscious-perception:

* John Fiske.

The Unconscious conditions the Conscious.—" Physiological psychology starts with physiological facts and seeks to discover the psychological facts which are connected with them. It begins without and seeks to penetrate within by varying the external conditions of internal phenomena. A mind is a thing that reasons. A faculty is a distinct mode of psychical activity. Consciousness is the faculty of internal vision, and the point of clear consciousness may be called ap-perception. Ap-perception, or the consciousness of perceiving external objects, takes place in the frontal regions of the brain. Ap-perception is the internal activity that unitizes our experiences. But the agent that is conscious knows only results worked out in the unknown laboratory of the unconscious. In the hidden foundations and springs of mental life take place the important mental operations which fit things to appear in the field of consciousness. The conscious is always conditioned upon the unconscious."

Self-Consciousness and Physiological Psychology.—" Phenomena," says Lotze, " imply things which appear and a self-conscious being to whom they appear. The unitizing function of consciousness is an incontrovertible fact, absolutely inexplicable on any physiological hypotheses." "The scope of physiological psychology is necessarily limited to bodily functions and the physical concomitants of mental actions." "A psychology without a soul," at its best, has "the brain secreting thought just as the liver secretes bile." From this standpoint, the existence of a self-conscious soul is a metaphysical assumption, and self-activity is inconceivable. Man is merely a mechanism, and mind a mode of motion.

The Inner-Sense.—" We have the power," says President Hopkins, " of knowing immediately the processes and products of our own minds. Through this we not only know ourselves but also our fellow-men. That this knowledge is immediate all agree. Inner-sense is the best name for this power, as it corresponds with outer-sense. But, call this power what you may, we have revealed through it an inner world more wonderful even than that which is without— a world of intelligence, of comprehension, of feeling, of will, of personality, and of moral instead of physical law. It is a world whose phenomena we can study and arrange as we do those of the external world; but, as in the external world, the phenomena themselves must be immediately given. We must in some way intuitively and necessarily know them to be."

SUGGESTIVE STUDY-HINTS.

Review.—Write out a topical analysis of sense-perception. Discuss by topics. How do messages pass between the outer and the inner world? Define mind, faculty, sense-perception. Etc.

What is meant by consciousness? Tell what comes to us from the wonder-world around us? What do you mean by the inner world?

What power enables us to look directly into the inner world? Explain the meaning of each name given to this faculty. Which name do you prefer? Why?

Analyze two of your acts of consciousness. Give the three great facts you discover. Look once more. Are you conscious of abstract sadness, or of self feeling sad? What do you mean by self-consciousness? What will you call the ideas you gain through consciousness?

Give the office of consciousness. What does self perceive? What does self do with his experiences? Illustrate by the connective tissue.

Name the four characteristics of consciousness. Explain each.

Give the author's definition of consciousness; your definition: McCosh's definition; Wundt's definition.

Define conscious-percepts. Give the marks of a conscious-percept. Give the distinction between a conscious-percept and a sense-percept. Illustrate.

State as clearly as you can the distinctions between attention, consciousness, and memory.

Trace the growth of consciousness. Mention some of the difficulties in studying mental phenomena.

What do you mean by clear consciousness? by sub-consciousness? by unconsciousness? What does Fiske say about unconscious cerebration? What does McCosh say about unconscious mental action? What does Wundt say about the unconscious? What do you say?

Letter.—You may make a neat analysis of Chapter VII, and include it in your letter to your friend. It will pay you to "hasten leisurely" here. Put in your letter what you perceive about yourself. Mastery here means victory all along the line.

Topical Analysis of Chapter VII.—Self-Consciousness.

I. Two Worlds.
  Matter-world—Sense-perception.
  Mind-world—Conscious-perception.

II. Names.
  Conscious-perception, or conscious-intuition, etc.

III. Analysis of Acts of Consciousness.
  Mental phenomena.   Self-knowledge.
  Self-consciousness.

IV. Office of Self-consciousness.
  To gain self-knowledge.   To know self acting.
  To unitize our experiences.

V. Characteristics of Self-consciousness.
  Sees self acting.   Enters into all knowing.
  Gives certainty.   Is present knowing.

VI. Definitions of Self-consciousness.
  Author's definition.   McCosh's definition.

VII. Conscious-percepts.
  Concrete notions of mental   Individual notions.
    acts.   Definition.

VIII. Attention, Consciousness, and Memory.
  Office of each.   Confusion inexcusable.
  Each a disitnct activity.

IX. Growth of Consciousness.
  Acts feebly in childhood.
  Reaches full activity in youth.

X. Education of Self-consciousness.
  Incidental in childhood.   Difficulties.
  Direct in youth and manhood.

XI. Comparative Psychology.
  Brutes are not self-conscious.   Man is self-conscious.

XII. Degrees of Consciousness.
  Clear self-consciousness.   Unconsciousness.
  Obscure consciousness.

XIII. Unconscious Cerebration.
  Fiske.   McCosh.   Wundt.

CHAPTER VIII.

NOUMENAL-PERCEPTION, OR NOUMENAL-INTUITION.

By this is meant our power to perceive necessary realities. The soul is endowed with the capability to know directly and immediately necessary realities. Our elementary notions of the realities that underlie phenomena are called necessary ideas.

PERCEPTIVE KNOWING.

```
┌─────────────────────────────────────────────┐
│             3. Noumena.                     │
│   NOUMENAL-PERCEPTION—NOUMENAL-PERCEPTS.    │
├─────────────────────────────────────────────┤
│          2. Mental Phenomena.               │
│   CONSCIOUS-PERCEPTION—CONSCIOUS-PERCEPTS.  │
├─────────────────────────────────────────────┤
│          1. Physical Phenomena.             │
│     SENSE-PERCEPTION—SENSE-PERCEPTS.        │
└─────────────────────────────────────────────┘
```

We find ourselves endowed with three perceptive faculties giving us direct insight into the three elementary worlds. Sense-perception and consciousness are our powers to gain immediate knowledge of the two phenomenal worlds. Noumenal-perception is our power to intuitively behold the noumenal world. This power is known by the following and still other

Names.—
{ Noumenal-Perception.
Noumenal-Intuition, or Intuition.
Rational-Perception, or Reason.
Truth-Perception, or Common-Sense.

Noumena and Phenomena.—Gold is yellow, malleable, ductile; yellow, malleable, ductile, etc., are phenomena, but the enduring substance of which we affirm the phenomena is called noumenon. I think; thinking is phenomena, but the enduring self who thinks is called a noumenon. (*Noeo*, I perceive; *nous*, the mind; *noumenon*, the very essence, the enduring entity, the necessary.) Noumena, the plural, is now used to include necessary entities and necessary relations, as matter, mind, space, time, causation, existence, right, beauty, resemblance, truth, number, and infinity. The necessary realities that underlie and condition phenomena, and endure unchanged through all change, are termed noumena. Because we can find no better expression, we call the power to perceive these realities noumenal-perception or noumenal-intuition. Our concrete notions of these realities are termed necessary ideas, or noumenal-percepts.

Necessary Ideas.—The table is here and the stove is there. What is this in which things exist? The child answers, "It's where things are." The philosopher calls it space. In order that things *may* be, space *must* be. Space is a necessary reality. Space endures—is noumenon and not phenomenon. Take this bar of iron. I find that it possesses the phenomena of extension, divisibility, weight, porosity, compressibility, elasticity. That these properties or phenomena *may* be, a substance possessing these properties *must* be. Material substance is a necessary reality underlying physical phenomena. Material substance endures, is noumenon, and not phenomenon. In the same way we find that mind, time, cause, etc., are noumena and not phenomena. Our direct notions of these realities are noumenal-percepts. Because these ideas underlie and condition all other ideas, they are called *necessary ideas*.

Acts of Noumenal-Perception analyzed.—I turn my hour-glass. My little girl patiently watches till the last grain of sand has fallen, and says, "Papa, it took a long time." Intuitively the child perceives concrete time. The capability to know noumena immediately is called *noumenal-perception*. In the same way you may examine space, cause, etc., and discover for yourself the nature of this marvelous power. You find that you perceive noumena as well as phenomena. Your analysis gives the

Conditions of knowing Necessary Ideas.—The apple falls. "What made it fall?" asks the three-year-old Newton. The question involves the three conditions of knowing necessary truths:

1. *Objective reality.* Space exists, though you may not perceive it. Space is an objective reality. The notion, cause, would be impossible but for the objective reality of causes. Gravity is an objective reality. Time is a reality independent of self. Matter and mind are objective realities. We perceive necessary realities.

2. *Phenomena involving necessary realities.* The falling apple involves cause. Phenomenal experience does not give the idea, this cause, but is necessary to the perception of it. Seeing the falling apple was necessary in order that Newton might perceive gravity. No one gains the idea, right, until he perceives right acts. Phenomena condition the perception of noumena. Without phenomena we can not know noumena.

3. *A capability to perceive necessary realities.* A being not endowed with noumenal-perception might know phenomena but could never cognize noumena. Even the little child knows at once concrete space and concrete cause, just as it knows color and sound and odor. Self, as noumenal-perception, directly beholds concrete necessary realities. Your analysis gives you also the

Tests of Necessary Ideas.—How do we know a necessary idea? There are four safe tests:

1. *Self-evidence.* Self stands face to face with necessary realities. Mediate proofs are not only not needed—they are an insult to the mind. Think of attempting to prove that something made the apple fall! We *know* that we perceive these noumena. We do not and can not define our necessary ideas nor prove them. They are *self-evident.* Axioms are abstract necessary truths, elaborated from necessary ideas, and, like these ideas, are self-evident.

2. *Necessity.* The mind must start with something. There must be primary ideas before there can be secondary ones. Noumenal ideas must be, in order that phenomenal ideas may be, just as noumena must be that phenomena may be. Space must be, in order that extended objects may be. Mind must be, that thought may be. I must perceive the necessary reality, concrete being, before I can say, "He is." We perceive these foundation ideas to be ultimate and final. We discern their necessity in all knowing. They are *necessary* ideas.

3. *Universality.* Necessary ideas are accepted by all. One or more necessary ideas are present in each

act of the mind. Necessary ideas are the universal ideas that underlie and condition all other ideas.

4. *Independence.* Like a chemical element, a necessary idea is ultimate. A necessary idea can not be derived from other ideas. Each necessary idea is absolutely independent of other necessary ideas. An idea that is self-evident, necessary, universal, and independent, is a necessary idea.

Noumenal-Percepts are singular, concrete, necessary notions. Keep in mind that only our concrete notions are called percepts. I perceive this large tiger, but I do not perceive vertebrate. The notion, this tiger, is a sense-percept. I perceive self remembering the story of Tell, but I do not perceive abstract memory. The idea, this memory, is a conscious-percept. I perceive that heat causes this water to boil, but I do not perceive that every effect must have a cause. The idea, this cause, is a noumenal-percept. Sense-percepts, conscious-percepts, and noumenal-percepts, are individual concrete notions. We perceive the concrete, not the abstract; the individual, not the general. Noumenal-percepts are concrete notions of necessary realities.

We perceive the individual, not the general. I perceive this space, not infinite space; this cause, not universal cause; this time, not eternity; this infinity, not the unlimited. What a world of confusion would be avoided by heeding this plain psychological fact! Noumenal-percepts are concrete notions of necessary entities and necessary relations. Most of the designations of these ideas are now merely historic. The following are some of the

Names.— {
Noumenal-Percepts, or Noumenal-Intuitions.
Necessary Ideas, or *a priori* Ideas.
First Truths, or Necessary Truths, or Intuitions.
Categorical Ideas, or Regulative Ideas.
Innate Ideas, or Connate Ideas.
}

Through the centuries these expressions have confused philosophers, but need not now confuse you. You find that you are endowed with the capability to know intuitively substances and necessary relations. You call the concrete ideas thus gained noumenal-percepts, or noumenal-intuitions, or necessary ideas. Perhaps, for the present, it will be well to disregard the other names. Later you will be interested in tracing their history. Necessary judgments, elaborated from necessary ideas, are called axioms, first truths, and necessary truths.

Necessary Realities, Necessary Ideas, Necessary Judgments.—You need to clearly distinguish these expressions. To help you to do so, this connected view is given:

1. *Necessary realities* are the realities that make phenomena possible. Mind, matter, cause, space, time, infinity, truth, beauty, right, and a few other realities, are classed as necessary realities because they must be in order that phenomena may be.

2. *Necessary ideas* are our immediate notions of necessary realities. My notion, this space, is necessary to my knowing that the table is here and the stove there. My idea, this space, is a necessary idea. Our elementary notions of necessary realities are termed necessary ideas because they underlie and condition all other ideas.

3. *Necessary judgments* are truths elaborated from necessary ideas. Cold *causes* this water to congeal. My idea, this cause, is a necessary idea; but, that every effect must have a cause, is a necessary judgment, a necessary truth. Axioms are necessary truths elaborated from necessary ideas.

Tree of Necessary Ideas.*—As the tree of life bore twelve kinds of fruit, so this tree bears twelve kinds of necessary ideas. These ideas are involved in all knowing. Self, as noumenal-perception, immediately knows these ideas in individual and concrete cases. Self, as reason, infers general truths from particular truths.

* Bascom's enumeration of necessary ideas is adopted.

NOUMENAL-PERCEPTION, OR NOUMENAL-INTUITION.

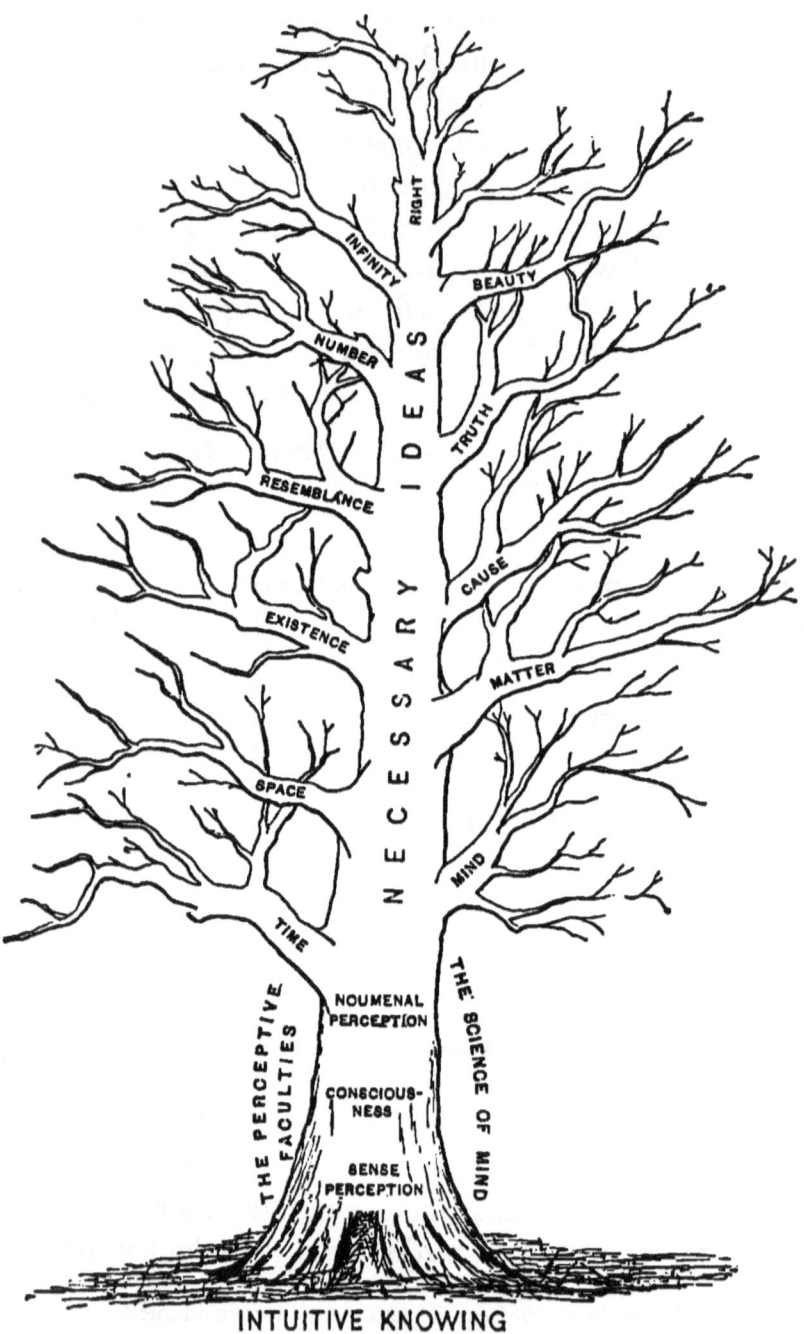

Axioms are necessary truths generalized. You will critically apply the four tests given above, and remove from the tree spurious fruit.

Build on the Rock.—Truth must be seen with sunlight clearness. You can afford to linger here. A few hours of penetrating thought may save you from a life of groping.

1. *Space.* I walk a mile. What is this through which I walk and in which all things are? The child perceives the idea, *where things are*, and learns to call this reality space. As space is not a phenomenon, we can not gain the idea through outer or inner-perception. As space is elementary, we can not infer this idea from other ideas. Self, as noumenal-perception, knows immediately this space, and this, and this. Let us try the four tests: (1) I stand face to face with this space. I know that I perceive this space; this is self-evidence. (2) That things may be, space must be. Space is a necessary reality. (3) I think of things as in space. Everything is somewhere. The space-idea pervades all thinking—is universal. (4) I find it impossible to derive this idea from other ideas, just as it is impossible to derive gold from the baser metals. Space is a necessary reality, and the space-idea is a necessary idea. Most of the axioms of geometry are intuitive truths generalized from space-percepts.

2. *Time.* I take the train at Philadelphia and go to New York. I spend from breakfast to dinner with a friend. What passes? "Mamma, you stayed a long time." The child has the idea—time. How did it gain this idea? You answer that the child intuitively perceives this time, and this, when its experiences involve

time. You reason as follows: The idea, this time, must be a phenomenal-percept, a specific truth under some general truth, or a noumenal-percept. It is not a phenomenal truth. No one claims that it is a specific idea under some general idea. We can not avoid the conclusion: the idea, this time, is a noumenal-percept. Apply the four tests of necessary ideas. What kind of truths are the axioms of algebra? Is an axiom a necessary idea or a necessary truth?

3. *Existence.* The mountain is—exists. *It is* is the only affirmation applicable to everything. That existence is a necessary idea will be readily seen. Indeed, this idea seems to underlie all other ideas. Self, as noumenal-perception, intuitively knows things as existing. Prove that the notion "concrete existence" is a necessary idea.

4. *Right.* The bad boy strikes his mother. His little sister says to him, "You ought not—wrong; naughty." The child reads the story of the good Samaritan: its "bad Pharisee" and "good Samaritan" show that the child has the idea of right and wrong. In fact, whenever the child observes acts involving right, it at once perceives the idea of right. From experience and education it finds out what is right, and soon learns to say, "That is right." Show that the notion "concrete right" is a necessary idea.

5. *Beauty.* "The babe is beautiful." The child perceives something pleasing in things. Before it learns to say "Beautiful bird!" it knows concrete beauty. Self, as sense-perception, sees the yellow primrose, and, as noumenal-perception, knows it as beautiful. Apply to beauty the tests of necessary ideas.

6. *Truth.* The blood circulates. The earth is spherical. These are statements of truths, for they assert realities. Arnold was a traitor. This is true—it asserts a fact. Washington was a traitor. This is not true—it asserts a falsehood. The child intuitively beholds the truth-idea in individual truths.

7. *Matter.* I press the table; it resists me. I see that it has extension. I find that I can move it. I place it on the scales; it has weight. The enduring thing having these attributes I learn to call matter. Self, as sense-perception, knows immediately physical phenomena. Self, as noumenal-perception, knows immediately matter—things having properties. It is self-evident that the substance sugar *must* be, in order that the property sweet *may* be. We know things as having attributes. I see the tree. This mental act involves sense-perception, for I intuitively cognize the tree as tall and green. It involves self-consciousness, for I cognize self perceiving the tall, green tree. It also involves noumenal-perception, for I intuitively cognize the entity, which is tall and green, as a material substance.

8. *Mind.* I think, I admire, I decide. I am conscious of thinking, feeling, willing. That mental acts *may* be, a mental entity *must* be.

> " I think we are not wholly brain,
>   Magnetic mockeries; casts in clay;
> Let science prove we are, and then
>   What matters science unto men ? "

I know by direct insight that the noumenon underlies the phenomenon. The spirit entity that thinks, I intuitively know as self. I perceive self thinking, feeling, and willing. I am conscious of noumenal-intuition just as I am conscious of sense-intuition. "I am, therefore I think," is the true psychology. "The mind," says Wundt, "is the entity that reasons."

9. *Cause.* Why does the ball fall? The child says, "Cause." Why does the clock tick? "Cause." The child notices changes, and asks you, "What makes the changes?" You answer, "Cause." That effects *may* be, cause *must* be. Causation is a necessary idea. We perceive concrete cause, and think the general: "Every effect must have a cause." The idea, this cause, is intuitive. As mind originates activity—possesses spontaneity—we may say that a mind is a self-cause. The absolute self-cause is God.

10. *Number.* Is number a necessary idea? Try it. In case you remove number from the truth-tree, endeavor to replace it by a genuine necessary idea. How will liberty do? How do you like spontaneity?

11. *Resemblance.* The likeness in the two things observed is not in the one or in the other. Every case of comparison is but an application of the idea—resemblance. As experience can not give the idea, and as it can not be a product of induction, we class resemblance as one of our necessary ideas.

12. *Infinity.* Take $\frac{1}{3} = \cdot 3333333 +$; however far I carry the process, I know I do not and can not reach a limit. I perceive this infinity. Take two parallel lines. I extend them two feet. They are still the same distance apart. I have the direct insight that they would never meet, however far extended. Intuitively I know this infinity. I imagine a limit to space. What lies beyond? Space. Space is its own environment. Space is self-related. Space is limitless. Space is infinite.

Show that you intuitively know infinite time and infinite cause.

Noumenal-Perception defined.—Self, as noumenal-perception, perceives necessary ideas. This is about all that can be said. The fact is so simple that we can find nothing simpler into which to resolve it.

1. *Noumenal-perception is the mental power to gain intuitively concrete necessary ideas.* It is understood that noumenal-perception is an ultimate endowment of the soul, and that we perceive necessary ideas only in the singular and in the concrete.

2. *Original.* You have done your best to understand this faculty. Now embody your conclusion in a good definition.

Various Definitions.*—1. BASCOM: The capability to know directly intuitive ideas. 2. SCHUYLER: The power of apprehending necessary ideas. 3. LAWS: Noumenal-intuition is the power to know immediately and instantly noumenal ideas. 4. HOPKINS: The power to know immediately first ideas. 5. PORTER: The power to acquire first ideas intuitively. 6. HAMILTON: The power the mind has of being the native source of *a priori* cognitions. 7. WHITE: Intuition is the power to know directly and immediately necessary relations; as, space, time, being, substance, cause, design, etc.

Agnosticism.—To know is to be certain of something. No mysticism must be admitted into the operations of

---

* *Explanatory.*—In these definitions the expression *necessary truth* is used in the sense of *necessary idea*. To avoid confusion we have substituted "ideas" for "truths" in the following definitions. A necessary truth is a generalization from necessary ideas. We perceive necessary ideas, and elaborate them into necessary truths. The notion that these equals added to these give equal sums, is a necessary idea; but the generalization that equals added to equals give equal sums, is a necessary truth. We gain necessary ideas intuitively, but infer necessary truths. Axioms are necessary truths, not necessary ideas. The distinction is deemed important.

the intellect. We begin with certainty, and not doubt. We know ourselves thinking and perceiving material objects. Not only do all men admit necessary ideas, but they *must*. Agnosticism is intellectual suicide. Only "cranks" deny their own existence. "We know matter as existing, but we also know, and this directly, that it has relations to other things known, that it is in space, and that there is causation in its action. We also know mind as existing, and we know it to have being, potency, spirituality, and relations to things." Endowed with intuition, we build on the rock. "Philosophy," says Carlyle, "can bake no bread; but she can procure for us God, freedom, and immortality." Psychology can build no railroads, but she can give us certainty. A knowledge of our own capabilities renders agnosticism impossible.

Growth of Noumenal-Perception.—Each act of sense-perception involves noumenal-perception. I perceive, not abstract properties, but things having properties. I perceive, not abstract mental acts, but self knowing, feeling, acting. Thus it is evident that the child gains necessary ideas as involved in the perception of phenomena. They are seen dimly at first. While all men accept and act upon necessary ideas, few distinctly state them to themselves. No one denies his own existence, or that he is in space, or that he grows old, but few grasp distinctly and fully these ideas. This power, though early active, is probably the latest of all the faculties in reaching full activity and development. These necessary or ultimate ideas seem to develop in the following order: Our first noumenal-percepts are concrete notions of objective realities. We know things having properties. The ideas, time and space, appear in connection with our ideas of things. Next we observe change, and directly gain the cause-idea. Next we gain the idea—law—through our knowledge of the uniform ways in which energies act. Finally, we gain the idea—this unity—from our knowledge of the co-ordination of things. Thus, step by step, we advance to the conception of the universe as the perfect unity. Tennyson, holding the tiny flowering plant, well expresses this idea:

" I pluck you out of the crannies;
  Hold you here, root and all, in my hand,
  Little flower—but if I could understand
  What you are, root and all, all in all,
  I should know what God and man is."

SUGGESTIVE STUDY-HINTS.

Review.—Place on the board your diagram of conscious-perception, and also the diagram of sense-perception. Compare by topics with your analyses of noumenal-perception.

What is meant by noumenal-perception? by noumena?

Mention the names applied to noumenal-perception. Which name do you prefer? Why? Give the distinction between noumena and phenomena. Illustrate. Give the etymology of noumenon and the meaning of noumena. Why do we use this hard word?

What do you mean by necessary ideas? Name several necessary ideas. Prove that time is a necessary idea.

Analyze two of your acts of noumenal-perception. What do you discover?

Name the three conditions of cognizing necessary ideas. State the first test of a necessary idea. Illustrate. Give the second test and illustrate. Give the third; the fourth.

What is a noumenal-percept? Are percepts general or particular notions? Illustrate. Give some of the names applied to noumenal percepts. Explain. Criticise the expression "innate ideas." Are powers innate? Are all ideas acquired?

Place the tree of necessary ideas on the board. Test the fruit. State the author's definition of noumenal-perception; your definition; definition of Dr. Laws; Hamilton's definition; White's definition.

Show that agnosticism disappears in the light of the true psychology. What is agnosticism? Why do some persons claim to be agnostics? Is absolute agnosticism possible?

Letter.—You will need to explain and illustrate very clearly. Though not more difficult to understand than sense-perception, your friend may not be familiar with noumenal-perception, and will need very full explanations.

Topical Analysis of Chapter VIII.—Noumenal-Perception.

I. Position.
    3. Noumenal-perception.
    2. Conscious-perception.
    1. Sense-perception.

II. Names.
    Noumenal-perception.   Truth-perception.
    Noumenal-intuition.   Intuition, common-sense,
    Rational-perception, or reason.   etc.

III. Conditions of Cognizing Noumena.
    Objective reality.   Noumenal-perception.
    Phenomena.

IV. Tests of Necessary Ideas.
    Self-evidence.   Universality.
    Necessity.   Independence.

V. Noumenal-percepts.
    Definition.
    Marks .... { Singular notions.
                      Concrete notions.
                      Notions of necessary realities.
    Names.
        Noumenal-percepts and necessary ideas.
        Noumenal-intuitions and ultimate ideas.
        Necessary truths and first truths.
        A priori ideas and intuitions.
        Innate ideas and connate ideas.
        Categorical ideas, etc.

VI. **First Truths (grouped by Bascom).**

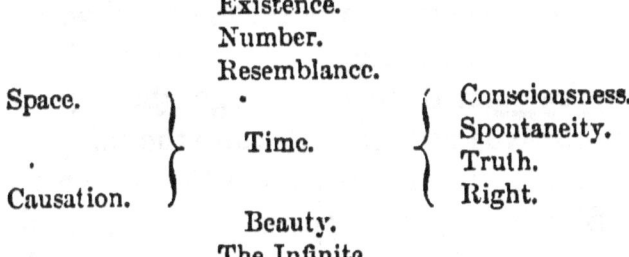

      Existence.
      Number.
      Resemblance.
 Space.   Consciousness.
      Time.   Spontaneity.
             Truth.
 Causation.   Right.
      Beauty.
      The Infinite.

VII. **Noumenal-perception defined.**
 Author's definition. Various definitions.
 Original definition.

VIII. **Agnosticism.**
 Define.   Disprove.

IX. **Growth and Development of Noumenal-perception.**
 1. Time. 2. Means. 3. Methods.

CHAPTER IX.

PERCEPTIVE KNOWING—GENERAL VIEW.

Perceptive Knowing is simply Direct Insight.—Self stands face to face with noumena as well as with phenomena. I do not prove to you that the sun is bright, that you despise cowards, or that something makes the apple fall. You know these things at once. All immediate concrete knowing is intuitive. Perceptive knowing is intuitive knowing, is immediate knowing, is presentative knowing, is simple cognition.

Names.—
 Perceptive Knowing.
 Presentative Knowing.
 Intuitive Knowing.
 Simple Cognition.

The Perceptive Faculties are the Capabilities to know immediately.—Because we are endowed with direct insight, these powers are called intuitive faculties. As we acquire immediate knowledge, these are also called the acquisitive faculties. Because the things known are made present, some term these the presentative faculties. Simple cognitive powers is also a good name, as these faculties give us knowledge in its simplest form.

Names.— { The Perceptive Powers.
The Intuitive Powers.
The Acquisitive Powers.
The Presentative Powers.
The Simple Cognitive Powers. }

We perceive Noumena as well as Phenomena.—We have direct insight into the matter-world, the mind-world, and the world of necessary realities. We are endowed with three intuitive powers, each opening to us a distinct world. In each perceptive act each of the three forms of perception supplements the others.

The Perceptive Faculties.— { Sense-Perception.
Conscious-Perception.
Noumenal-Perception. }

Sense-Perception is the Capability to gain Elementary Sense-Knowledge.—We acquire knowledge through the senses. Sense-perception is the best possible name for this faculty. As we know at once the outer world, this faculty is properly called outer-perception, external-perception, and objective-perception. Perception is brief but indefinite.

Names.— { Sense-Perception.   Objective-Perception.
Outer-Perception.   Perception.
External-Perception. }

Consciousness is the Capability to perceive Self acting.—I have direct insight into the mind-world. I perceive myself knowing, feeling, willing. Because we have direct insight into the inner-world, this faculty is called inner-perception. As we know immediately mental phenomena, this power is also termed conscious-perception and conscious-intuition. The mind looks on itself working, hence Kant named this capability apperception. McCosh calls it self-consciousness. To correspond with objective-perception, some name it subjective-perception. Each name has its merits, but self-consciousness and conscious-perception are preferred.

Names.—
{
Consciousness and Conscious-Perception.
Inner-Perception.
Self-Consciousness.
Conscious-Intuition.
Ap-Perception.
Subjective-Perception.
}

Noumenal-Perception is the Capability to know intuitively Necessary Realities.—Noumena means the ultimate and the necessary. Such ultimate realities as space, time, cause, are noumena. "Noumenon," says Herbert Spencer, "is the antithesis of phenomenon. Appearance without reality is unthinkable. Noumenon is necessary actuality." Because we have direct insight into the necessary truth-world, this faculty is called truth-perception. As we know at once necessary ideas, some call this power intuition, or rational-intuition. In this sense, intuition is indefinite and misleading. Each perceptive faculty is an intuitive faculty. Sense-intuition, conscious-intuition, and noumenal-intuition, are correct and definite names. This faculty is also called reason and rational-perception, because rational beings alone perceive necessary realities. But, as reason is now almost uniformly used to designate the power of inference, these names are objectionable. Noumenal-perception and noumenal-intuition are unobjectionable.

Names.— $\begin{cases} \text{Noumenal-Perception.} \\ \text{Noumenal-Intuition and Intuition.} \\ \text{Truth-Perception.} \\ \text{Rational-Perception and Reason.} \end{cases}$

Products of Perceptive Knowing.—Self gains some ideas at once. These singular, concrete ideas are percepts. As we gain these ideas by direct insight, they are called intuitions. As these ideas are the elements of all knowing, they are simple cognitions.

Names.— $\begin{cases} \text{Percepts.} \\ \text{Intuitions.} \\ \text{Simple Cognitions.} \end{cases}$

Classes of Percepts.—A mind acts as a unit. Each mental power is supplemented by all the other powers of the soul. A mental product results from self acting in all his capabilities. We are conscious of our noumenal as well as of our phenomenal perceiving. Through phenomena we perceive noumena, and we perceive noumena as necessary to phenomena. Still, our elementary ideas form these well-marked groups. Those gained through the senses are sense-ideas, or sense-percepts; those gained through consciousness are conscious-ideas, or conscious-percepts; and those gained through noumenal-perception are noumenal-ideas, or noumenal-percepts.

Percepts.— $\begin{cases} \text{Sense-Percepts.} \\ \text{Conscious-Percepts.} \\ \text{Necessary Truths.} \end{cases}$

Intuitions.— { Phenomenal { Sense-Intuitions.
                                { Conscious-Intuitions.
                 { Noumenal—Necessary Ideas.

1. *Sense-percepts* are simple cognitions of material objects. We perceive material objects as external, extended, and as exerting force.

2. *Conscious-percepts* are simple cognitions of self acting. We perceive self existing and exerting power.

3. *Noumenal-percepts* are simple cognitions of necessary realities. We perceive necessary entities and necessary relations. Our concrete notions of these necessary realities gained by direct-insight are termed noumenal-percepts. Nothing could be plainer. Strange, that antiquated darkness and misleading theories should so long hide the truth! But modern psychologists have brushed away the cobwebs. It is the old story of Columbus and the egg.

SUGGESTIVE STUDY-HINTS.

Place the diagrams of sense-perception, conscious-perception, and noumenal-perception side by side on a sheet of paper, or on blackboards. Compare them topic by topic.

With the diagrams before you, study Chapter IX. Do not for a moment lose sight of the fact that self acts as a unit. Dr. Laws insists that the *intuitive faculty* is simple in its nature but complex in its functions, and presents it as follows:

Intuition.— { Phenomenal-Intuition. { Sense-Perception.
                                        { Consciousness.
              { Noumenal-Intuition.

Some writers claim that sense-perception and consciousness give us noumenal as well as phenomenal percepts. To me it seems every way better to treat each perceptive function as a distinct faculty.

References.—Those wishing fuller information are referred to Porter's "Human Intellect"; Sully's "Psychology"; McCosh's "Pyschology"; Hopkins's "Outline Study of Man"; Bascom's "Science of Mind," etc.

PART III.

THE REPRESENTATIVE POWERS.

CHAPTER X.—Memory.
      XI.—Phantasy.
      XII.—Imagination.
      XIII.—Representation.—General View.

PSYCHOLOGICAL PYRAMID.

	THE WILL.	THE WILL POWERS.		
THE CAPABILITIES OF THE MIND.	THE FEELINGS.	THE EMOTIONS.		
		THE PHYSICAL FEELINGS.		
		THE INSTINCTS.		
	THE INTELLECTUAL FACULTIES.	THE THINKING POWERS.		
		THE REPRESENTATIVE POWERS.	IMAGINATION. PHANTASY. MEMORY.	IDEALS. PHANTASMS. MEMORIES.
		THE PERCEPTIVE POWERS.	NOUMENAL-PERCEPTION. CONSCIOUS-PERCEPTION. SENSE-PERCEPTION.	NOUMENAL-PERCEPTS. CONSCIOUS-PERCEPTS. SENSE-PERCEPTS.

PRODUCTS.

THIRD PART.

THE REPRESENTATIVE POWERS.

By these we mean our capabilities to *re*present our experiences in old or new forms. Now you stand beneath the fragrant orange-tree, and see and handle and smell and taste its delicious fruit. You present, or *make present*, to yourself the orange-tree, with its environments. Weeks have passed. An orange-blossom in a bouquet suggests that orange-tree. You see yourself again standing beneath the tree and enjoying its fragrant fruit. You *re*present, or *make present again*, to yourself the orange-tree. The power to *re*present things to yourself just as you presented them the first time is called *memory*. You fall asleep. You see yourself standing beneath an orange-tree. The fruit is pure gold. You fill your basket with gold oranges, and dream of boundless wealth. The picture seems to you an objective reality. The power thus spontaneously to *re*present things to yourself, changed but seeming to be realities, is called *phantasy*. You plan an orange-grove. All the rows are circles. In the midst you place a lovely cottage for yourself, "with one fair spirit for your minister." The power to thus intentionally *re*present your experiences, modified into ideals, is called *imagination*.

The Representative Faculties.—{ Memory. Phantasy. Imagination. }

You recall the landscape just as you saw it; self, as *memory*, recalls. You drift into dream-land, linking fancy unto fancy; self, as *phantasy*, builds air-castles. You plan an ideal cottage; self, as *imagination*, creates ideals. Our representative faculties are our powers to reproduce and change the forms of our acquisitions.

CHAPTER X.

MEMORY.

By this is meant the power to reproduce our acquisitions just as we experienced them. Years ago you saw an eclipse of the sun. Now you reproduce the scene exactly as you perceived it. You say you *re*member. Yesterday you felt angry. You are now conscious of the fact that you were angry, and of the insulting note that occasioned your anger. You recall your past experience.

Acts of Memory analyzed.—Some time since I attended a lecture on the solar spectrum. I now recall the spectrum as it appeared on the canvas. I recall the lecturer, and myself enjoying the lecture. The whole scene, just as presented, is again made present— is *re*presented. Thus recall your visit to your childhood home; your first teacher. What do you do when you remember?

Elements of Acts of Memory.—You discover in a complete act of memory four elements—retention, recollection, association, and recognition.

1. *Self, as memory, stores his acquisitions.* I know the multiplication-table. I do not keep it in consciousness, but I can recall it at will. This element of memory is called retention. I meet a stranger; some resemblance calls to mind a friend. That some characteristic of that friend was retained seems a reasonable inference. Otherwise, how could the resemblance suggest the friend? How these keys of memory are kept we have no means of knowing. The mind is not Plato's tablet, nor Cicero's storehouse. Neural changes, fleeting as the ripples on the bosom of the lake, give no hint of past mental acts. That self, as memory, in some unknown way *retains* so as to be able to recall his acquisitions, is all we can yet say.

2. *Self, as memory, reproduces his experiences.* I was conscious of seeing General Grant. I am now conscious of recalling that experience. Again the silent man is present. This element of memory is termed recollection, reproduction, or remembrance. It is the essential element, and hence is often used as equivalent to memory.

3. *Self, as memory, restores things with their associations.* The rose with its fragrance, the singer with the song, the lover with his love, Grant with his staff, are *re*presented just as they were presented. The magic changes wrought by phantasy and imagination are absolutely distinct from the work of memory. Here past experiences with all the objective conditions are *re*presented without change. This element of memory is called *association*, because things with their associations are made again present.

4. *Self, as memory, identifies memories and experiences.* I recall my visit to Niagara; I recognize the remembrance as a former experience. I meet an acquaintance; I *recognize* him. This element of memory is called recognition. The soul retains the keys to its acquisitions. Present mental acts, by means of these keys, restore the past. The object, with its environments, is *re*presented. Finally, the remembrances are recognized as identical with former experiences. The act of memory is complete. You may distinguish the four elements of memory in the following lines:

"How dear to my heart are the scenes of my childhood,
   When fond recollection (*re*)presents them to view!"

Office of Memory.—Self, as memory, stores, reproduces, and recognizes his experiences. This, in the mental economy, is the sole function of memory. What was originally present in consciousness is made present again—is *re*presented. Memory is the mind remembering past experiences. Retention, association, and recognition are incident to complete reproduction, and are merely elements of memory.

It is the function of memory to reproduce all forms of knowledge, and to know the representations as former acquisitions. Memory utilizes the results of all previous cognitions. Without memory, we should be as oblivious of the past as we are ignorant of the future.

Characteristics of Memory.—You can readily distinguish between memory and other faculties by noting two marked peculiarities of this power of the soul:

1. *Self, as memory, recalls the past.* Take away memory, and all the past would be a blank. Memory is our only power to make the past reappear.

2. *Memory identifies.* Memory links the present with the past, and thus we maintain our personal identity. Memory identifies recollections as former experiences.

3. *Memory enters into all mental activity.* Self, as consciousness, unitizes all mental acts; self, as memory, treasures and recalls all. Like attention and consciousness, memory enters into all knowing, all feeling, all willing. You attend. You perceive the coming train. You hasten with throbbing heart to meet a long-absent brother. You are conscious of each act. Years pass. Now you vividly *re*present the scene. You are now conscious of recalling a past experience. Thus is woven the web of mental life.

Memory defined.—The soul is endowed with powers or faculties. Wundt tells us that "faculties are distinct modes of psychical activity." Sense-perception is self perceiving material things. Memory is self recalling past acquisitions:

1. *Memory is the power to store and reproduce experiences.* We recall our acquisitions in the old forms in which we experienced them, and we recognize them as former experiences.

2. *Original.* Put your conception of memory in your own words. Until made your own, and translated into your own language, the thoughts of others are oftener an injury than a benefit. So familiar seems to you the memory notion that there is danger of superficial work.

3. **Various Definitions.**—MANSEL: Memory is the power of the mind to reproduce its own acts. SCHUYLER: Memory is the power to recall previous cognitions. BASCOM: Memory is the power of recalling the phenomena of consciousness. McCOSH: Memory is self remembering. WHITE: Memory is the power to reknow objects previously known. EVERETT: Memory is the power to reproduce and recognize former knowledge.

Memory-Knowledge.—The products of memory are called memories, recollections, remembrances. "Memories of other days," "sweet recollections," and "kind remembrances," are some of our most familiar expressions. Original mental products are called percepts, concepts, ideals, and judgments. Memory-products are termed *re*-percepts, *re*-concepts, and *re*-judgments:

1. *A remembered percept is a re-percept.* Yesterday I saw a dove. Self, as sense-perception, intuitively formed the percept—this dove. To-day I recall this

percept. Again the dove is present. The idea—this dove—is now a remembered percept, a *re*-percept.

2. *A remembered concept is a re-concept.* From the percepts, this triangle, and this, and this, I discern the general notion, three-angledness. I embody this abstract general notion or concept in the word triangle. When I recall the concept triangle it is a remembered concept, a *re*-concept.

3. *Memories are intellectual products.* Emotions and volitions are strung on ideas, as pearls on threads of gold. Last week a friend did me a kind act. I perceived the kind act and felt gratitude. I now recall that kind act, and also the fact that I felt gratitude. The *re*-percept—that kind act—occasions a feeling of gratitude, but it is a new feeling. We can not make present again past feelings or past volitions. We recall intellectual products only. Memories are intellectual products.

Experiences and Memories.—We recall our former experiences. Our remembrances are unmodified transcripts of our experiences. Memory *re*presents acquisitions in the old forms of experience. Some relations, however, deserve careful study:

1. *Remembrances suggest but do not resemble the original objects.* The soul creates the mental objects which it recalls. The landscape, the odor, the song, are remembered as former experiences. There is a correspondence, but we can make no comparison between a percept or *re*-percept and a material object. We do not form images of sounds, or odors, or flavors, or textures, or weights, or temperatures.

Sense-perception does not give copies of external

objects. Self interprets the qualities or signs of material objects and groups these into percepts. When recalled, these *re*-percepts suggest but do not resemble the original objects. By keeping this fact in mind you will avoid much error and confusion.

2. *Remembrances consist of fewer details than the original objects.* But these skeletons are better in most cases for thought purposes than the real objects. The mind seizes on the essentials, and is not confused by multitudinous details. In thought and imagination we deal with our revived *notions* of things.

3. *Remembrances ordinarily awaken less intense emotion than experiences.* Some are more deeply affected by recollections than others, because of their ability to reproduce more vividly past experiences. Some even intensify memories by thought and imagination, and thus deepen the feelings. But, as a rule, memories create less and less emotion, until we are able to contemplate even the death of a mother with composure.

Attention, Consciousness, and Memory.—Penetrating and prolonged attention gives clear consciousness and good memory. These three activities enter into all distinct mental work. Self, as attention, concentrates his efforts; self, as consciousness, perceives himself knowing, feeling, and willing; self, as memory, reproduces without change his past acquisitions. We are conscious of what is passing around us and within us when we give attention. We remember only those things of which we have been conscious. Slight attention, dim consciousness, and faulty memory go together. The more complete the attention the more distinct will be the consciousness and the more tenacious will be the memory.

Laws of Memory.

A law is a uniform way in which an energy acts. The uniform ways in which the soul acts in recalling past acquisitions are called the laws of memory. It is not an accident that I remember this and not that. Law reigns in the world of mind. Three memory-laws are well recognized: the law of the brain, the law of acquisition, and the law of suggestion.

I. Law of the Brain.—*Memory depends on the condition of the brain.* When my brain is in good condition, I remember readily; but when tired out, or suffering from a severe attack of sick-headache, I recollect with difficulty and very imperfectly. The Rev. John Applegate received a blow which indented a small portion of his skull. For a year the past was blotted out, but, as soon as the indented portion of the skull was removed, he remembered as he did before receiving the injury. Each one can verify this law by his own experience and observation. However explained, we can not deny the fact that good digestion favors good memory.

1. *Vigorous health* is the first requirement of the law of the brain. As a rule, the cerebrum, the immediate organism through which the mind acts, is a fit instrument for mental activity in the ratio of physical vigor. It is certain that good memory and good health are closely related. Other things being equal, the better your physical condition, the better will be your memory.

2. *Frequent change* is the second requirement of the law of the brain. Different mental acts call into activity different ganglionic areas. The study of physical science calls into activity some portions of the cerebrum, while mathematics, literature, and art call into activity other parts. A profound physiological and psychical law underlies the practice of all schools, from the primary to the university,

in giving daily lessons in each of the four great departments named. Thus all the mental faculties are judiciously exercised, and different ganglia are successively called into activity. Continually thinking on one subject inflames the portion of the brain so overworked. Memory, as well as thought, becomes confused. It is not so much the wear of a single effort, but it is the monotonous beat upon beat, stroke upon stroke, always in the same place. As drops of water wear away stones, so a long series of reiterated mental blows will shiver the golden bowl.

3. *Effort must stop short of exhaustion* is the third requirement of the law of the brain. Exhaustion weakens. Nearly all the evil effects of hard study come from carrying effort to exhaustion. Let the student work vigorously for forty minutes, and rest and recreate twenty minutes out of each hour. He will grow stronger, and will in the end learn double as much as the student who pores over his books hour after hour. Memory will become accurate and distinct. Most young children in our schools suffer severe injury from the constant violation of this requirement. *A recess each hour, or some equivalent, is imperative.*

II. Law of Acquisition.—*The mind tends to recall what is thoroughly known.* Self tends to repeat his acts. What we have done we tend to do again. The mind tends to act as it has acted before. When we know things thoroughly we can recall them readily and accurately. Each repetition gives increased facility in recalling. Thus habits are formed.

1. *This law requires interested attention.* In order to know thoroughly, we must feel a deep interest in the subject and give our entire attention to its mastery. The more complete the attention, the greater the tendency to recall. We remember in the ratio of our attention. When we concentrate all our energies upon a subject and examine it closely for a considerable time, we *fix* the matter in our minds. Such acquisitions are readily recalled. The wise teacher creates and sustains intense interest, and thus secures complete attention and good memory. The wise student bends all his energies to the work in hand. What he thus acquires he knows thoroughly and recalls readily.

2. *This law requires vividness of apprehension.* The mind most readily recalls that which it vividly apprehends. What is indistinctly and partially grasped will soon be forgotten. The more vivid and complete the apprehension, the better will be the recollection. Listless persons are notorious for poor memories. Wide-awake persons rarely complain of forgetfulness.

3. *This law requires frequency of repetition.* What is often recalled, and in various relations, is easily reproduced. When the intervals are short, each repetition deepens the impression and strengthens the tendency to persist. The wise teacher makes each lesson a review of previous lessons. The wise student never becomes "rusty," but keeps his acquisitions bright by use. The old man remembers things of his childhood so vividly because he has reviewed them so often.

III. Law of Suggestion.—*Present experiences tend to suggest past experiences.* "By a wonderful process, which is sometimes called mental suggestion or association, we find that every thought and action in a long life links itself with some other thought or action. No mental act is completely isolated. No act, even of perception, takes place without associating itself with some previous thought, or suggesting a new one." *

Methods of association and suggestion. There are five ways in which experiences are associated, and in which ideas tend to suggest one another. "These seem to me to be original and irreducible; at least, no reduction of them can be made that will be of practical value. They will remain the separate working methods of suggestion, and must be studied as such." † By five circles we may fitly represent our experiences as linked together in five distinct ways. By having each circle cut all the other circles, it is intended to indicate the truth that the suggestion may occur in

* Fiske. † Hopkins.

any one of these five ways. The possibilities of recalling are thus multiplied many fold.

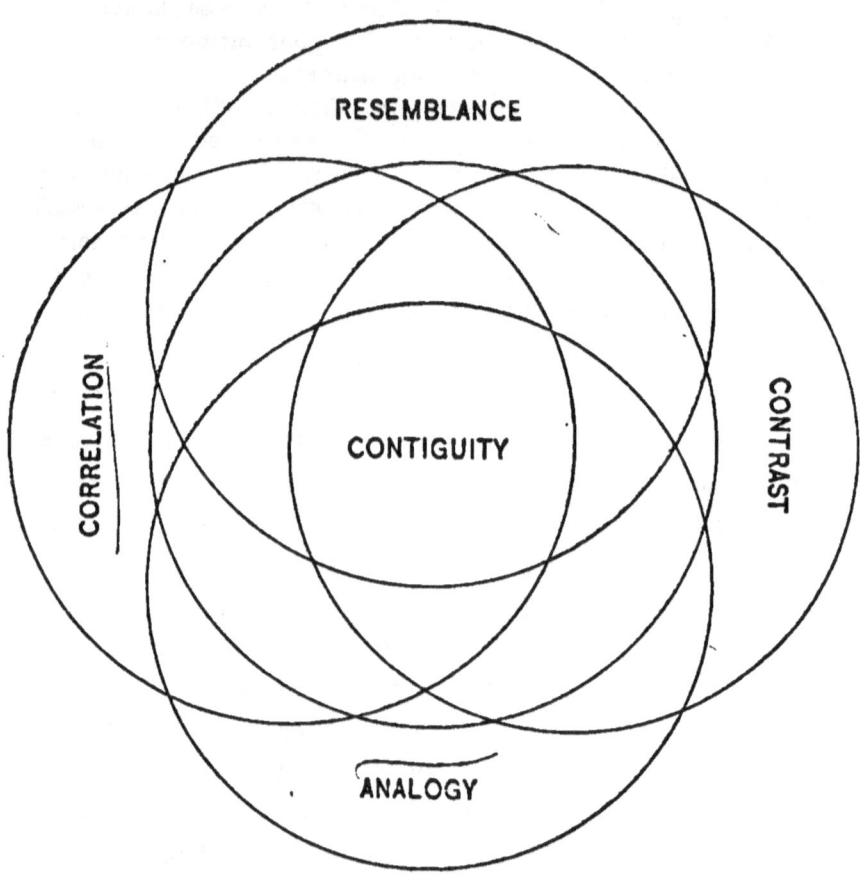

1. Resemblance.—*Resembling objects tend to bring up each other.* Like tends to recall like. This cottage reminds me of my childhood home. The youth I just met called back to mind my college friend. Similar sounds and odors and flavors and emotions tend to suggest each other. But it is needless to multiply examples. Each moment you may observe the workings of this law. You may give several illustrations from your own experience.

2. Contrast.—*Contrasted objects tend to bring up each other.* Dissimilars recall dissimilars. Darkness suggests light, pain suggests pleasure, evil suggests good, death suggests life. You may give examples in your own experience.

3. **Contiguity.**—*Experiences which occur together tend to suggest each other.* This is the great central method of association and suggestion. Places and things near together suggest each other. Versailles suggests Paris, Brooklyn suggests New York. Places also suggest events occurring at or near them. Philadelphia suggests the Declaration of Independence, West Point suggests Arnold's treason. Contiguous occurrences tend to bring up each other. Ideas which have been in the mind at the same time tend to recall each other. Experiences which occur together or in immediate succession tend to suggest each other. You see two persons together. The sight of one will tend to suggest the other. Association of words, of sounds, of thoughts, of forms occurring together are of this kind. Events occurring near together are thus associated. Waterloo suggests St. Helena. Of a group of contemporaneous events, each suggests the adjacent links, and so on. You may give illustrations from your experience.

4. **Correlation.**—*Correlated ideas tend to bring up each other.* Dependent and related ideas tend to suggest each other. The end suggests the means, the effect the cause, the conclusion the premises. Things related suggest each other. Signs suggest the signification, as the mathematical signs. The sword suggests power. What is suggested by the flag, the cross, the crown, the altar, the pulpit, the platform?

Certain sounds or sights have come to awaken in our minds ideas, and they are ideas which have been associated by the eye and by the ear. In other words, things seen and things heard suggest not themselves, but something else that stood in connection with them. Human language, whether spoken or written, is an extended illustration of this law of suggestion. We have come by this law to have certain thoughts arise in the mind when certain words are presented to us. There is no reason why *horse* should instantly bring up the picture of a horse, except that we have associated with that word that animal.

5. **Analogy.**—*Things analogous tend to bring up each other.* The river rolling on for ever suggests the endless flight of time; spring suggests youth, and winter old age. White suggests purity, and purple suggests royalty. Analogies more or less striking pervade the thought-world.

Marvelous, almost infinite, are the associations of ideas, emotions, actions. The law of suggestion works wonders, and the most wonderful of all is the power to call back to consciousness the experiences of a long life.

Forgetting.—It is a beneficent law that evil, painful, and unimportant things shall fade from memory. We refuse to recall what would give us pain or uselessly burden memory. This is the true Lethe. On the other hand, we live over and over again our joyful experiences, and they stay with us forever. Forgetting is as necessary to a happy life as remembering.

Growth of Memory.—The early activity of memory is a familiar fact. When a few weeks old the infant recognizes its nurse, and when a few months old it recognizes words as the signs of ideas. Objective, or concrete memory be-

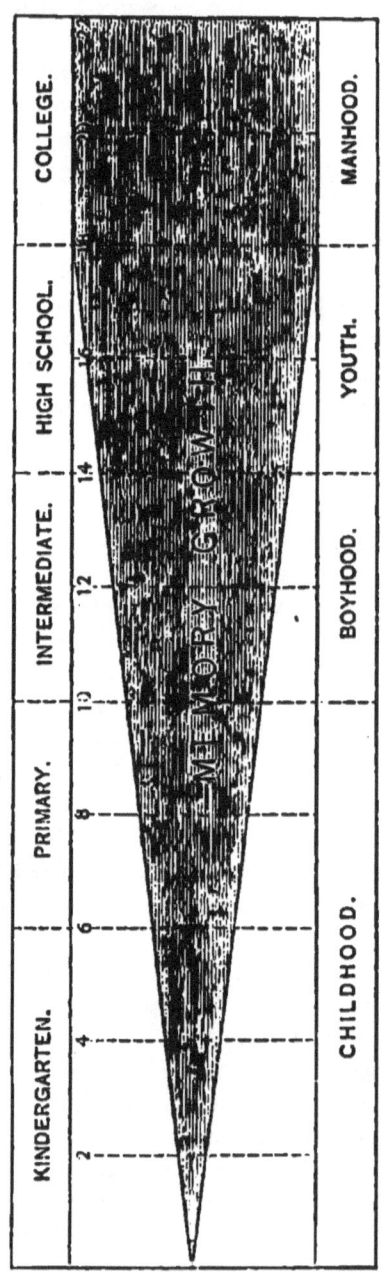

comes quite active during the second year, and reaches full activity about the tenth year. Childhood is peculiarly the time to cultivate concrete memory, or memory of things and concrete facts. About the tenth year the pupil begins to acquire and recall readily semi-abstractions, or the concrete and the abstract combined. By the fourteenth year abstract memory, or memory of classifications, principles, and inferences, is quite active, and seems to be fully active at eighteen. From the tenth year to the eighteenth year is pre-eminently the period for the higher forms of memory-culture. In manhood, memory is kept vigorous by use, and certainly may be greatly strengthened in special directions. Even the aged may, by systematic effort, keep memory strong. The tendency to live exiled in the past should be resisted. The world is full of new beauty and new truth. Let the aged keep *en rapport* with the present, and keep memory vigorous by constantly recalling recent acquisitions.

Development of Memory.*—We recall most readily what we apprehend most clearly. Persistent effort in faithfully reproducing our past experiences educates memory. A good memory is of incalculable value. It enables us to compare, combine, and firmly interlock past and present acquisitions. One with a poor memory gropes in the dark. Because he can not command his facts, he can not do effective thinking. Great men have almost invariably possessed great memories.

[As a magnet will increase its force if a slight increase is made daily to the weight it supports, so the memory of numbers, dates, facts, and principles may be indefinitely increased by committing

---

* See "Education of Memory" in "Applied Psychology and Teaching."

an additional one or two each day to memory, and taking care by frequent reviews that nothing once memorized shall escape. But equal care should be taken not to overburden the power of recollection by undertaking too many new items at a time. Let the student make a special effort with precisely the kind of recollection that he is most deficient in, be it names, dates, shapes, or whatever it be, and he will find that, by persistent practice for a few months, he can bring the special power to the front. The habit of attention to likeness and difference, so that the mind at once takes in the species and differentia involuntarily, is the habit that secures good memory.]

Systematic and persistent exercise in recalling tends to develop memory. A plan of work that secures such exercise may be called a method of educating this power. Good study and good teaching promote the growth of memory.

Comparative Psychology.—The brute associates impressions, and present impressions suggest to it former impressions. The brute recalls its past experiences. As animal experience is limited to the sensuous, so brute recollection is limited to recalling sensuous impressions. Impressions are vague intellectual products lower than ideas. That present impressions tend to suggest past impressions is the great law of brute memory.

SUGGESTIVE STUDY-HINTS.

Review.—Explain intuition. Why are the perceptive faculties called intuitive powers? Define each of the perceptive powers. Distinguish sense-percepts, conscious-percepts, and noumenal-percepts. Give two examples of each. Etc. Take your examples and illustrations largely from the studies you are now pursuing. One example from your own experience may be worth more to you than ten from other sources.

What is meant by representation? By representative powers? What other names are applied to these powers? Name the three representative faculties. Give an example of each activity.

Analyze an act of memory. What four points do you discover? Why do you call these elements of memory? Does each complete act of memory involve these elements?

Explain retention. Illustrate. What is retained? Explain recollection. Give synonyms. Illustrate. Explain association. Illustrate. Explain recognition. Give examples.

Describe the office of memory. What do you mean by the function of a faculty? What do you mean by a faculty? Give two characteristics of memory. Give a distinction between consciousness and memory.

State the author's definition of memory; your definition; Everett's definition.

Give synonyms of memories. Illustrate each. What is a percept? A re-percept? Why do you call recollections intellectual? Give three points of difference between experiences and memories.

What do you mean by energy? by soul-energies? by law? by laws of memory? Give the law of the brain. Give and explain its three requirements. Give the law of acquisition. Give and explain its three requirements.

Explain association and suggestion. Give the five ways in which ideas suggest each other. Illustrate by circles. Give the law of resemblance. Give three examples. Explain the law of contrast. Illustrate the law of contiguity. Give the law of correlation; also of analogy. Give examples of each.

What do you mean by the growth of memory? Explain the diagram showing the stages of memory-growth. What is meant by educating memory? How may you improve your memory?

Give your explanation of brute memory. How does brute memory differ from human memory?

State the law of forgetfulness. Why is it important to be able to forget? What should we forget? How do we forget?

Letter.—Show your friend that graphic and other devices are designed to aid him to gain clear views of self; but insist on his verifying everything for himself by constantly looking within. Try to interest him in the improvement of his memory.

Topical Analysis of Chapter X.—Memory.

I. Elements of Memory.
    Retention.   Representation.
    Recollection.   Recognition.

II. Office of Memory.

III. Characteristics of Memory.
    Memory reproduces.
    Memory attends all knowing.

IV. Memory Defined.
    Author's definition.   Various definitions.
    Original definition.

V. Memory-Knowledge.
    Names.
        Memories.   Recollections.   Remembrances.
    Re-percepts and Re-concepts.
    Intellectual products.

VI. Experiences and Memories.

VII. Memory and other faculties.

VIII. Laws of Memory.
    Law of the brain.
    Law of acquisition.
    Law of suggestion.
        Resemblance.   Contiguity.   Analogy.
        Contrast.   Correlation.
    Law of forgetting.

IX. Growth of Memory.
    In childhood.   In youth.   In manhood.

X. Development of Memory.
    Time.   Means.   Methods.

XI. Comparative Psychology.
    Human memory.   Brute memory.

CHAPTER XI.

PHANTASY.

By this is meant the power to represent spontaneously our experiences in new forms which seem to be realities. Without purpose, the soul weaves into curious shapes its experiences. Self, as phantasy, does not create ideals, but merely conjoins experiences in new ways.

The soul is ever active. Intentional activity exhausts the physical organism. The brain needs rest. When I cease to think, and float off into dream-land, the brain rests, recuperates, but the soul continues its ceaseless activity. Self for his own amusement images an endless panorama. In revery, as in sleep, an endless chain of phantom-forms is ever passing. These pictures we call phantasms, and the power to produce them we term phantasy.*

Self, as memory, reproduces his past experiences unchanged. However faint our recollections, we recognize them as past experiences. But, in revery and in dreams, our experiences, strangely modified, are *re*-presented. Memory and sensation furnish materials. Self,

---

* This form of representation has been slighted by many psychologists. Most have treated it as a phase of imagination. I consider phantasy a distinct form of representation. This view seems to me to greatly simplify the subject. This orthography is preferred, because phantasy in this sense is a definite term. Webster says: "A phantasm is an image formed by the mind and supposed to be real." Phantasy, as here used, is the power to form phantasms. Fancy, a contraction for phantasy, is now used in so many senses as to be extremely objectionable.

as phantasy, weaves the materials into grotesque and fantastic groups called phantasms. At the time these seem to us objective realities. They often seem so real that we are surprised to find them phantoms of our brains.

Acts of Phantasy Analyzed.—We are conscious of the acts of self as phantasy. We are able to recall and examine some of these acts. Nothing is more common than dream-telling. Let us examine a day-dream. I was resting in my easy-chair. I ceased all intentional effort, and my senses ceased to bring me messages from the outer world. I drift into revery-land. "A beautiful flower-garden surrounds me. A sparkling fountain is near me. Floating on the little lake are three swans. A bevy of lovely girls, seated in a boat, cheer me with laughter and song. One"—the door-bell aroused me, and the scene vanished. At the time all seemed real. When aroused, I knew that the picture was the work of phantasy. Relate a day-dream and also a night-dream. Show the work of phantasy.

Office of Phantasy.—Phantasy is the power to weave our experiences into phantasms.

1. *Self, as phantasy, aggregates his experiences.* In this form of representation self, as memory, merely recalls without recognizing experiences. Phantasy conjoins experiences, immediate and revived. The material is not analyzed; it is merely joined together, or aggregated. Phantasy *represents* experiences in new forms.

2. *Phantasy gives hints to memory, imagination, and thought.* In discerning class-notions, the vague, shadowy phantasm dimly outlines the concept. We see three-sidedness, but the corners are blurred. We see

the soldier, but shadows conceal his uniform and armor. Hints of phantasy doubtless help imagination to some of its grandest achievements. Phantasms often suggest realities.

3. *Phantasy is the safety-valve of the soul.* Death of brain-fiber follows each thought, emotion, and purpose. A few hours of vigorous study exhaust the working brain. The soul is ceaselessly active. Phantasy, we infer, acts through brain-areas not exhausted by intentional activity. While the working brain recuperates, the soul amuses itself with vivacious picture-groups.

Characteristics of Phantasy.—We study the phenomena of mental action in revery and dreams. We discover a new world called dream-land. We find that the soul is endowed with the capability to produce phantasms.

1. *Phantasy is undirected representation.* To give the weary brain rest, self, ceasing to acquire and direct, drifts off into the land of shadows. Spontaneously the mind forms grotesque and shadowy panoramas. Self, as phantasy, is a kaleidoscope.

2. *Phantasy is lawless representation.* The real world disappears and the shadowy world seems the real world. The soul feels joy or sorrow in view of these phantasms. The laws of time and place and sequence are ignored. The sea is crossed in a moment. Snow-castles are as warm as summer bowers.

3. *Phantasy is self-drifting.* We seem to be spectators. We see ourselves sicken and die. We attend our own funerals. We do not usually remember our dreams because we do not consciously connect the waking and the shadowy worlds. Self, as phantasy,

drifts, scribbles. The record is indistinct, for there is little or no attention. These phantasms are not worth preserving. They do not connect with our waking activities. They fade away like the morning mists. It is well.

4. *Phantasy pleases and refreshes.* It is the play faculty of the soul. When we are at peace with our stomachs, ourselves, our neighbors, and our Creator, we have refreshing sleep and pleasant dreams.

Phantasy Defined.—As phantasy, self blends the objective and subjective. The soul drifts. Without effort and without intention it links fancy unto fancy. During revery and sleep our phantasms seem to us to be objective realities. The products of phantasy are concrete, and have in all cases a material basis. Our phantasms are limited to our experiences. The phantasms of the blind are colorless; those of the deaf, soundless.

1. *Phantasy* is the capability of self to *re*present spontaneously his experiences in new forms called phantasms. A phantasm is a crude picture-group which seems to be an objective reality. At the time we are conscious of our phantasms, but not of self making them out of his revived experiences. As phantasy is the dominant activity in dreams and revery, this form of representation is called phantasy.

2. *Original.* Give your definition of this power. Try to sharply distinguish memory and phantasy.

3. **Various Definitions.**—PORTER: Phantasy is the power to bring before the mind images severed from all relations. SCHUYLER: Phantasy is the power to produce a series of images of which it is itself a spectator. HOPKINS: The soul as phantasy is the spontaneous source of reveries and dreams. WHITE: Phantasy is the power to spontaneously make phantasms which seem realities.

Relations of Phantasy to the other Faculties.—The psychologist ventures modestly here. The phantom-world is the real wonder-land. Many problems remain unsolved.

1. *Phantasy and memory.* Self, as memory, revives his experiences; self, as phantasy, weaves these experiences into new forms called phantasms. In dreamland we recognize former dreams as ours, but recognition of our waking activities is wanting. Phantasms are designed for temporary amusement, and it is not the business of memory to retain them.

2. *Phantasy and the emotions.* The sleeping child laughs or weeps. The criminal undergoes the agonies of execution in his dreams. Phantasms stir the emotions only less than the realities. "I felt glad when I awoke and found it all a dream."

3. *Phantasy and will.* During revery and dreams, the soul, as will, is ordinarily almost passive. The activity of phantasy is unintentional and undirected. The absence of attention accounts largely for our inability to recall phantasms.

4. *Phantasy and the thinking faculties.* In revery and dreams, fortunately, the thought-element is deficient. The exhausted thought-ganglia need rest. Phantasy sometimes aids thought by vaguely picturing concepts, judgments, and arguments, and thought is sometimes abnormally active during disturbed sleep.

5. *Phantasy and imagination.* Phantasy is slightly active during our waking hours, and its imagery constantly furnishes hints to imagination and thought. Imagination is more or less active during sleep, and sometimes develops phantasms into ideals.

These are general statements. In fact, the soul in all its powers may be active in some degree during sleep. The character of our phantasms depends largely on the relative activity of our various capabilities. When reason is active, our phantasms become debates. When will is active, our phantasms become actions. When emotion is active, our phantasms become love-scenes.

Phantasy in Dreams.—It is certain that nutrition of brain and nerves is at its maximum during sound sleep. The dead tissue caused by mental effort is removed and replaced by living tissue. Retarded cerebral circulation renders the brain unfit for thought purposes. Self ceases from volitional activity. The body reposes and recuperates. This is sleep. With awe and doubt the psychologist attempts to explore dream-land. He finds amid much uncertainty some well-established truths:

1. *Self never ceases to act.* During sleep the activity is almost purely automatic. Because of its evident activity in dreams, because there are no indications of dreamless sleep, and because we never find it inactive, we infer the continued activity of the soul during the profoundest slumber.

2. *Self is not conscious that dreams are psychical acts.* Dreamland seems to be real land. We are conscious of dream phenomena, but are not conscious at the time that our dreams are creations of the mind. To this statement there are apparent exceptions. In profound sleep dreams are not usually remembered, but is not the soul conscious at the time of the passing phantasms?

3. *Self, as will, acts feebly, if at all, in sleep.* The soul floats in the mists of dream-land. No attention, no directed effort, no voluntary action disturbs deep sleep.

4. *Self, as thought, is quiescent.* In disturbed sleep, the thinking faculties may be more or less active, and sometimes are very active. We even solve problems that we could not solve while awake. The

rule, however, holds good: thought is largely absent from our refreshing dreams.

5. *Organic sensations modify dreams.* The special senses cease to report ordinary excitations. The ears and the nose, as well as the eyes, are closed. But the conditions of the stomach and other organs strangely affect our dreams. How do late suppers affect our dreams?

6. *The emotions are more or less active.* In sweet, healthful sleep, our feelings are pleasant, and a feeling of satisfaction pervades our being. All goes well. But exciting dreams stir our anger, excite our mirthfulness, or move us to tears. In all forms of phantasy there seems to be a connecting current of feeling.

7. *Memory as suggestion is active.* One thing suggests another in an endless chain, but recognition is wanting. Thus self, as memory, from his experiences recalls the materials out of which he makes his phantasms. Phantasms pass as a rapidly moving panorama before the eye of consciousness. There is little or no attention. The medley lacks all system. Our waking experiences fail to suggest these fleeting specters. It is well that we do not remember dreams. We can hardly conceive a greater misfortune than to have the myriad phantasms of the night obtruding upon our waking life. We are conscious of our dreams at the time, and we often in our sleep recall and recognize former dreams. Here we find one of the great marvels of dream-land.

8. *Phantasy revels in dream-land.* While the work-a-day brain reposes and recuperates, self, as phantasy, calls into action the portions of the brain that repose during directed effort. This hint of infinite wisdom can not be mistaken. The never-wearying soul conforms to the needs of a material organism.

Phantasy in Somnambulism.—One or more of the sensor organs is excited. The motor organs are stimulated to action by the phantasm. Sleep-walking is the ordinary form of somnambulism. Sometimes the thinking faculties are intensely active, and difficult problems are worked out. The phantasm seems reality, and the dreamer becomes an actor. Seldom do somnambulists remember their exploits.

Phantasy in Mesmerism, Clairvoyance, etc.—Mesmerism and clairvoyance are forms of induced revery. While the will is passive, some of the faculties are stimulated to intense activity. Phantasms seem realities, and the muscular organs respond to the excitation. Through suggestions, the operator induces phantasms, and thus leads the mesmerized to do strange things.

Phantasy in Insanity, Drunkenness, etc.—Insanity is such an affection of the brain as renders it an unfit organism for mental action. Insanity is a disease of the brain. Phantasms possess the soul. An insane man is no longer a self-directing person. The creations of phantasy occasioned by a diseased brain are to him the only realities. The phantasms assume every possible form. To the soul embodied in a whiskey-soaked brain, snakes and demons are fearful realities.

Phantasy in Nerve-Diseases.—Internal excitations of the sensor organs are referred to external causes. Waking dreams are believed to be external realities. Illusions of this kind are myriad.

1. *Vision.* Internal excitations of the optic apparatus occasion the appearance of external images. The victim believes these mental images to be real, external objects. Many honestly believe that they have seen friends long dead. Vision is admirably explained by Shakespeare in the dagger-scene in Macbeth. He gives the exact physiological explanation, in language which, for accuracy and brevity, can not be surpassed. He calls it
"A dagger of the mind, a false creation,
   Proceeding from the heat-oppressed brain."
Intense emotion, driving the blood to the brain, heats and oppresses the nerve-centers, producing "a heat-oppressed brain." By a brain so oppressed, phantasms—daggers of the mind—are created and projected into space. Nerve-diseases produce similar results. Auditory illusions, tactile illusions, gustatory illusions, and olfactory illusions may be accounted for in the same way.

2. *Hysteria is hydra-headed illusion*, occasioned by nerve-diseases. The victim believes the illusion reality. Phantasy dominates reason. Disillusion is difficult and sometimes impossible.

Happy Dreams.—It may be well to ponder some of the conditions favoring pleasant dreams:

1. *Physical.* Suitable food and warmth, good digestion, sufficient exercise, and proper recreation are essential to refreshing dreams. Avoid exhaustion.

2. *Psychical.* A good conscience, with cheerful, earnest work and rational recreation, prepare us for happy dreams. Avoid worry as you avoid sin.

3. *Things to cherish.* During our waking hours we should acquire knowledge and cherish everything beautiful and pure. We should labor unselfishly for human good. We should cherish every high and ennobling ideal. Our phantasms will thus become refreshing, pure, and elevating.

4. *Things to avoid.* As we avoid deadly poisons, so should we avoid low and impure companionship, literature, or thoughts. If cherished, such things become nests of vipers and hosts of fiends to trouble us in our dreams. Avoid telling dreams. Even when they recur to you, drive them away by earnest work. Encourage no one to tell dreams in your presence. Avoid associating much with persons so weak as to believe in dreams and presentiments. So may your dreams be pleasant.

Comparative Psychology.—Numerous indications authorize the conclusions that brutes are endowed with the power to form phantasms. The dog, like some men, talks in his sleep. The horse evidently sees ghosts. The brute perceives, remembers, forms phantasms. But these representations are sensual and indescribably crude.

SUGGESTIVE STUDY-HINTS.

Review.—Give the difference between presentative and re-presentative powers. Why are the perceptive faculties called presentative powers? Give the distinction between a percept and a re-percept. Do we recall emotions? What is the office of sense-perception? Consciousness? Memory? Define each. Etc.

Analyze an act of phantasy. Out of what are phantasms made? Does self as phantasy create? Mention some characteristics of phantasy. State the office of phantasy. Specify. What is a phantasm?

Give author's definition of phantasy; yours; Porter's.

State the relation of phantasy to memory; to the emotions; to will; to thought; to imagination.

Tell what you know about dreams. What has phantasy to do with dreams? Why do we not remember dreams? Explain somnambulism; mesmerism; drunkenness; insanity; visions; hysteria.

Name the conditions of happy dreams. Should we often tell dreams? Why?

Diagram and Letter.—You may now make an analysis of Chapter XI, and embrace this in your letter to your friend. Write a careful letter. Most persons have confused notions of phantasy, strangely mixing memory and imagination with phantasy. If in your power, make the distinctions clear to your friend.

CHAPTER XII.

IMAGINATION.

By this is meant our power to intentionally represent our acquisitions in new forms. Out of our experiences, recalled and immediate, we make new wholes. As the potter molds clay, so we mold our acquisitions into new forms. As perception, self perceives things having properties. As memory, self represents his past experiences unchanged. Out of materials furnished by perception and memory, the mind, as imagination, constructs a new world called the ideal world.

Acts of Imagination Analyzed.—This block is a cubic foot. Now it is a cubic yard, now a cubic rod, now a cubic mile, now a cubic world. Now it is a rhomboid, now a cylinder, now an ellipse. Now it is wood, now iron, now gold. Now it is red, now yellow, now green. Self, as imagination, changes size, changes form, changes material, changes color. You may now make out of materials furnished, a tree. You have gold, iron, copper, silver. Your tree has copper roots, iron trunk and branches, silver leaves, and gold fruit. You may make five different trees out of the same material. You may also make of the same materials five chairs. Here you observe self, as imagination, constructing new wholes out of materials furnished.

You may now blot out St. Louis and make a city to suit yourself. The Gulf now extends to St. Louis, and the city is built at the foot of a snow-capped mountain. But you are the creator of this new St. Louis. You find that self, as imagination, erases old forms and constructs new forms out of materials furnished by memory.

Office of Imagination.—Imagination is the creative power of the soul. It is our power to give shape to our acquisitions. Self, as imagination, so changes and combines his acquisitions as to form new wholes. These new combinations are called creations of the mind. In this sense, self, as imagination, creates.

1. *Self, as imagination, modifies his acquisitions.* The size, the form, the color, and the materials are in-

finitely varied. Now the book could be placed in a mustard-seed; now it would fill a church. You may give many illustrations.

2. *Self, as imagination, creates and destroys.* Creation is used in the sense of making new wholes out of materials given. Imagination creates no new elements. Far out beyond the bounds of all worlds I create a new world and people it with new orders of intelligent beings. Not satisfied, I destroy my creation and make another vastly more magnificent. Try it.

3. *Self, as imagination, projects the future.* Napoleon fought his battles in imagination many times before he led his battalions to victory. The lover proposes again and again in imagination before he ventures his fate. Demosthenes addressed a thousand imaginary audiences before he captivated the Athenians. Often, in imagination, the teacher organizes and conducts her school before she enters the school-room. The youth lives many lives in imagination before he achieves success. The bride-elect goes through her part in the marriage-ceremony many times before the wedding-day.

4. *Self, as imagination, creates ideals.* This is pre-eminently the office of imagination. The painter determines to portray a noble heroism. This is the idea. As an object, he pictures a brave young man battling with oppression and misfortune in his heroic efforts to become a pre-eminent benefactor. The picture in his mind is his ideal. Now with pencil and brush he toils. Now he sees on the canvas his ideal realized, embodied. Ideals are the working-models for inventors, artists, poets, and character-builders. Our highest ideal is perfect manhood, realized only in Christ.

"Lives of great men all remind us
We can make our lives sublime."

From all noble lives we gather materials for the creation of our ideal life. Then, by every act, thought, and emotion, we struggle to realize and embody this ideal. This is character-building.

Characteristics of Imagination.—Certain peculiarities mark imagination as a distinct faculty.

1. *Imagination is our power purposely to represent our acquisitions in new forms.* Out of its cognitions, immediate and remembered, the soul intentionally constructs new forms. Inventors, artists, poets, educators, and scientists are gifted with vigorous imaginations.

2. *Imagination is the intentional picturing power.* All its products are individual and have a material basis. We call our capability to purposely make images, imagination. The successful student uses his imagination almost as much as he uses his reason.

3. *Imagination is the creative power of the soul.* In its highest form, it virtually creates. Its creations are new because experiences are set *in new lights*. "Poetry is truer than history." A fable may contain more truth than a biography, because the permanent meaning of things is set in general forms. Because they represent universal human nature, the creations of Homer and Plato and Shakespeare and Emerson will continue to live through the centuries.

Limits of Imagination.—Lofty as are his flights, self, as imagination, works within well-defined limits.

1. *As to physical phenomena, imagination is limited to sense-percepts.* I can place in my creations only

what I have experienced. The creations of the blind are colorless; of the deaf, soundless; of those destitute of smell, odorless.

2. *As to psychical phenomena, imagination is limited to conscious-percepts.* I endow my rational creations with my own conscious powers. I can do no more. My angels simply know, feel, and will. God knows infinitely, feels infinitely, wills infinitely, but it is impossible for me to endow even Deity with additional powers, though convinced that His capabilities are infinite in number as in degree.

3. *As to noumena, imagination is limited to noumenal percepts.* The creations of Homer and Shakespeare are limited to matter, mind, space, time, and cause; but, within the charmed circle, what wonders are wrought! Imagination, "bounded in a nut-shell, is king of infinite space."

4. *Imagination is limited to the concrete and the individual.* I think vertebrate, but my ideal is a beautiful gazelle. I think triangle, but my image is a specific equilateral triangle. Triangle can not be imagined, because it would have to be at once right-angled, equilateral, and isosceles. You can think the abstract and the general, but you can imagine only the concrete and the particular.

Imagination defined.—Self, as imagination, out of his experiences constructs new wholes. Because you are endowed with this power you can make an original essay, a new invention, or a new poem. The ideas in Hamlet are old, but the play is new. Imagination is our capability to purposely make new combinations.

1. *Imagination is the power of self purposely to*

put his experiences into new forms. Self, as memory, recalls the experiences out of which he creates his ideals. As the creative activity predominates, this form of representation is called imagination.

2. *Original.* You may now use your imagination in constructing an original definition of this power. Try to make clear distinctions between memory and imagination, and between phantasy and imagination.

3. **Various Definitions.**—BASCOM: Imagination is the power of the mind to present to itself vividly new phenomenal forms. SULLY: Imagination is the power to work up our experiences into new forms. GARVEY: Imagination is the power to make new combinations. HOPKINS: Imagination is the capability of the mind to rearrange its acquisitions and create new wholes. PORTER: Imagination is the power to recombine and construct anew materials furnished by experience. DAY: Imagination is the faculty of form, and is the power to construct ideals. WHITE: Imagination is the power to modify and recombine the products of memory. DEWEY: Imagination is the capability to embody an idea in an image.

Products of Imagination — Ideals. — We recognize *memories* as representing real experiences, as when the maiden recalls the parting scene with her lover. *Phantasms* seem to be objective realities, as when heart-breaking sobs awaken the maiden as she dreams of her lover untrue. But self intentionally creates *ideals* and cognizes them as his own workmanship, as when the maiden plans a reception-party for her returning friend.

1. *Ideals are creations of self, as imagination.* Any new form into which we purposely put our experiences is termed an *ideal*. The architect plans a model school-building; his plan is his ideal. The lady plans her flower-garden; her plan is her ideal. You plan an oration; your plan is your ideal. The artist plans a pict-

ure; his plan is his ideal. The teacher plans a model school; his plan is his ideal. You plan a noble life; your plan is your ideal.

2. *Ideals are creations in which ideas and objects blend in harmony.* An ideal embraces three elements: ideas, objects, and the blending act. The sculptor's idea is injured innocence; his object is a pure but slandered maiden. In imagination, he so blends the idea and the object as to arouse indignation toward her traducers and sympathy for herself. He now embodies his ideal in marble.

3. *Ideals are intentional creations.* Milton's Satan was not an accident, nor was Edison's ideal electric lamp. Inspiration and hard work are intimately associated. We work up to higher and still higher ideals. Purposely we embody ideas in images, and call the products ideals.

Imagination and other Faculties.—Each mental power is supplemented by all the other faculties of the soul. Self, in all his capabilities, is present in each intentional act. Thus memory supplies materials, thought suggests and criticises, emotion stimulates, will concentrates effort, determines and executes, but imagination is the master workman in constructing ideals.

1. *Memory supplies materials.* Self, as memory, opens up the store-house of past acquisitions. Immediate percepts also seem to enter into our creation. Out of these materials, self, as imagination, constructs ideals. Because the imagining activity predominates, this form of representation is termed imagination.

2. *Thought keeps imagination within bounds.* The idea and the object must blend in harmony. No law

must be violated. Means must be adapted to ends. Reason is said to clip the wings of a wild imagination.

3. *Emotion gives wings to imagination.* The lover becomes a poet. The enthusiast becomes an inventor, an orator, an artist, a scientist, a missionary, a reformer.

4. *Will directs imagination and works ideals into actuals.* Self, drifting fancy-free, forms crude phantasms but creates no ideals. Eads concentrated his efforts for weary months before he perfected his ideal of the St. Louis bridge; worked for weary years before his ideal became the actual bridge.

Kinds of Imagination.—Self, as imagination, creates ideals. When the ideals tend to move the emotions, we call this power

1. *The emotional imagination.* Its ennobling ideals are of the beautiful and the good. Its debasing ideals are of appetite and passion.

The beautiful adorns the universe. God is beauty and he has scattered beauty everywhere. He has endowed us with the rational emotion to appreciate and enjoy the beautiful. He has also endowed us with emotional imagination—the power to create the beautiful. Song and eloquence, painting and sculpture, poetry and literature, architecture and landscaping, manners and dress—these are some of the ways in which man seeks to create the beautiful. Pause and reflect! How large a section of life is devoted to the beautiful and the sublime!

2. *The ethical imagination.* The good gives rise to our highest ideals. All good results from obedience to law. Goodness is intentional conformity to law. We

are endowed with conscience, the rational emotion to appreciate and enjoy the right. Ethical imagination is the power to create ideals of the good. The idea is goodness, or conformity to law; the object is a rational being; the ideal is a rational, law-abiding life. The duty world is the highest. Happiness is the result of law obeyed. One whose soul is filled with pure and lofty ideals becomes the noble man.

Low and impure ideals degrade and ruin. Ideals born of appetite and passion tend to brutalize.

3. *The philosophic imagination.* We idealize the thought-world. My thoughts take shape. The topics so arrange themselves as to follow each other logically and effectively. An oration is created. My knowledge of the plant-world takes shape. The myriad forms of plant-life arrange themselves into orders, families, classes, genera, species, individuals. The science of botany is created. Points, lines, surfaces, and solids appear in various space relations. The science of geometry is created. The power, control, and application of steam takes shape. The engine is invented. But it is needless to specify. The philosophical imagination is essential to invention, discovery, and system. Imagination is no less necessary to the scientist, the philosopher, the statesman, and the practical man, than to the poet or the architect. The student who is deficient in imagination fails to master science.

Imagination and Phantasy.—Both are dependent on perception and memory for materials, and both construct new forms. In other particulars they differ so widely that careful thinkers are constrained to regard them as distinct faculties. It is well to reiterate here "that a faculty is a power of the soul to do acts distinguishable in kind from other acts."

1. *Imagination is intelligent activity;* phantasy works in the dark. Thought guides imagination, but is measurably inactive during the play of phantasy.

2. *Imagination is determined activity;* phantasy is drifting. As imagination, the soul plans, makes working models, organizes. As phantasy, the soul floats down the stream and weaves a gossamer web.

3. *Imagination creates ideals;* phantasy forms phantasms. The one gives us the "Star-spangled Banner," the other a medley; the one gives us the Parthenon, the other a grotesque ruin. Imagination is the mental artist; phantasy is the mental kaleidoscope.

4. *In imagination, we know that our ideals are our own creations;* in phantasy, our phantasms appear to us to be objective realities. In imagination, the soul knows itself constructing new forms; in phantasy, the soul seems to itself a spectator.

5. *Ideals are remembered;* phantasms appear for a moment, then disappear forever. We treasure our ideals as we do our ideas, but our dreams and reveries fade into utter forgetfulness.

Growth of Imagination.—The feeble beginnings of imaginative activity may be noticed at an early period. Phantasy reigns in these early years. The effort of the three-year-old to make new stories indicates slight imagination but much phantasy. Fairy-tales delight young children because they are to them realities. As our experiences multiply, and thought and will begin to grow active, nursery-stories cease to satisfy. Now boys and girls begin to enjoy the products of imagination, and show a disposition to do things for themselves. Imagination becomes decidedly active during youth, but rarely reaches its highest activity before the twentieth year.

Education of Imagination.*—Culture of imagination immeasurably increases human achievement and human

---

* See "Applied Psychology" for full discussion.

happiness. "Imagination is capable of steady growth, and requires constant cultivation. The creative imagination, when most gifted, can at first rise only to a certain height above the materials which its experience gives. Its succeeding essays are founded upon those which have been made before, and it proceeds by successive steps, more or less long and high, till it attains the most consummate achievements that are ever reached by man. That there is a striking diversity of original endowment can not be doubted, but that this is the common law of the development of this power can not be denied." * Education makes the difference between a feeble and a vigorous imagination.

"Human nature, with its joys and sorrows, its achievements and disappointments, is better fitted to stir up our higher faculties than the grandest objects fashioned out of matter. History and biography reveal incidents which incite the imagination, and youth should be made acquainted with them. They bring under our notice characters which transcend in grandeur the greatest of the works of nature—its mountains and its vales, its streams, its cataracts, and its precipices. Those who would train the mind to its highest capacity must furnish to the young the record of deeds of heroism, of benevolence, of self-sacrifice, of courage to resist the evil and maintain the good. Friendship, fidelity, patriotism, and piety must be presented in their most attractive forms." †

Comparative Psychology.—The brute creates no ideals and is incapable of appreciating creations of imagination. It gains no ideas, much less does it embody ideas in images. Brute representation includes memory and phantasy, but not imagination. Even the phantasms of brutes are the lowest form of sensuous combinations. So far as I can see, the brute is not endowed with even rudimentary imagination.

* Porter.   * McCosh.

SUGGESTIVE STUDY-HINTS.

Review.—Give the office of memory; of phantasy. What has attention to do with memory? Give the five laws of suggestion. Etc.

Does the soul, as imagination, create new ideas? What does it create? Do you like the word construct better than the word create? Why?

Analyze an act of imagination. What do you discover? Where does self get his materials? What does he do with them?

Show the limits of imagination as to matter; as to mind. Give the office of imagination. Specify. Give the characteristics of imagination.

Repeat the author's definition of imagination; your definition; Garvey's definition; Dewey's definition.

Show, by examples, the work of memory; of phantasy; of imagination. What are creations of imagination called? Why? What is an ideal? Illustrate. Give the three elements of an ideal.

What is the relation of imagination to memory? to thought? to emotion? to will? Illustrate.

What do you mean by the emotional imagination? æsthetical imagination? philosophical imagination? ethical imagination?

In what respect do imagination and phantasy resemble each other? How do they differ? Prove that they are separate faculties.

Tell what you know about the growth of imagination. When does this power become fully active? Give examples.

What is the law of the development of imagination? Why is the education of imagination so important? Show that the study of human nature stimulates imagination even more than the study of nature and art.

Are brutes endowed with imagination? How do you account for new combinations made by brutes?

Letter.—You will now write an interesting letter to your friend. Use your imagination. Let all your illustrations be original. Advise the earnest culture of imagination by the study of nature, art, and literature. Urge the vigorous use of this power.

IMAGINATION.

Topical Analysis of Chapter XII.—Imagination.

I. Acts of Imagination Analyzed.
   Ideal tree.   Ideal cottage.   Ideal school-room.

II. Office of Imagination.
   Modifies acquisitions.   Projects the future.
   Creates new wholes.   Creates ideals.

III. Characteristics of Imagination.
   Constructive power.   Ideal-making power.
   Picturing power.

IV. Limits of Imagination.
   As to matter.   As to necessary realities.
   As to mind.   As to concrete things.

V. Definitions.
   Author's.
   Original.
   Various definitions.
   Bascom's.   Garvey's.   Porter's.
   Sully's.   Hopkins's.   White's.

VI. Ideals.
   Creations of imagination.
   Elements.
   Ideas.   Objects.   Harmonious blending.
   Intentional creations.

VII. Imagination and
   Memory.   Thought.   Emotion.   Will.

VIII. Kinds of Imagination.
   Emotional.   Ethical.   Philosophic.

IX. Imagination and Phantasy.
   Agreements.   Differences.

X. Growth and Education of Imagination.
   Growth.   Culture.   Means.

XI. Comparative Psychology.

CHAPTER XIII.

REPRESENTATION—GENERAL VIEW.

REPRESENTATIVE knowing is making present again past experiences. *Presentation* is the capability of the mind to make things present to itself for the first time. *Representation* includes the capabilities of self to represent his past experiences in old and new forms. Self *re*presents his experiences unchanged or in modified forms. Representation is a general name including a group of related but distinct activities. This group of soul-energies is known by the following

Names.—
{ The Representative Powers.
The Reproductive and Constructive Imagination.
The Conceptive Powers.
Representation.—Memory. Phantasy. Imagination. }

Because images are most prominent in representation, some writers consider these powers as merely forms of imagination. This view tends to confusion, as nearly all writers treat memory and imagination as distinct powers. "Representative powers" best expresses the meaning, and is now one of the best-established expressions in mental science.

1. *The representative powers are our capabilities to make present again, in old or new forms, our past experiences.* Representation is *memory* when we recognize the representations as past experiences. Representation is *phantasy* when the new forms of our past experiences are phantasms. Representation is

imagination when the new forms of our past experiences are ideals.

The Representative Powers.— $\begin{cases} \text{Memory.} \\ \text{Phantasy.} \\ \text{Imagination.} \end{cases}$

2. *Memory is the power of self to represent in old forms, called memories, his past experiences.* Memory is the capability to recall past experiences unchanged. As images are the most prominent features of our recollections, memory is sometimes called reproductive imagination. Memory is every way preferable. It neither misleads nor confuses. It is specific, and is in universal use. Treating memory as a group of faculties can serve no good purpose. Self, as memory, does all recalling. Take away memory, and our past would be a blank. The soul, as memory, reproduces its past experiences. Retention, recollection, association, and recognition are merely elements of complete acts of memory.

Names.— $\begin{cases} \text{Memory.} \\ \text{Reproductive Imagination.} \\ \text{Reproduction.—} \begin{cases} \text{Retention.} \\ \text{Recollection.} \end{cases} \begin{matrix} \text{Association.} \\ \text{Recognition.} \end{matrix} \end{cases}$

3. *Phantasy is the power of self to represent spontaneously his past experiences in new forms called phantasms.* Self, as memory, recalls his experiences; self, as phantasy, spontaneously weaves these experiences into new forms called phantasms. Phantasy is the capability to manufacture these new forms. In this form of representation the soul, at the time, is not conscious of making these pictures out of its revived experiences; it is only conscious of the phantasms. Phantasy is undirected or drifting activity; hence it is called the

drifting imagination. Fantasy, fancy, and phantasy are merely different forms of the same word. Fancy is used in many senses, and is extremely indefinite. Drifting imagination is specific, but tends to confuse. As phantasy is never used but to designate this faculty, it is given the preference. Because images are so conspicuous in recollections, some use phantasy and recollection as synonyms. But the soul, as phantasy, does no recollecting; it merely weaves its recollections, without intention or effort, into new forms. Representation, as phantasy, conjoins revived experiences, forming phantasms.

Names.— { Phantasy.
Fantasy, or Fancy.
Drifting Imagination. }

4. *Imagination is the power of self to represent intentionally his past experiences in new forms, called ideals.* Self, as memory, reproduces his experiences; self, as imagination, manufactures out of these experiences ideals. Memory, in this form of representation, is subordinate, merely furnishing materials; imagination is the master builder. Imagination is the capability to evolve the ideal from the actual. All agree in calling the power of the soul purposely to create, or construct, or form ideals, imagination. To distinguish imagination proper from reproductive imagination or memory, and from drifting imagination or phantasy, it is sometimes called the creative or constructive imagination. Imagination, unmodified, best designates this power.

Names.— { Imagination.
Constructive Imagination.
Creative Imagination. }

5. *Representative knowledge is re-knowledge.* Knowledge gained directly is intuitive knowledge, or original knowledge, or presentative knowledge, or perceptive knowledge; but when we re-know, our cognitions are called re-knowledge, or representative knowledge, or revived knowledge.

Forms of Representative Knowledge.— { Memories. Phantasms. Ideals. }

6. *Memories are reproduced experiences.* The original experiences or old forms are recalled just as they were experienced. Products of memory are reproduced acquisitions. When we recall our experiences unchanged, we call them memories, recollections, or remembrances. Remembered percepts are simply re-percepts. Remembered concepts are merely re-concepts. Remembered judgments are re-judgments.

Misleading.—To call memory-products concepts or conceptions is misleading. This relic of the old psychology tends to confuse the learner. A concept is a general notion, and conception is the power to discern general notions. These terms are thus used in logic and literature as well as in modern psychology.

Memory-Products are called— { Memories. Re-percepts. Recollections. Re-concepts. Remembrances. Conceptions (obsolete and misleading). }

7. *Phantasms are crude mental pictures which seem to be realities.* Webster says: "A phantasm is an image formed by the mind and supposed to be real." The soul, out of its revived experiences, spontaneously forms a panorama for its own amusement. These moving scenes appear to be objective realities,

and self seems to be a spectator. The products of phantasy take various

Names.— { Phantasms.
Phantasies and Fancies.
Dreams and Reveries.
Air-castles, etc.

8. *Ideals are ideas and objects blended.* Out of its revived experiences the soul, as imagination, constructs new forms, called ideals. Ideals are created out of reals, and may become realities. Out of his experiences the inventor creates an ideal steam-engine. When he builds the engine, the ideal becomes a reality. The products of imagination take various

Names.— { Ideals.
Imaginations.
Creations of Imagination.
Etc.

SUGGESTIVE STUDY-HINTS.

Place on your left the diagrams of the three perceptive powers, and on your right the diagrams of the three representative powers. With these before you study Chapter XII. Compare the faculties named, topic by topic.

Keep constantly in mind the important fact that in its action, as in its nature, the mind is a unit, and that a faculty is merely a distinct capability of the soul.

State the office of each of the presentative and representative powers. Give the characteristics of each. Define each. Name the products of each of these powers.

Could there be representation without perception? Could there be phantasy without memory? Does imagination imply memory?

References.—For a more elaborate treatment of representation, the student is referred to "Human Intellect," Porter; "Simple Cognitive Powers," McCosh; "Outlines of Psychology," Sully.

PART IV.

THE THOUGHT FACULTIES.

CHAPTER XIV.—CONCEPTION.
   XV.—JUDGMENT.
   XVI.—REASON.
   XVII.—THOUGHT-KNOWING—GENERAL VIEW.

PSYCHOLOGICAL PYRAMID.

THE CAPABILITIES OF THE MIND.	**THE WILL.**	THE WILL POWERS.	
	THE FEELINGS.	THE EMOTIONS.	
		THE PHYSICAL FEELINGS.	
		THE INSTINCTS.	
	THE INTELLECTUAL FACULTIES.	THE THINKING POWERS.	REASON. JUDGMENT. CONCEPTION.	REASONS. JUDGMENTS. CONCEPTS.
		THE REPRESENTATIVE POWERS.	IMAGINATION. PHANTASY. MEMORY.	IDEALS. PHANTASMS. MEMORIES.
		THE PERCEPTIVE POWERS.	NOUMENAL-PERCEPTION. CONSCIOUS-PERCEPTION. SENSE-PERCEPTION.	NOUMENAL-PERCEPTS. CONSCIOUS-PERCEPTS. SENSE-PERCEPTS.

PRODUCTS.

FOURTH PART.

THOUGHT-KNOWING, OR THE COMPARATIVE POWERS.

THESE are our capabilities to discern relations. Self, as perception, gains the elements of knowledge; and self, as thought, *elaborates* these elements into higher forms. That we may discover relations, we *compare;* and that we may digest elementary notions, we *reflect.* This group of faculties is known by the following

Names.—
- The Thought-Powers.
- The Comparative Powers.
- The Elaborative Faculties.
- The Logical Powers.
- The Reflective Faculties.
- The Understanding (indefinite).

Each name is expressive and specific. Omitting the last, these names may be used interchangeably.

The universe is a unit. Each individual, each group of individuals, and each system of groups, is a related part of one stupendous whole. Thinking is discerning relations.

First, we discover relations of similarity, and think individuals into classes. Our capability to discern class-relations and thus gain general notions is termed our classifying power, or *conception.*

Second, we discover truth-relations, and think notions into sentences. Our capability to discern and predicate truth-relations is termed *judgment*.

Third, we discover that each thing is in some causal way related to every other thing. Causes and effects, means and ends, conditions and dependencies, antecedents and consequents, ratios and proportions, elements and compounds, in myriad forms unite all things into infinite series of cause-relations. We discern cause-relations and think conclusions. Our power to discern cause-relations and think judgments into arguments is called *reason*.

The Thinking Faculties.— { Conception. Judgment. Reason. }

You observe this figure, and this, and this. You discern that they are alike in being rectangular and having four equal sides. You discern the group-notion, square figures. Your power to do this is called *conception*. You know the meaning of the notions vertebrate and horse. You discern the agreement of these notions, and say the horse is a vertebrate. Your power to discern the agreement of notions is called *judgment*. As all animals are endowed with instinct, and as the dog is an animal, you discern the conclusion that dogs are endowed with instinct. Your power to infer conclusions is termed *reason*.

Self, as conception, elaborates percepts into concepts; self, as judgment, elaborates concepts into judgments; and self, as reason, elaborates judgments into reasons.

CHAPTER XIV.

CONCEPTION.

By this is meant the power to think individuals into classes. Our percepts are notions of individual things. Between individuals we discern relations. I perceive this block, and this, and this, and this. They differ as to size and proportion, but I see that they are related as to the number of sides. I think these three-sided figures into one class. As the notion *three-sidedness* is common to all three-sided figures, it is called a general notion or a concept.

We discern general notions through individual notions, as

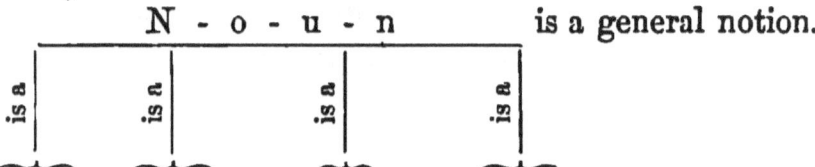

N - o - u - n is a general notion.

John and Ohio and (a) boy and (a) book are individual notions. Percepts are our scaffolding to enable us to think up to concepts. We discern the name-relation between John, Ohio, etc., and think all name-words into one class. Noun is a concept. Verb is a concept. All class-notions are concepts.

Acts of Conception Analyzed.—You observe these blocks of various forms and sizes. You decide to consider them with reference to the number of sides. You abstract the property, number of sides. You leave out of view everything else. You now compare the several figures. You discern common properties. This, and this, and this, have three sides; this, and this, and this, four sides. You generalize—discern a general property. You now classify the figures with reference to the common property. You collect them into groups. This group of three-sided figures you call triangles. You discern the group-notion or the concept, triangle. This group of four-sided figures you call quadrilaterals. You discern the group-notion or the concept, quadrilateral. So with the concepts pentagon, hexagon, etc. Draw the scaffolding, and analyze the act of forming the concept *pencil;* also, the concept *tree;* also, the concept *lake;* also, the concept *quadruped.*

Elements of Conception.—From the analysis you discover the steps or processes by which the mind reaches concepts. Analytic observation, abstraction, generalization, and classification are processes of thinking things into classes. Self, as conception, advances by these steps in gaining group notions.

1. *Analytic observation.* You perceive things having properties. Here you have a collection of leaves. This leaf is oval, its veins are parallel, its edges are dentate. You observe this leaf, and this, and this, and note peculiarities. Observing things as having properties and parts is called analytic observation. The first step in elaboration is necessarily analytic. We must discriminate before we can assimilate.

2. *Abstraction.* You decide to consider leaves with reference to shape. You abstract *shape* and disregard the veins, edges, etc. Drawing out one quality and considering things with reference to this, regardless of other qualities, is called abstraction. Above, we considered figures with reference to number of sides. You may give other examples of abstraction. You discover how you get your notions of attributes. These notions you call abstract ideas, as redness, hardness, dullness, roundness, goodness, etc.

3. *Comparison.* Putting leaves side by side, you compare them,

and thus discern relations of likeness. As you have abstracted shape, you compare the leaves as to shape, and find points of agreement as well as of disagreement. Discerning resemblances is called comparison.

4. *Generalization.* You discover a common something; you generalize; you find a general property. This leaf, and this, and this, are ovate. Ovateness is general to these leaves. This leaf, and this, and this, are lanceolate. Lanceolateness is general to these leaves. Finding a property common to several objects is called generalization. Above we generalized and found the common properties of the figures to be three-sidedness, four-sidedness, etc.

5. *Classification.* You now arrange the leaves in groups with reference to the general property, shape, and name the groups. This group you call ovate; this, lanceolate; this, cordate. You gain the class notions—ovate, lanceolate, cordate—and designate them by these names. The act of conception is complete. Grouping objects into classes with reference to general properties is called classification. The second step in elaboration is synthetic; we first discriminate, and then assimilate. You may classify books with reference to color of binding, and point out and define the five elements of conception. You may classify these roses with reference to color, and point out the steps.

Office of Conception.—Self, as conception, discerns relations of similarity between things, and thus thinks many individuals as one class. You perceive this tree, and this, and this. You compare them, and find that they have the common property—apple-bearing. You think them into one class—apple-tree. The mind, as thought, can not well deal with the trees of the forest or the inhabitants of the sea as individuals; but, endowed with conception, we are able to think myriads of individuals into a few classes. As sensations are the materials out of which sense-percepts are made, so percepts are the elements out of which concepts are made. *Discerning concepts, through percepts, is the office of conception.*

Characteristics of Conception.—We perceive particular notions, but think general notions:

1. *As conception,* self discerns many as one. The millions of acorn-bearing trees are oaks. The billions of back-boned animals are vertebrates.

2. *As conception,* self elaborates percepts into concepts. From the percepts, this bird, and this, and this, I elaborate the concept *bird.* I discriminate various kinds of fruit, and assimilate such as have common properties into classes, and call these group-notions peach, apple, pear.

3. *As conception,* self gives names to general notions. Thus, the general notion, four-footedness is embodied in the word quadruped. Things are realities, and the relations between things are realities. Things and relations exist independent of the mind. We discern the relations of resemblance, and think things into groups. We call these group-notions concepts. We give to our general notions names; as noun, verb, adjective.

4. *As conception,* self discerns, but does not picture, group-notions. We think three-sidedness, but we can not picture a triangle at once isosceles, equilateral, and right-angled. We can picture only the concrete individual thing. We can picture this cow, but we can not picture mammal.

Conception defined.—Conception is the power to discern group-notions.

1. *Conception is the soul-energy to think many into one.* We think many individuals into one class. We discern class-relations, and elaborate percepts into concepts.

2. *Original.* Express clearly in your own words your view of conception. Illustrate.

3. **Various Definitions.**—1. Schuyler: Conception is the capability to form general notions. 2. Porter: Conception is the power to form concepts. 3. Sully: Conception is the power to form general notions. 4. McCosh: The power to discover relations of resemblance. 5. Day: Conception is the power of the intelligence itself to conceive general notions.

Products of Conception.—
{ Concepts.
General Notions or General Ideas.
Group-Notions or Group-Ideas.
Class-Notions. }

Concept, that which is grasped or held together, admirably expresses the meaning. We discern the relations of resemblance between these animals, *grasping* them together as one class; we call this class of animals dogs. As the notion is common to all these animals, it is a *general* notion; and as it grasps together all these animals, it is a class-notion or group-notion. All class-notions are concepts. *A concept is a notion of objects grasped together through common properties.*

Concepts of Objects and of Attributes.—You observe this red rose, this red bird, and this red sky. You gain two concepts: red objects and redness. You test this hard wood, this hard iron, and this hard glass; you gain the concepts, hard objects and hardness. Redness, hardness, brightness, etc., are general notions of properties of objects. As the properties are abstracted from the objects, these terms are called abstract concepts, abstract ideas, abstract nouns. But the distinction is not deemed material. A concept is ever a general notion.

Properties of Concepts.—Self, as conception, discerns group-notions, and gives names to these notions. I discern the group-notion three-sidedness, and call this notion triangle. General notions take general names:

1. *Denomination* is the giving to a class-notion a class-name. I

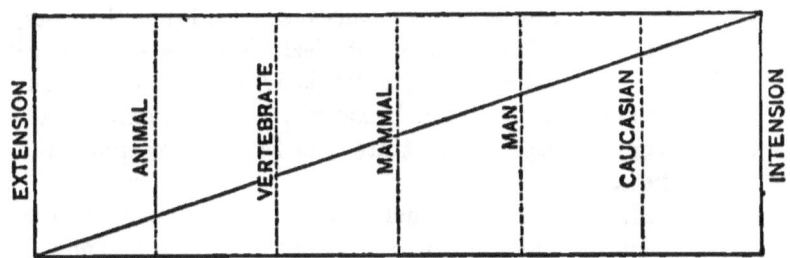

think many resembling things into one class. I gain a class-notion. I now give the notion a name, which is used as a sign to represent the class-notion. I think wheat, corn, oats, barley into oneness. I call the concept grain. The notion of an individual object is a percept, but a general notion always extends to several individuals. The concept may be embodied in a general term. Mineral is a general name representing a general notion.

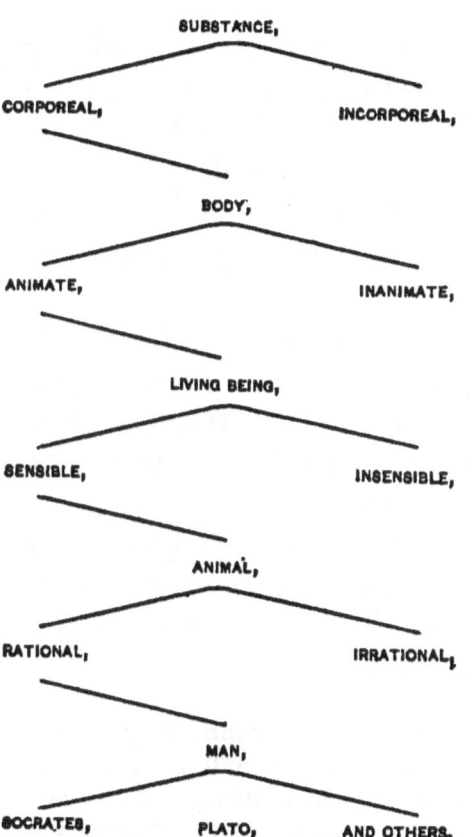

2. *Extension* has reference to the number of individuals embraced in the concept. The concept *man* extends to more individuals than the concept *Caucasian*. Animal has much greater extension than mammal. A general notion always extends to several individuals, and, the more individuals embraced, the greater the extension. Fruit has greater extension than lemon.

3. *Intension*, or *inclusion*, has reference to the number of common attributes included in the concept. A concept includes a greater or less number of common properties. The

attributes of the individual are very numerous. The lower the class, the greater the number of common attributes. Birds have few common attributes; vertebrates fewer; animals fewer. As the extension becomes greater, the intension becomes less. As intension increases, extension decreases. Illustrate this by the preceding and the following figures.

Remark. The concept man includes more common characteristics than the concept animal; but the concept animal extends to many more individuals. Man has the greater intension; animal the greater extension.

Terms used.—
{
1. Individuals.
2. Species.
3. Genera.
4. Families, Orders, etc.
}

Individual, Species, and Genus.—General notions may include larger and larger generalizations. In the classified sciences, botany, zoölogy, geology, and chemistry, special nomenclatures are used. But *individual*, *species*, and *genus* are terms common to all sciences and all literature. With the thought-pyramid before you, study and illustrate these terms.

1. *An individual is one of a species.* Notions of individual things are always percepts. Through percepts we discern concepts. All class-notions are concepts. The individual is simply one of a class of things. Name the individuals in the figures.

2. *A species is a group of individuals having one or more common characteristics.* The right-angled triangle is a species of triangle. The greyhound is a species of dog. The pippin is a species of apple.

Species, in zoölogy and botany, is a class sprung from a common stock. A species of animals is a group that has or may have descended from a single pair. In this work, as in logic and literature, a species means one of the classes into which a higher class or genus may be divided; as, vertebrates, articulates, mollusks, and radiates are species of the genus animal.

3. *A genus is a group of species having one or more common characteristics.* Man is the genus of which Caucasian, Mongolian, Ethiopian, American, and Malayan are species. Metal is a genus of which gold, silver, copper, iron, etc., are species. Triangle is a genus of which equilateral triangle is a species.

4. *A lower genus becomes a species of a higher genus.* Apple is a genus of which pippin is a species; but apple is a species of the genus fruit. Man is a species of mammal. Illustrate by the cut.

5. *Comprehension.* I perceive this orange. I apprehend it as an object. I gain the notion, this orange. Self, as perception, apprehends or gains percepts. I discern the general notion—orange. I also discern the higher notion—fruit—and say the orange is a fruit. I now know the orange in its relations—I *comprehend* it. Self, as conception, comprehends or knows things in their relations. Illustrate by the thought-pyramid.

6. *Nomenclature of a special science.* Zoölogy gives us—
Animal Kingdom,
    Branches,
        Classes,
            Orders,
                Families,
                    Genera,
                        Species,
                            Individuals.

Botany, geology, chemistry, etc., must necessarily have special nomenclatures.

Science deals only incidentally with this apple or that rose; it deals with individuals merely to discover relations of similarity. The individual is an objective reality. In the individual are found the common features of the class. The class-notion or concept is a thought-product. Science deals with concepts.

Classification and Definition.—We analyze when we separate a whole into its parts, but we synthesize when we put the parts together to make a whole. You at every step break up complex wholes into simpler parts, that you may conquer in detail. You crown your victory by recombining the parts into old or new wholes. You observe that these processes supplement each other, and enter into all thinking. Ascending, we discriminate as well as assimilate; descending, we assimilate as well as discriminate; but in the first, the process is pre-eminently synthetic, while analysis predominates in the second. Beginning at the base, let us cautiously ascend and afterward descend the

THOUGHT-PYRAMID.*

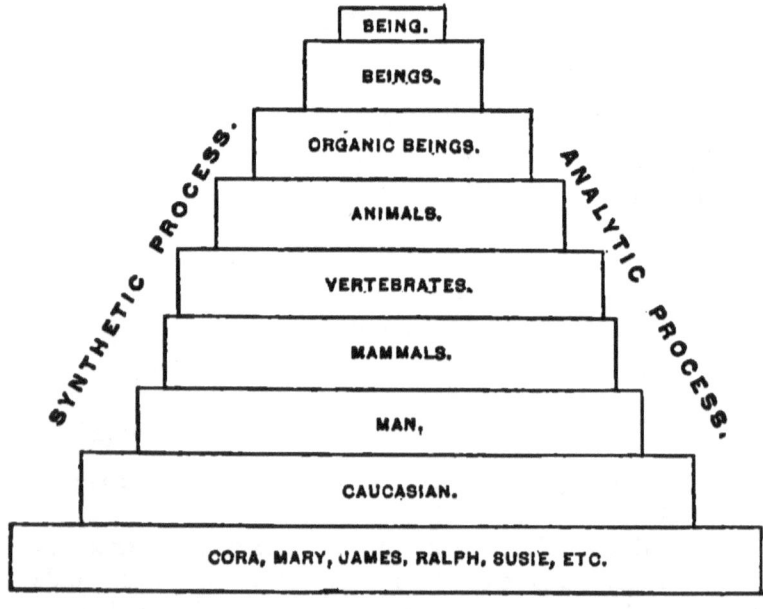

* Hopkins.

Conception is our classifying power. We perceive individuals and discern resemblances. Through resemblances we think individuals into classes. We form concepts and give names to these class-notions. This is classification.

Definition is referring the thing defined to a higher class, and giving the characteristic differences. Each step upward necessitates definition as well as classification. Logical definition alone is considered here.

1. *Caucasian.* You perceive Cora, Mary, James, etc. You notice that they resemble one another in color, and you think of them as white persons. You thus get the concept, white race, and you express this general notion by the word Caucasian. You now define this word by referring it to its genus and giving its distinctive feature. Caucasian is the white race, or

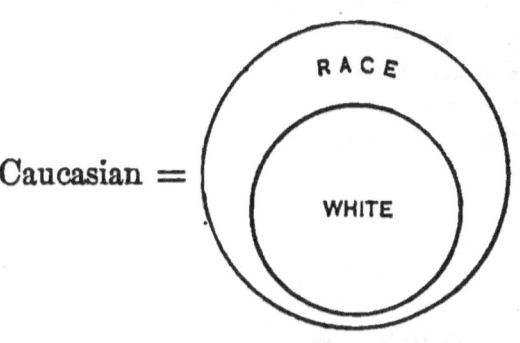

Caucasian =

Now work out and define the concepts Mongolian, Ethiopian, American, and Malayan.

2. *Man.* You find that the several races resemble one another in being rational. You discern the notion, rational animals, in which you include all the races. You call this notion human race, or man. Wider analytic observation leads to the discovery that the highest order of animals, including man, give suck to their young. You now comprehend, and hence can define, man. Man is a rational mammal; or

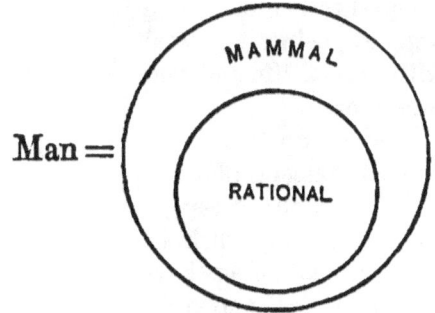

Man =

3. *Mammal.* By wider synthesis you group into one class all suck-giving animals. These

you term mammalia. A still wider analysis brings out the fact that all mammals are vertebrates. Then mammals are suck-giving vertebrates, or

Mammal =

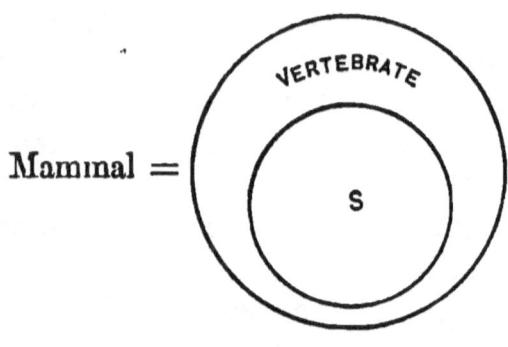

Grouping with reference to distribution, you may work out and define the concepts aërial mammals, aquatic mammals, and terrestrial mammals. Define biological species; logical.

4. *Vertebrates.* You find out that other beings as well as mammalia are backboned. Thus related, you think all creatures having spinal columns into one class—vertebrates. You here discover that vertebrates belong to a great kingdom. You now define: Vertebrates are backboned animals, or

Vertebrate =

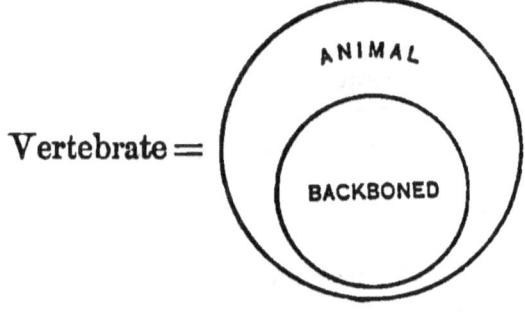

You may now work out and define the concepts articulates, mollusks, radiates, and protozoans. Give examples of each.

5. *Animals.* By a comprehensive synthesis you unite all creatures endowed with animal life into one class, called the animal kingdom, or animals. But you discover beings besides animals possessing organs. Now you comprehend animal as an organic being endowed with animal life and sensation, or

Animal =

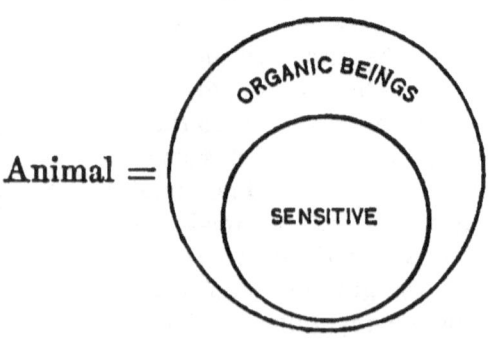

Work up to and define the concept, plant.

6. *Organic beings.* By a sweeping synthesis you unite all beings having life, animal and vege-

table, into a single class. You think—organic world. You discover also an inorganic world. But you discern a relation between organic and inorganic things—being. You comprehend organic being as beings having life, or Organic Being =

You may work up and define the concept, inorganic.

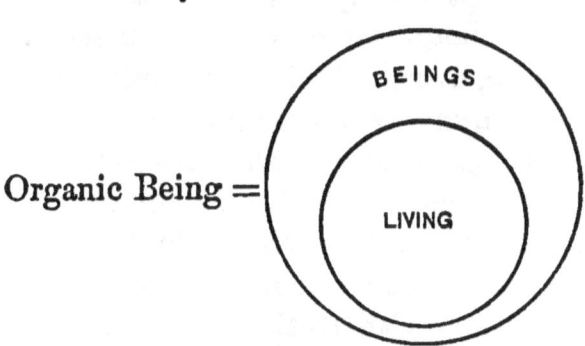

7. *Beings are.* This is all that can be said. Extension can be carried no further. You can not comprehend, and hence can not define, being. You have reached the limits of thought. You have for the base of your pyramid sense-percepts, and for its apex a necessary idea. All thought-cycles are similar, beginning in phenomena and ending in noumena.

Conception and other Faculties.—The soul is a unit. A faculty is merely a capability of the soul. Conception is simply self classifying things:

1. *Perception* supplies raw material; conception elaborates crude percepts into finished concepts. Percepts *must* be, in order that concepts *may* be. Here we find a key to correct teaching.

2. *Memory* makes present again our percepts, enabling us to view them side by side. We can thus discern resemblances and think sameness. Without memory, conception would be impossible. When we recall our percepts, we call them re-percepts; so when we recall our concepts, we term them re-concepts, or remembered concepts.

3. *Imagination and phantasy* obscurely outline general notions; but the triangle appears without corners and the soldier without weapons. Still, these vague

outlines assist us to clear notions. We can not imagine a concept. Why? Illustrate.

4. *Judgment and reason* make large contributions. Indeed, every act of classification, as will be seen further on, involves these powers.

Comparative Psychology.—Can the brute discern general notions? The brute perceives things and notices resemblances, but can it think sameness? The brute discerns concrete objects, but does it discern abstract qualities? Can it think the many into one? Is the brute endowed with even rudimentary conception? Does any brute use intelligently abstract words to express general ideas? Science, at the present time, can only give negative answers to these questions.

1. Man thinks individual notions into concepts; the brute perceives individuals, but is incapable of forming general notions.

2. Man uses language; the brute is dumb. The instinctive cry of the brute is not language. Only man is endowed with the power to form and express abstract notions.

Growth of Conception.—Children, when two or three years old, make crude classifications. Boys and girls classify the objective world. Youths master the classifications of sciences. Men master systems. The steady growth of this power is manifest from year to year.

Education of Conception.*—Development of conception extends mental power almost infinitely. I think mammal, and it is equal to perceiving millions of individuals. You are able easily to think myriads into a few classes. Thus you make science. "The training

---

* See "Applied Psychology."

of conception should begin in connection with sense-observation. Objects should be laid in juxtaposition, and the child invited to discover their similarities of form, color, etc. And here his active impulses may be appealed to by giving him a confused multitude of objects and inviting him to sort them into classes. By such a direct inspection of a number of examples together, notions of simple classes of natural objects, as species of animals and flowers, as well as of geometric forms and numbers, may be gained. A sufficient variety of instances must be supplied in every case, but the number required will differ according to the character of the notion to be formed. This operation of comparing and classifying should be supplemented by naming the objects thus grouped together, and pointing out in the form of a definition the more important of the traits they have in common." * "The material objects, chalk, salt, coal, and the common metals, will afford us numerous lessons; and so will the series of inquiries into the nature, properties, and action of water. For form we may use the regular solids, surfaces, and lines, while botany and natural history will provide an inexhaustible supply of lessons on life. The main thing will be to make sure that the child states, in clear, unambiguous language (which *he* understands), *only such facts as he has really observed.*" †

SUGGESTIVE STUDY-HINTS.

Review.—Climb the tree (p. 56) and ascend the pyramid (p. 152) to conception, giving definition, office, and product of each faculty. Give the distinction between perception and representation, etc.

* Sully. † George P. Brown.

What is thinking? Why are the thinking faculties called the comparative powers? Why the logical powers? The elaborative faculties? The reflective faculties? Give the meaning of discern. (We perceive things having properties, and discern relations between things.)

What is meant by conception? Analyze two of your acts of conception. Tell what you do. Place on the board a diagram showing how you think up to general notions.

First step. What do you mean by analytic observation? Illustrate. Why does this come first? *Second step.* What do you mean by abstraction? Illustrate. Give etymology of the word. What kind of concepts are hardship? beauty? goodness? *Third step.* What do you mean by comparison? Illustrate. What do you discern? *Fourth step.* What do you mean by generalization? Illustrate. Which do you do first, abstract or generalize? *Fifth step.* What do you mean by classification? Illustrate.

State the office of conception. Illustrate. Out of what are sense-percepts made? Concepts?

Name the first characteristic of conception; the second; the third. How do imagination and conception differ?

Give author's definition of conception; yours; Schuyler's. Why do you object to Day's?

What are the products of conception called? What is a concept? Illustrate. Why are concepts called general notions? group-notions? class-notions? Give distinctions between percepts and concepts. Are the terms, idea and notion, synonyms?

What are the properties of a concept? What do you mean by denomination? Give five examples. What do you mean by extension? Illustrate by the thought-pyramid, beginning at the bottom. What do you mean by intention? Illustrate by the thought-pyramid, beginning at the top.

What do you mean by an individual? by a species? by a genus? Give five examples of each. Give the distinction between apprehension and comprehension. Give five examples. In what sense is species used in zoölogy? in logic?

What distinction do you make between analysis and synthesis? Why do you analyze? Synthesize? What is a logical definition? Write on the board, in two forms, definitions of Ethiopian, man, mammal, vertebrate, vegetable, inorganic. Why can not being be defined?

Give the relation of conception to perception; to memory; to imagination; to judgment.

Letter.—Write with great care a letter to your friend, giving a clear account of conception. As this is the most difficult of the mental powers to master, you may ask your friend to study it patiently and work it out.

Analysis of Chapter XIV.

I. **Illustrations.**
    Percepts.   Concepts.

II. **Acts of Conception analyzed.**
    Pencil.   Tree.   Lake.

III. **Elements of an Act of Conception.**
    Analytic observation.   Generalization.
    Abstraction.   Classification.
    Comparison.

IV. **Office of Conception.**
    To gain concepts.   To name concepts.

V. **Characteristics of Conception.**
    Discerning concepts.   Thinking, but not picturing.
    Naming concepts.

VI. **Definitions of Conception.**
    Author's.   Original.   Various.

VII. **Names of Products of Conception.**
    Concepts.   Group-notions.
    General notions.   Class-notions.

VIII. **Properties of Concepts.**
    Denomination.   Intention or inclusion.
    Extension.

IX. **General Nomenclatures.**
    Individual.   Species.   Genus.

X. **Definition.**
    Refers to a higher class.   Gives the differentia.

XI. **Comparative Psychology.**

XII. **Growth and Education of Conception.**

CHAPTER XV.

JUDGMENT.

By this is meant the power to discern the agreement or disagreement of ideas. You say the mountain is high; here you discern and declare the agreement between the notions high and mountain. Perceptive-knowledge and thought-knowledge differ in two respects: 1. We gain perceptive-knowledge intuitively but reach thought-knowledge by processes of elaboration. 2. Perceptive-knowledge is concrete, while thought-knowledge is abstract. Concepts are our first thought-products. We think things into classes by discerning relations of resemblance. As the reaper binds the wheat in bundles, so we think individual things into groups. Judgments are our next higher thought-products. We discover that ideas are so related as to agree or disagree. Self, as judgment, discerns and asserts the agreement and disagreement of notions. We discern truth-relations, which we express in sentences.

Analysis of Acts of Judgment.—The horse is a vertebrate. 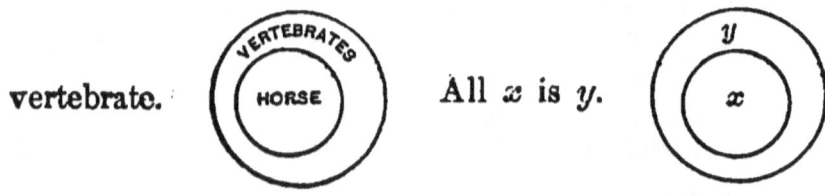 All x is y.

I discern and assert the agreement of the notions vertebrate and horse, and also that of x and y. Discerning and asserting the agreement of notions is called judging. Bees are not vertebrates; w is not x.

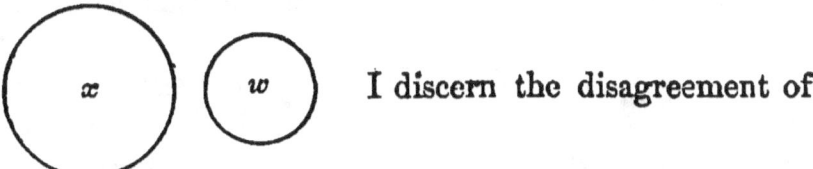 I discern the disagreement of
the notions bee and vertebrate; also of w and x. Discerning and asserting the disagreement of notions is called judging. The capability to discern the agreement or disagreement of notions is termed judgment.

The oyster is a mollusk.

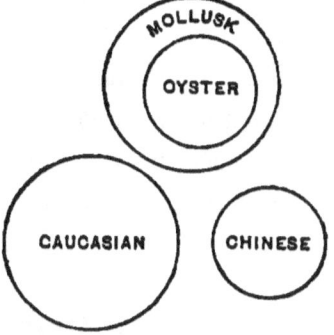

The Chinese are not Caucasians.

I discern agreement between the notions oyster and mollusk, and that the former is included in the latter. I express this agreement by saying the oyster is a mollusk. I discern disagreement between the notions Chinese and Caucasian, and that one is not included in the other, and I express this disagreement by saying that the Chinese are not Caucasians.

Office of Judgment.—Self, as judgment, elaborates percepts and concepts into truths; as, Pope was a poet; Burr was not a patriot. In discerning the agreement and disagreement of notions we discern truths.

1. *The mind, as judgment*, discerns the agreement or disagreement of notions. This is primary. We

find that ideas are so related as to agree or disagree. We discern agreement between the notions wise and Bacon.

2. *The mind, as judgment,* asserts the agreement or disagreement of notions. We not only discern the relation between the ideas, but we also assert agreement; as, Bacon was wise.

3. *The mind, as judgment,* elaborates notions into truths. The evolution of truth is pre-eminently the office of judgment. In discerning the agreement of two notions you discern a truth; as, the earth is round.

Characteristics of Judgment.—The following marks distinguish this capability:

1. *Self, as judgment, discerns truth-relations.* Notions agree, as, silver is a metal. The agreement is real, is true. Judgment is our capability to discern this agreement. Beings destitute of judgment are incapable of cognizing truth.

2. *Self, as judgment, thinks notions into propositions.* Judgment is our sentence-making power. We discern and predicate truth-relations. Each declarative sentence expresses an act of judgment.

3. *Self, as judgment, accepts his predications as true.* When the predication accords with reality, we accept the proposition as true; but when the predication does not accord with reality, we reject the proposition as false. Judgment is an essential element of belief. I believe, or accept as true, that Columbus discovered America; but I disbelieve, or reject as false, that Washington was King of England. Because I have the power to discern truth relation, I accept as true my predications.

Elements of Judgment. { Discernment of truth-relations. Assent to truth discerned. }

1. *As judgment, self discerns truth-relations.* Notions agree; this agreement is termed truth-relation, since the assertion of the agreement is either true or untrue. Space is infinite; Cæsar was perfect; as judgment, the soul discerns the truth of the first proposition, and the untruth of the second.

2. *As judgment,* self assents to truth discerned. The soul discerns truth and accepts it. Truth is harmony with reality. The soul is so constituted that it believes its predications of truth-relations. I discern the agreement of the notions man and biped, and I accept as true that man is a biped. I believe it.

Judgment defined.—Judgment, judging, and a judgment represent the faculty, the act, and the product. Judging is the act of predicating the agreement or disagreement of notions. A judgment is the expression of the agreement or disagreement of notions. A judgment is called a proposition or a sentence.

1. *Judgment is the mental power to discern and predicate the agreement or disagreement of notions;* as, I discern the agreement of the notions man and animal, and make the predication that man is an animal. I also discern the disagreement of the notions bird and mammal, and make the predication that birds are not mammals.

2. *Original.* You may write your definition of judgment and give illustrations. What is judging? What is a judgment?

3. **Various Definitions.**—1. STORMOUTH: Judgment is the faculty to discern truth. 2. McCOSH: Judgment is the power to compare

notions as to agreement or disagreement. 3. SULLY: Judgment is the capability to predicate one idea of another. 4. HAMILTON: Judgment is the power to recognize the relation of congruence or conflict between notions. 5. DEWEY: Judgment is the power to refer ideas to realities, and affirm truth-relations. 6. DUNTON: Judgment is the faculty of the mind by which we know the relation between two objects of knowledge.

Terms of a Judgment.—We discern the congruence or incongruence of notions, and predicate these truth-relations. A judgment embodied in language is called a proposition or a sentence, and consists of three parts: subject, predicate, and copula. The terms (from *termini*, extremes) are the subject and predicate.

1. *The subject is the basis of the judgment.* It is that of which we assert the agreement or disagreement. The subject is always a noun, or some word or expression used as such. It may be a percept, as, Arnold was a traitor; or a concept, as, some girls are studious.

2. *The predicate is that which is affirmed or denied of the subject.* The copula and predicate are often condensed into one term; as, God is. When expanded, we have the regular form, God is existing. *The predicate is always a concept.*

3. *The copula expresses the act of judging.* Because it unites the terms of the judgment, it is called the copula. It is present in every act of judgment, either expressed or included in the predicate.

Properties and Classification of Judgments.—In logic, judgments are classified with reference to quantity, quality, relation, modality, etc. For full treatment of this topic, the student is referred to works on logic. Psychology seeks merely to unfold the nature of the judging activity.

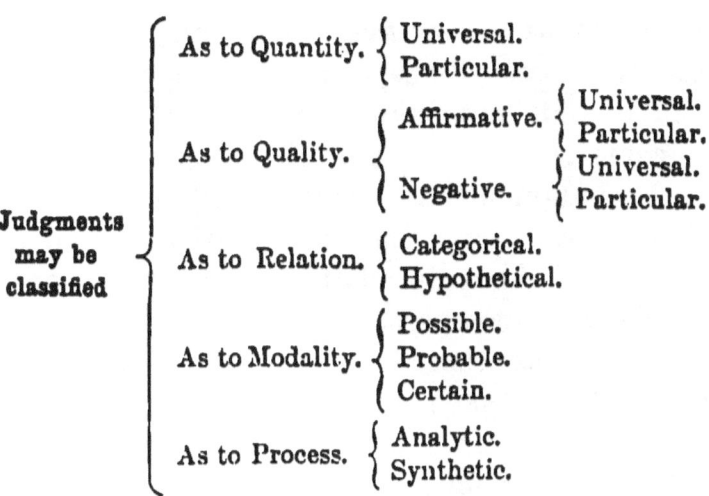

1. *Quantity refers to the extension of the subject.* As to quantity, judgments are universal or particular. (1.) Universal judgments are those in which the predication is of the entire class; as, all men are fallible; all x is y; no man is perfect; no w is x. (2.) Particular judgments are those in which the predication is of a percept or of a part of a class; as, Mary is wise; some boys are studious; some y is x; some boys are not studious; some y is not x. Give five examples, and illustrate by figures.

2. *Quality refers to the congruence or incongruence of notions.* As to quality, judgments are affirmative or negative. (1.) Positive judgments predicate the congruence of notions; as, all elephants are quadrupeds; some men are wise. Give five universal affirmative judgments and five particular affirmatives. (2.) Negative judgments predicate the incongruence of notions; as, no bird is a mammal; some men are not wise. Give five universal negative and five particular negative judgments, illustrating by figures.

Judgment and other Faculties.—In gaining concepts we necessarily judge. Percepts and concepts are the materials out of which we make judgments. Re-percepts and re-concepts are simply remembered percepts and concepts. Re-judgments are remembered judgments. Imagination helps in arranging the materials. Self, as judgment, discerns the truth-relations between notions. Reason enables us to compare judgments and infer conclusions. It is clear that judgment enters in some form into all distinct knowing; and it is equally certain that judging involves all the other intellectual powers. The soul is a unit in knowing.

Comparative Psychology.—The brute is incapable of abstraction, hence can not form concepts. As the predicate of a judgment is necessarily a concept, it is evident that the brute is not endowed with judgment in the sense of the capability to discern truth-relations. Many brute acts seem to indicate the exercise of judgment, but it is believed that all brute activity can be accounted for without supposing the brute to be endowed with this power.

Axioms are Necessary Judgments.—Generalizations from necessary ideas are necessary judgments. These judgments are self-evident truths. They may be verified, but can not be proved. All axioms are necessary judgments. The parts of this apple are equal to this whole. So of this orange and this cube. From my intuitive insight into the relations of the parts to the whole, I discern the general truth—the parts are equal to the whole. The soul perceives directly necessary ideas, and from these elaborates self-evident truths.

Growth of Judgment.*—Conception is exercised ear-

---

* See "Education of Judgment," "Applied Psychology."

lier than judgment, but at a very early age children form crude judgments about food and surroundings. At first they use percepts as the subjects of their judgments. When about three years old, the child begins to use concepts as subjects. Now the child becomes more careful about his statements as the truth-idea begins to be realized. Judgment gradually develops, and in youth seems to reach full activity, though continuing to grow throughout active life.

SUGGESTIVE STUDY-HINTS.

Review.—Give your definition and illustration of conception; of concept; of abstraction; of generalization; of definition. What is the material of which we make concepts? concepts? ideals?

What is meant by judgment? Give the distinction between perceptive-knowledge and thought-knowledge. What are our first thought-products? What relations of things enable us to think individuals into groups? into sentences?

Analyze several of your acts of judgment. What do you discern? What relations of notions enable us to think ideas into propositions? Give five examples.

Give the author's definition of judgment; your definition; McCosh's definition; Hamilton's definition. Define a judgment.

What are the terms of a judgment? Define and illustrate. Give the properties of a judgment. Define and illustrate.

Out of what are judgments made? What do you call a remembered percept? concept? judgment? How does memory help in judgment? What aid does imagination give?

Does the brute judge? How do you account for the remarkable acts of dogs? foxes? horses? elephants?

What is a necessary judgment? Are axioms necessary judgments? What distinction do you make between a necessary idea and a necessary judgment?

Do we perceive necessary truths in the abstract? Illustrate.

Letter.—You may now write a letter, giving your friend your views of judgment. Let all the illustrations be yours.

ANALYSIS OF CHAPTER XV.

I. Analysis of an Act of Judgment.

II. Office of Judgment.
    Discerning agreement.   Predicating.
    Discerning disagreement.

III. Characteristics of Judgment.
    Present in all knowing.   Believed or disbelieved.
    True or false.

IV. Elements.
    Discernment of truth-relations.
    Assent to truth discerned.

V. Definitions of
    Judgment.—Original.   Quoted.
    Judging.   A judgment.

VI. Terms of a Judgment.
    Subject—may be a percept or a concept.
    Predicate—must be a concept.
    Copula.

VII. Properties and Classes.
    QUANTITY.—Universal.   Particular.
    QUALITY.—Positive.
                Universal affirmative.
                Universal negative.
        Negative.
                Particular affirmative.
                Particular negative.

VIII. Judgment, and other Faculties.
    Perception, Conception, and Memory furnish materials.
    Reason tests the judgment.
    Judgment contributes the truth-element to all knowing.

IX. Comparative Psychology—Brutes not endowed with Judgment.

X. Necessary Judgments.

XI. Growth and Education of Judgment.

CHAPTER XVI.

REASON.

By this is meant our power to reach conclusions. As all intentional violation of law is sin, and as fraud is intentional violation of law, we reach the conclusion that fraud is sin. You reason when you use intelligently such terms as "*hence,*" "*therefore,*" "*because,*" etc. You arrive at conclusions through judgments. You so combine two propositions as to discern, or infer, or draw, or reach a conclusion. Your capability to do this is called reason.

Acts of Reason analyzed.—Self, as reason, infers conclusions from premises, and hence is sometimes called the power of inference. Let us examine some easy acts of reason.

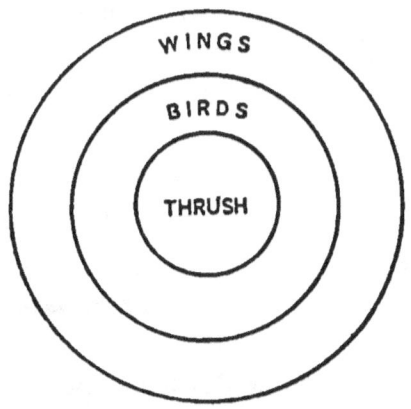

All birds have wings,
The thrush is a bird,
∴ The thrush has wings.

Rational beings are accountable,
Man is rational,
∴ Man is accountable.

We accept the first and second judgments as true, and through these judgments discern the conclusion.

Self, as reason, discerns conclusions. Change one term, and we have:

All birds are vertebrates,
Doves are birds,
∴ Doves are vertebrates.

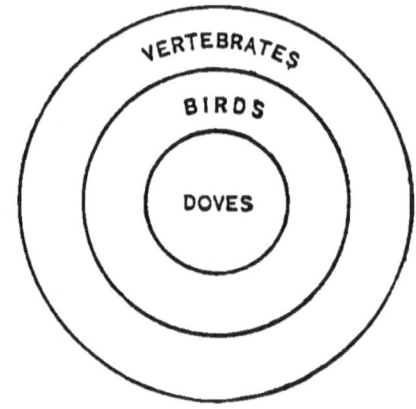

y is x,
z is y,
∴ z is x.

Since doves are birds, and birds are vertebrates, we discern the conclusion, doves are vertebrates. So, since z is included in y, and y in x, we discern that z is included in x. We call the act reasoning when we discern conclusions, and we call the power to discern conclusions reason.

Cause-Relations.—Self, as reason, discerns cause-relations. The relations of causes and effects, means and ends, conditions and interdependencies, antecedents and consequents, wholes and parts, proportions and analogies, etc., are discerned through the medium of interlocked judgments. Cause-relations are all-pervading. From the atom to the Infinite First Cause, cause-relations bind together all things. The universe is a cause-unit. Reason is our capability to discern cause-relations and cause-unity.

Office of Reason.—Self, as reason, discerns cause-relations. When we discern class-relations, we *conceive;* when we discern truth-relations, we *judge;* but, when we discern cause-relations, we *reason.*

1. *Self, as reason, infers particulars from generals.* All things are so related that these inferences are safe:

All minerals are valuable,
Bismuth is a mineral,
∴ Bismuth is valuable.

All M is P,
All S is M,
∴ All S is P.

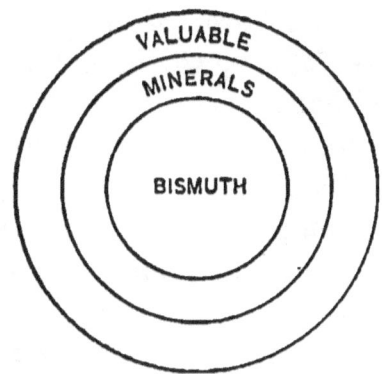

Granted that all minerals are valuable, we may safely infer value of any mineral, however unfamiliar.

2. *Self, as reason, infers generals from particulars.* Since the universe is a cause-unit, and since laws are ever the same, we may safely infer general truths from particular truths. In this case, and this, and this, light diminishes as the square of the distance increases, and we safely infer this as a general law. The sum of the three angles of this triangle is equal to two right angles; but this triangle represents all triangles; therefore we infer the general truth—the sum of the three angles of a triangle is equal to two right angles.

3. *Self, as reason, verifies his conclusions.* By analysis we reduce our arguments to judgments, our judgments to concepts, and our concepts to percepts. By synthesis we reconstruct our arguments. By these processes we subject our conclusions to the tests of law and reality.

Characteristics of Reason.—The soul, as reason, so combines two propositions as to reach a more remote truth:

1. *Reason is the power of inference.* As all men are fallible, we infer that kings are fallible. A being without reason is unable to derive truths from other truths. Only rational beings draw conclusions.

2. *Reason is the science-making power.* In discerning truths in their causal relations, we discover laws and systematize knowledge. Man is a science-maker.

3. *Reason is the power to accept conclusions.* Self, as reason, accepts his inferences as true. This is called intellectual assent or belief. Through the medium of the proofs we discern the conclusions that Washington was President; that the earth revolves around the sun; that the square described on the hypotenuse is equal to the sum of the squares described on the other two sides of a right-angled triangle; and we accept these conclusions as true. We assent to these conclusions; we believe these truths.

Definitions of Reason.—Self, as reason, discerns new truths by comparing other truths. Truths are so related that we can infer conclusions from premises.

1. *Reason is the capability to discern conclusions.* Reason is the power to discern cause-relations. *Reasoning* is inferring conclusions from premises. *A reason* is the expression of an act of reasoning.

2. *Original definition.* Write out and illustrate your definition. What do you do when you reason? What relation do you discover between the proof and the conclusion?

3. Various Definitions.—1. SULLY: Reason is the power to derive conclusions from premises. 2. PORTER: Reason is the power to discern the agreement or disagreement of judgments. 3. McCOSH: Reason is the power to compare two notions by means of a third. 4. BASCOM: Reason is the capability to reach conclusions by means of related judgments. 5. EVEREST: Reason is the capability to combine two propositions, and thus reach a proposition more remote. 6. WUNDT: Reason is the power to unite two judgments in a new judgment. 7. DUNTON: Reason is the faculty to gain new truth through truths already known.

Logic is the science of the laws of thought. Just now you are struggling to understand the thinking powers. Later you will study the laws of thought and their applications. That we may better understand the reasoning process, we will briefly examine the products of reasoning:

1. *Names.* A product of reason is termed a reason, an argument, or a syllogism. An argument stated in regular logical form is called a syllogism.

Products of Reason.—
- 1. Names.—
  - Reasons.
  - Arguments.
  - Syllogisms.
- 2. Terms.—
  - Major Term.
  - Middle Term.
  - Minor Term.
- 3. Propositions.—
  - Major Premise.
  - Minor Premise.
  - Conclusion.

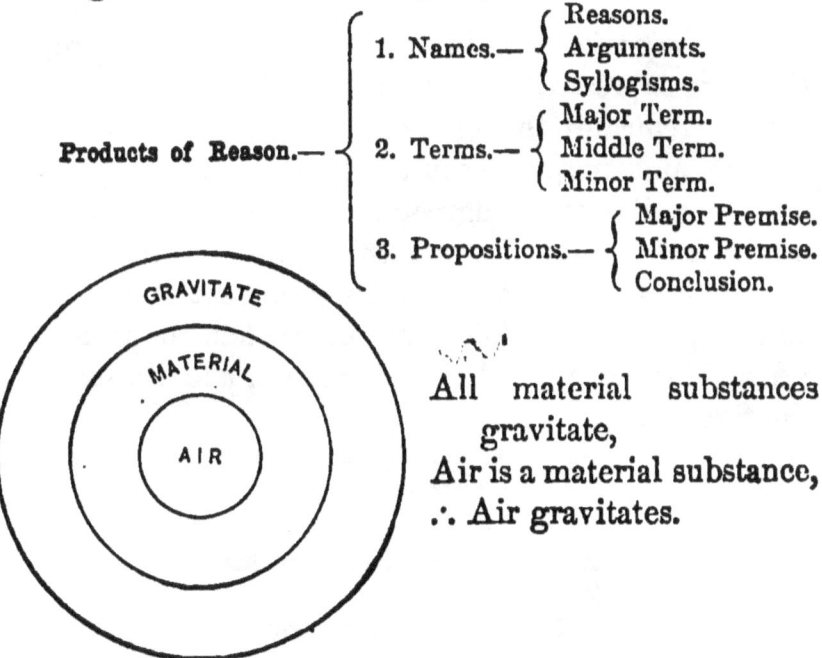

All material substances gravitate,
Air is a material substance,
∴ Air gravitates.

Ordinarily, arguments are informal, as, "Iron is a material substance ; ∴ iron gravitates."

2. *Terms.* A syllogism is an argument in regular form, and contains three terms. The major term is the predicate, and the minor the subject of the conclusion. The middle term is the medium of comparison.

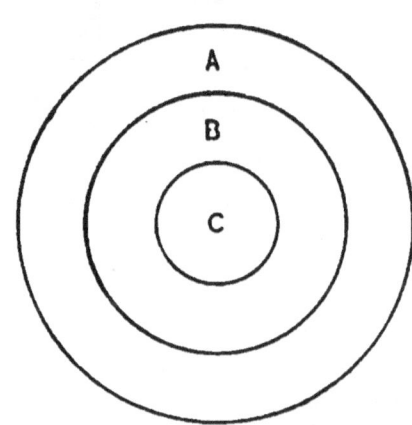

All B is A,
All C is B,
∴ All C is A.

3. *Propositions.* In every argument three propositions are expressed or implied: (1) the major premise, which predicates the agreement or disagreement of the middle and major terms; (2) the minor premise, which predicates the agreement or disagreement of the minor and middle terms; (3) the conclusion, which predicates the agreement or disagreement of the minor and major terms. Point out and explain the terms and propositions in the following reasons, and illustrate by the figures :

All responsible agents are free,
Man is a responsible agent,
∴ Man is free.

All metals are expanded by heat,
Zinc is a metal,
∴ Zinc is expanded by heat.

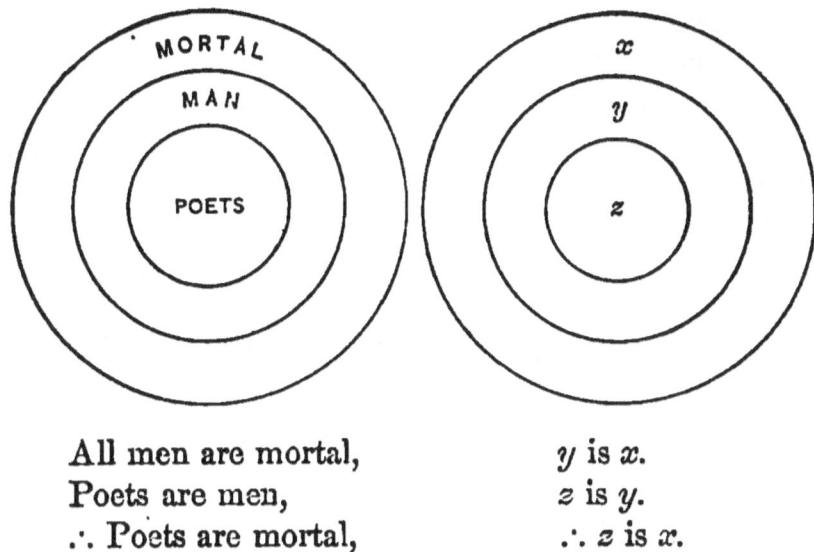

All men are mortal, y is x.
Poets are men, z is y.
∴ Poets are mortal,   ∴ z is x.

4. *Enthymeme.* Reasoning is discerning conclusions through the medium of premises. Rarely do we express both premises. The Americans are free, and therefore happy. The major premise, all free people are happy, is understood. A reason with one premise suppressed is called an enthymeme.

But is what we term syllogistic reasoning, reasoning at all? Yes, in the sense that all our reasonings, when we state the process in full, assume that form. Let the question be, Is this man a murderer? Certain facts being given, you determine by a process of reasoning that he killed the man. But did he do it with malice? You determine that also by a process of reasoning. You then say that—

> Murder is killing with malice prepense,
> This man killed with malice prepense,
> Therefore this man is a murderer.

The proof of the murder, and the force of the reasoning, does not turn on any manipulation of terms, or class relations, but on the facts which give us the right to use our terms, and which enable us to bring the individual into those class relations. It is not proved by the syllogism that the man committed the murder, but the syllogism is the form which the proof takes in our minds when we state it fully and in order.

REASON.

Reasoning Processes.—In our search after truth we infer generals from representative particulars—we *induct*. From generals we infer particulars—we *deduce*. Finally, we test correctness by a critical analysis and synthesis—we verify

1. *Inductive Reasoning* is inferring generals from particulars. Through the medium of particulars we discern generals:

(1.) Illustrations. Take the human hand. Let the fingers represent particulars and the arm the general. Also, place on the board converging lines.

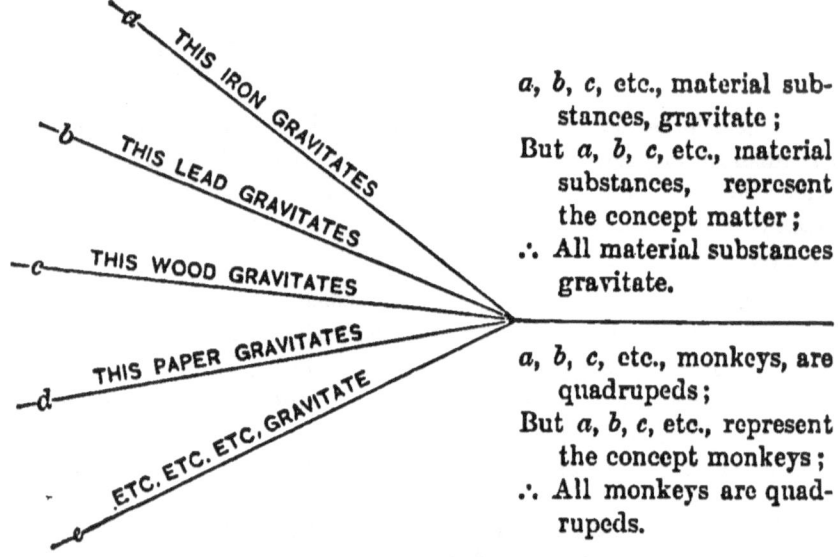

a, b, c, etc., material substances, gravitate;
But a, b, c, etc., material substances, represent the concept matter;
∴ All material substances gravitate.

a, b, c, etc., monkeys, are quadrupeds;
But a, b, c, etc., represent the concept monkeys;
∴ All monkeys are quadrupeds.

(2.) Nature is uniform. Forces not only persist, but also act uniformly. The reign of law is the sub-basis of all science. Induction is safe. You may illustrate as above:

In a, b, c, etc., cases, H_2O form water;
But a, b, c, etc., cases represent all possible cases;
∴ In all cases the union of one volume of oxygen and two volumes of hydrogen will form water.

(3.) Mathematical induction. One case is sufficient to justify the inference. Is this peculiar to mathematics?

The sum of the three angles of this triangle is equal to two right angles;
But this is a typical triangle;
∴ The sum of the three angles of any triangle is equal to two right angles.
(Give two examples, and show that a single typical case justifies a general conclusion.)

2. *Deductive reasoning* is inferring particulars from generals. Through the medium of general truths we discern particular truths:

(1.) Illustrations. Again study the human hand. Now you begin with the arm as representing the general truth, and you let each finger represent a particular truth. Also, place on board diverging lines as follows:

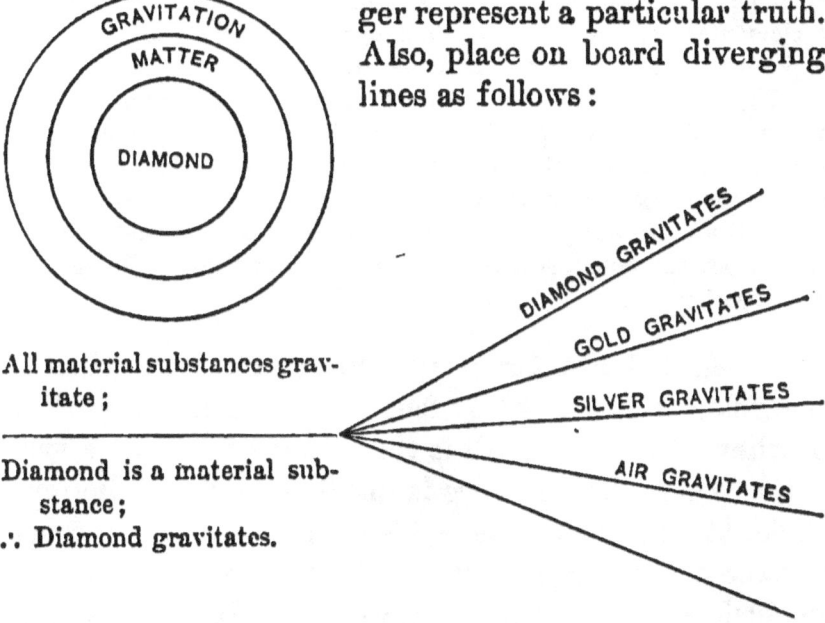

All material substances gravitate;
——————————————
Diamond is a material substance;
∴ Diamond gravitates.

(2.) Major premise. The conclusions of our inductions become the major premises for our deductions.

(3.) Deduction in science. By induction we discover laws, and by deduction we apply laws. Thus science is builded.

3. *Verification* is resolving arguments into their elements, and reuniting these elements into arguments. Syllogisms are reduced to judgments, judgments to concepts, and concepts to percepts. This is termed the

(1.) *Analytic test.* By analysis, we resolve arguments into elements. Thus we examine the foundations of reasoning and test the validity of our reasoning. Take this syllogism:
Men are rational,
Negroes are men,
∴ Negroes are rational.
We reduce the argument to judgments in order to examine each judgment separately. We reduce the major premise to the concepts men and rational. We reduce the concepts men and rational to elementary percepts to test their agreement. In the same way we reduce the minor premise and the conclusion.

(2.) *Synthetic test.* By synthesis, we combine elements into arguments. We think individual notions into the concepts men and rational. We discern the agreement of men and rational, and form the judgment men are rational.

In the same way we synthesize the minor premise and conclusion. Does the conclusion follow from the premises? This is the final question.

Disbelief, Doubt, Certainty.—Self, as reason, when a conclusion is disproved by facts, rejects it as false. We disbelieve that the earth is the center of the solar system. When the evidence is insufficient or conflicting, we doubt; but when the evidence is conclusive, we accept the conclusion as certain. Self, as reason, discerns conclusions and accepts them as true. We believe the earth is spherical, because the proofs satisfy reason. We believe Arnold was a traitor, because the testimony is conclusive. Assenting to conclusions as true is intellectual belief.

1. *Disbelief.* When a conclusion is not sustained by proofs, we disbelieve it. We disbelieve the story of Tell and the apple, because the proofs are wanting. Belief comes from evidence. "Faith comes by hearing." In the absence of evidence, belief is impossible. When the facts clearly disprove a conclusion, we disbelieve it and reject it as false. *Unbelief* is the absence of belief.

2. *Doubt.* When the proofs are insufficient, we doubt. Are the planets inhabited? We doubt, because the proofs do not satisfy us.

3. *Degrees of belief.* Belief varies as the proofs vary. We accept the nebular hypothesis as possible. We accept evolution in some form as probable. We accept the atomic theory as highly probable. Business men base their operations largely on estimated probabilities.

4. *Certainty.* Accumulative proof as well as demonstrative proof gives certainty. We know that the three angles of a triangle are equal to two right angles, for the mathematical proofs are demonstrative. We know with equal certainty that Washington was President, for the cumulative testimony renders doubt impossible. When proof is sufficient to establish the conclusion as absolutely certain, we accept it without the shadow of a doubt; we believe it absolutely.

Reason and Faith.—"To believe a thing is to regard it as true. Truth is harmony with universal intelligence." "Faith is the highest product of reason." Faith is not a faculty, but a complete act of faith involves all the faculties. The elements of practical faith are intellectual assent, confidence, trust.

1. *Intellectual assent.* The soul discerns the conclusion, "All

life comes from antecedent life." We assent to this proposition, accept it as true, believe it. Intellectual assent to truth discerned is the fundamental element in belief or faith. So far, belief is purely intellectual. This is what is meant by the cold logic of mathematics. But faith means much more than intellectual assent. It means also confidence and trust as well. It involves the emotions and the will as well as the intellect. Faith works by love, purifies the heart, and leads on to good lives. But the basis is truth discerned. Blind credulity is not faith. Only rational beings believe.

Belief or Faith.— $\begin{cases} \text{1. Antecedents of Assent.} \begin{cases} \text{Proofs.} \\ \text{Reasons.} \\ \text{Evidences.} \end{cases} \\ \text{2. Intellectual Assent.} \\ \text{3. Consequents of Assent.} \begin{cases} \text{1. Confidence—Emotion.} \\ \text{2. Trust—Will.} \end{cases} \end{cases}$

2. *Confidence.* We *confide* in the evidence as well as in our abilities to discern truth. We have not the means to make exhaustive experiments for ourselves, but we have confidence in Tyndall and other great scientists. We believe them to be honest and capable. We not only assent to the conclusion, "All life comes from antecedent life," but we accept it with confidence. We discern this stupendous truth and confide in it. We believe with the emotions as well as with the intellect.

3. *Trust.* We trust where we believe. The engineer believes the new bridge to be safe, and trusts his train upon it. We trust in Tyndall and other great scientists, and make the conclusion, "All life comes from antecedent life," the corner-stone of science. We assent we confide, we trust. Faith begins in intellectual assent, works by love, and culminates in action. Faith makes society possible, and life worth living. Faith is the condition of progress and achievement. Life is too short for one person to experience much, but by faith each one builds on the experience of others. By faith the vicarious experience of the race is appropriated by the individual. The scientist walks by sight in *one* case, but by faith in a *thousand* cases.

Growth of Reason.—The power of inference is the latest of all the intellectual faculties to reach full activity. When children not more than three years old startle their parents with troublesome *whys*, it is only budding reason, crude and concrete. The boy begins to solve problems and to debate, thus indicating a steady growth of this faculty. Reason does not often reach its highest activity before the twentieth year. Its growth throughout active life is everywhere evident. "Old men for counsel" attests the popular belief in this fact.

Education of Reason.*—"The culture of reason has been very generally neglected in our methods of teaching. The object of teachers seems to have been to fill the memory with the facts and truths of a subject, rather than to develop the power by which these truths were obtained. They have failed to develop the power of original thought and investigation. Even in teaching thought-studies, memory has been brought into activity more than thought. The mind has too often been regarded as a capacity to be filled, rather than an activity to be developed. Teachers have aimed to put knowledge into the mind, as we pour water into a vessel, or shovel coal into a coal-bin; while the power that originates knowledge, that works up ideas and thoughts into laws and principles, has been neglected.

"This culture should be carefully adapted to the age and development of the pupils. Children should be taught to compare objects, to inquire for causes, and to see the relation of things to one another. Inductive reasoning should precede deductive; causes should be presented before laws and principles; and deductive thought and the generalizations of science should be introduced as the mind becomes prepared for them." †

Comparative Psychology.—Does the brute reason? Does it discern cause relations? Does it infer conclusions from premises? Does any brute give indications of possessing even rudimentary reason? "There seems to be no proof," says Bascom, "that even the most sagacious brutes form judgments or induce or deduce conclusions from premises. The brute is endowed with sense-perception, memory, and phantasy. These faculties, we believe, fully account

---

* Brooks's "Mental Science and Culture."
† See "Education of Reason," "Applied Psychology."

for all brute phenomena. The animal has to do directly with things and their images. The animal can not form ideas, and hence can not be taught language. Man alone gains ideas, and deals with abstractions, generalizations, concepts, judgments, reasons." No process of development can ever make a reasoning animal out of a brute. The difference is in kind.

SUGGESTIVE STUDY-HINTS.

Review.—You may now climb the Psychological Tree (p. 56) and ascend the Psychological Pyramid (p. 152) till you reach reason. Define each faculty and its product, and give its office. In all cases give examples. What relations do you discern when you conceive? when you judge? when you reason? Point out the distinction between perceive and discern. Define faculty; perceptive faculties; representative faculties; thought faculties.

What is meant by reason? What is reason sometimes called? Why? Analyze an act of reason. What do you discover?

What is the office of a faculty? of reason? How do we find out particular truths? General truths? How do we verify conclusions? Illustrate.

Give the first characteristic of reason; the second; the third. What do you mean by belief? Show the distinctions between reason and conception; reason and judgment.

State the author's definition of reason; yours; Wundt's. Define reasoning and a reason.

What may we call the products of reason? What is a syllogism? an enthymeme? Give the terms of a syllogism. Give the propositions. Illustrate.

Give the two ways in which we reason. Define and illustrate deductive reasoning; inductive reasoning. Explain verification. Give three examples of each process. What do you mean by verification by analysis? by synthesis? What is belief? Name the three elements of belief. Illustrate.

How are reason and belief related? What is testimony? Give distinctions between unbelief, doubt, degrees of belief and certainty. Show that belief is an intellectual product.

Tell about the growth of reason. When does it reach full activity? Give some of the mistakes of the old education. What branches seem to be best for the culture of reason?

Does the brute reason? Give Bascom's views. What faculties has the brute? Do they account for all mental phenomena of brute-life?

Letter.—You may now tell your friend about the crowning intellectual power. Ask him to take plenty of time here. Everything must stand out in sunlight clearness.

Theories.—The antiquated theories of idealism, realism, and nominalism, which engaged thinkers of past centuries, are omitted. They might confuse and could not benefit the young psychologist.

Analysis of Chapter XVI.

I. **Acts of Reason analyzed.**
   Deduction.   Induction.

II. **Office of Reason.**
   Discerning particulars.   Verifying conclusions.
   Discerning generals.

III. **Characteristics of Reason.**
   Power to infer.   Power to believe.
   Power to systematize.

IV. **Reason defined.**
   Author's definition.   Various definitions.
   Original definition.

V. **Terms of a Syllogism.**
   Major.   Middle.   Minor.

VI. **Propositions of a Syllogism.**
   Major premise.   Conclusion.
   Minor premise.

VII. **Reasoning Processes.**
   Induction.   Deduction.   Verification.

VIII. **Reason and Belief.**
   Belief defined.   Degrees of belief.
   Disbelief.   Certainty.
   Doubt.   Blunders.

IX. **Growth and Education of Reason.**

X. **Comparative Psychology.**

CHAPTER XVII.

THOUGHT-KNOWING—GENERAL VIEW.

Reason crowns Cognition.—At the base of the psychological pyramid you find perceptive knowing. All cognition is founded on the rock of immediate knowledge. Representative knowing builds on perceptive knowing. Without representation there could be no comparison, and thought would be impossible. Crowning the pyramid of the intellectual faculties and their products, you find reason. Here, presented in one view, and, as far as possible, in the order of their dependence, are the nine cognitive powers:

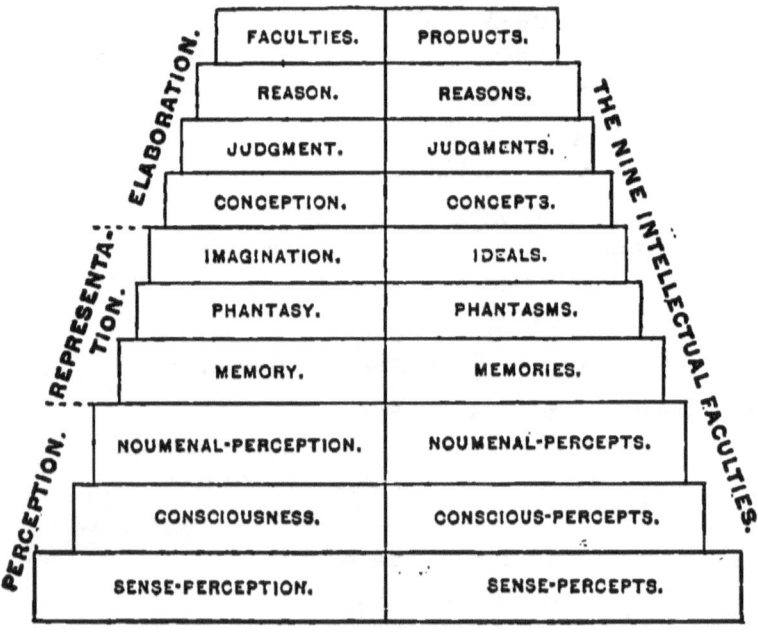

The Nine Intellectual Faculties.—The soul is the conscious self that knows, feels, and wills. The capabilities of the soul to exert acts of knowing different in kind are termed the intellectual faculties. A faculty is not an organ or an entity; nor is a faculty a myth. This bar of magnetic iron has not organs, but bound up in it are energies called magnetism, gravity, cohesion. The soul is an entity endowed with capabilities to know, to feel, and to will. *A faculty is a soul-energy to do acts distinguishable in kind from other acts.* You reproduce and recognize a past experience; the act is distinguishable in kind from all other kinds of mental acts; memory is a faculty; the soul is endowed with a reproductive energy.

1. *The intellectual faculties are the powers of the soul to perform different kinds of acts of knowing.* Discrimination and assimilation are processes involved in some degree in all knowing; but these are not faculties. Like the physical forces, faculties are distinct energies. A compound element is not a greater absurdity than a compound faculty. We have as many intellectual powers as we have distinct knowing energies, and no more.

2. *Groups of intellectual faculties.* The number three is not a sacred number in science, save so far as truth is sacred. Classification is scientific when it accords with reality. "How do we gain knowledge? How do we keep it? What can we do with it?" These questions indicate the natural grouping of the cognitive powers. Each group answers to one of these questions. Perception includes our three intuitive powers; representation includes our three representative powers; and elaboration includes our three thought-powers. This classification is considered true to reality, and is certainly exhaustive. No better classification seems possible for psychological, educational, or literary purposes.

3. *A uniform nomenclature needed.* Much of the confusion in the realms of mental science arises from an imperfect and ambiguous nomenclature. But psychologists and educators are rapidly approaching uniformity. The pyramid represents the substantial agreement of our latest and best authors.

Thinking is discerning Relations.—Thought-knowledge is a knowledge of relations. All knowing is immediate, representative, or mediate. Because we discern the unknown through the known, thought-knowing is called *mediate* knowing. Because we think crude percepts into polished concepts and judgments and reasons, we call thought-knowing *elaborative* knowing. Why is thought-knowing called reflective knowing? comparative knowing? logical knowing?

Names.— { Thought-Knowing.
Mediate-Knowing.
Comparative-Knowing.
Elaborative-Knowing.
Reflective-Knowing.
Logical-Knowing. }

Our thinking faculties are our soul-energies to discern relations. " The faculties of elaboration are variously denominated thus: *The elaborative or discursive faculties,* since they are employed in working up into higher forms the materials supplied by acquisition and reproduction; *the logical faculties,* since they are the faculties employed in logical processes; *the comparative faculties,* since comparison enters as an essential element into all their processes; *the faculties of relations,* since they deal with relations; *the thought faculties,* since their acts are styled thought; *the rational faculties, understanding,* or <u>*intelligence,*</u> since they are the faculties which characterize man as rational, and thus distinguish him from inferior beings." *

Names.— { The Thinking Powers.
The Comparative Powers.
The Elaborative Faculties.
The Reflective Faculties.
The Logical Faculties.
The Rational Faculties.
The Understanding (indefinite). }

· Understanding is used in various senses, and hence is objectionable. The other names are expressive and definite, and may be used interchangeably.

Thinking is based on Comparison.—Thinking is discerning relations between things. We perceive things and discern relations. The things perceived and the

* Schuyler.

relations discerned are objective realities, but concepts, judgments, and reasons are products of the mind.

1. *Conception* is the power to think things into classes. When we compare objects, we discern resemblances and form groups of resembling things. We gain general notions.

2. *Judgment* is the power to think notions into propositions. When we compare two notions we discern and predicate agreement or disagreement. We gain truths.

3. *Reason* is the power to think propositions into arguments. When we compare propositions, we discern conclusions or causal relations. Through interlocked judgments self, as reason, discerns causal relations, and thus builds science. We gain conclusions.

The Thinking Faculties—
{ Conception.
  Judgment.
  Reason. }

"**We distinguish Three Stages of Thinking.** First of all, there is the formation of general notions or concepts. This is an act of *conception*. Next to this comes the combining of two concepts in the form of a statement or proposition, as when we say, 'Material bodies have weight.' This is an act of *judgment*. Lastly, we have the operation by which the mind passes from certain judgments to certain other judgments, as when from the assertions, 'Material substances have weight,' 'Gases are material substances,' we proceed to the further assertion, 'Gases have weight.' This is an act of reason. These distinctions have been fixed by logicians, and not by psychologists. Nevertheless, since they roughly mark off the more simple and the more complex modes of thinking and products of thought, it is convenient to the psychologist to adopt the distinctions." *

Self, as Conception, thinks Many Individuals into One Class.—The product is called a general notion because

* Sully.

it is general to each individual of the class. Why are concepts called class-notions and group-notions? An idea may be a percept or a concept. Notion has been and is still used as synonymous with idea, but the tendency now is to use notion in the sense of concept.

Products of Conception— { Concepts. General Notions. Class-Notions. Group-Notions. Notions.

"To classify is no secret of science, no process reserved for the select few who are initiated into a magic art, but it is as universal and necessary as the act of thinking. The classifications of common life may be as rational and as useful for the ends of common life as are those of science for its special objects."*

"In our observation of the relation of resemblance, as of every other, we proceed through our knowledge, previous or present, of objects. From the knowledge we have of things we discern points in which they are alike. This enables us to put them into a class, to which we may attach a name. That class must include all the objects possessing the common attributes fixed on. The faculty to discern relations of resemblance is our power to manufacture our general notions or concepts." †

Self, as Judgment, discerns Truth-Relations.—The product of judging is called a judgment, because it is a decision of the mind. As it sets forth the agreement or disagreement of notions, it is called a proposition. We discern the agreement or disagreement of ideas—we judge. We express the agreement or disagreement—we form judgments. A proposition or sentence asserts the agreement or disagreement of notions. When the assertion corresponds with reality, the judgment is true. All judgments are either true or false.

* Porter. † McCosh.

Products of Judgment— { Judgments. Propositions. Sentences. }

Self, as Reason, discerns Conclusions through the Medium of Premises.—Because we think propositions together and thus discern conclusions, reasons are called syllogisms. Because we establish truth by proofs, reasons are called arguments and formal proofs.

Products of Reason— { Reasons. Arguments. Syllogisms. Formal Proofs. }

How simple and yet how wonderful are these powers! Man thinks—is rational. Man thinks—gains a mastery over the material world. Man thinks—tries to solve the problem of the universe. As the digestive organs elaborate food into bones, muscles, and nerves, so the thinking faculties elaborate our acquisitions into concepts, judgments, and reasons.

Forms of Thinking and Faculties of Thought.—"There are three distinct forms of thinking, and consequently three distinct faculties of thought, which may be defined as follows:

"Conception is the faculty of the mind by which we form our general abstract notions, or concepts.

"Judgment is the faculty of the mind by which we know the relation between two objects of knowledge.

"Reason is the faculty of the mind by which we gain new truth from truth already known."*

Original and Manufactured Knowledge.—All our knowledge is original or manufactured. Original knowledge has three sources: Sense-intuition, conscious-intuition, and noumenal-intuition. *Sense-intuition* is our power to gain original knowledge of the external world. *Conscious-intuition* is our capability to gain original knowl-

* Dunton.

edge of the mental world. *Noumenal-intuition* is our power to gain necessary ideas. Through these three sources we gain all the elements of knowledge.

The soul, out of original elements, manufactures higher forms of knowledge. We so combine these elements as to produce things unheard of before in earth or heaven; this is the work of self, as *imagination*. We discern class-relations and group resembling things into classes, and thus gain general notions; this is the work of self, as *conception*. We discern truth-relations and think notions into propositions; this is the work of self, as *judgment*. We discern cause-relations and reach conclusions through judgments; this is the work of self, as *reason*.

Self, as *memory*, reproduces, unchanged, all forms of knowledge. Memories are merely reproductions of our acquisitions, both original and manufactured.

Last Words of Physiological Psychology. — "Physiological Psychology investigates the phenomena of human consciousness from the physiological point of view. It finds a marvelous material mechanism called the nervous system, and it describes the effects of external and internal stimuli upon molecular nerve-substance. It is pre-eminently experimental, then speculative, but never demonstrative. Whatever changes take place in the nerve-substance, in the process of starting and communicating nerve-commotion, are invisible and impalpable. Connections between different cerebral areas and their functions are so complex and subtile that it may be doubted whether physiological psychology will ever succeed in completely disentangling them. We know certain of the physical conditions and concomitants of soul action, but mental phenomena can not be conceived of as identical with the molecular motion of the nervous mass; nor can the phenomena of consciousness be conceived of as the product of the brain. The conclusion is a logical as well as a psychological necessity: The subject of all states of consciousness is a real unit-being called mind, which is of non-material nature, and acts and develops according to laws of its own, but is specially correlated with certain material molecules and masses, forming the substance of the brain.

Physical Basis of Thought.—" A scientific physiology of the cerebral hemispheres does not exist, nor is it at the present a matter for even hopeful anticipation. In studying the higher mental phenomena, physiological psychology is obliged almost wholly to adopt the methods of the old psychology and accept the facts of consciousness. We decline to discuss the physical basis of the logical faculties, as there is absolutely no scientific ground on which to base such a discussion. The inability of psychological science to conceive of any physical process which can be correlated with the acts of conceiving, judging, and reasoning, is complete. We are forced to make the same humiliating admission as to memory and imagination and choice and intuition and conscience." *

Reason and Unity.—Infinite Reason planned the universe. Everything, from the atom to a system of worlds, is related by dependencies. Cause and effect, means and ends, antecedents and consequents, unite all into one unity. Endowed with Reason, we can think the thoughts of God after him.

Reason, through interlocked Judgments, discerns cause relations. In its work, Reason lays under contribution all our other capabilities. All are its servants, subject to its supervision. We fashion our percepts—Reason is there; we remember and imagine—Reason is there; we form judgments—Reason is there; we feel emotions of truth and beauty and duty—Reason is there; we choose and act—behold, Reason is there.

Not to educate Reason is to leave man to grope in a sea of hopeless mystery. To the unthinking, the universe is a maze without a plan, and life is not worth living. As reason grows, all things begin to assume proportion and harmony. Substances, forces, laws, conditions, dependencies; cause, space, duration; rational beings, brutes, plants, worlds; all things fall into rhythm and make for us the music of the spheres.

* Ladd, "Physiological Psychology."

PART V.

THE FEELINGS.

CHAPTER XVIII.—THE INSTINCTS.
        XIX.—THE PHYSICAL FEELINGS.—THE APPETITES.
        XX.—THE EMOTIONS.—EGOISTIC EMOTIONS.
        XXI.—THE EMOTIONS.—ALTRUISTIC EMOTIONS.
        XXII.—THE EMOTIONS.—TRUTH EMOTIONS.
        XXIII.—THE EMOTIONS.—ÆSTHETIC EMOTIONS.
        XXIV.—THE EMOTIONS.—ETHICAL EMOTIONS.
        XXV.—THE EMOTIONS.—GENERAL VIEW.

PSYCHOLOGICAL PYRAMID.

THE CAPABILITIES OF THE MIND.	THE WILL.	THE WILL POWERS.	
	THE FEELINGS.	THE EMOTIONS.	THE COSMIC EMOTIONS. THE ALTRUISTIC EMOTIONS. THE EGOISTIC EMOTIONS.
		THE PHYSICAL FEELINGS.	THE SPECIAL SENSES. THE GENERAL SENSES. THE APPETITES.
		THE INSTINCTS.	HUMAN INSTINCTS. COMMON INSTINCTS. STRICTLY BRUTE INSTINCTS.
	THE INTELLECTUAL FACULTIES.	THE THINKING POWERS.	REASON. JUDGMENT. CONCEPTION.	REASONS. JUDGMENTS. CONCEPTS.
		THE REPRESENTATIVE POWERS.	IMAGINATION. PHANTASY. MEMORY.	IDEALS. PHANTASMS. MEMORIES.
		THE PERCEPTIVE POWERS.	NOUMENAL-PERCEPTION. CONSCIOUS-PERCEPTION. SENSE-PERCEPTION.	NOUMENAL-PERCEPTS. CONSCIOUS-PERCEPTS. SENSE-PERCEPTS.

PRODUCTS.

FIFTH PART.

THE FEELINGS.

Feelings are agitations and impulses of the soul. I suffer hunger, I long for wisdom, I sympathize with my bereaved friend, I feel impulses to do what I believe to be right. These agitations and impulses are called feelings, or sensibilities, or susceptibilities.

Names. { The Feelings.
The Sensibilities.
The Susceptibilities.

A sensibility is a capability for a distinct kind of feeling. The power of thirst is a feeling or sensibility. The agitation and impulse of thirstiness is the activity of the capability to feel thirst. We are endowed with powers to feel, and we exert these powers, or we feel. A feeling implies a power to feel. We have as many sensibilities as we have distinct kinds of feeling. A feeling is usually agreeable or disagreeable; this general characteristic of the feelings will enable you to distinguish feeling from knowing and willing.

We enjoy and suffer. We enjoy sweet music, congenial society, success; but we suffer physical pain, want, disappointment. We discern truth, feel pleasure, and choose safety. We know, feel, and will.

Classes of Feelings. { The Instincts.
The Physical Feelings.
The Emotions.

Feeling is mental agitation and impulse. Some feelings are blind but guiding impulses—these we call instincts. Some feelings are occasioned by organic bodily excitations—these we name physical feelings. Some feelings are occasioned by ideas—these we term emotions. This easy classification of the feelings is thought to be exhaustive as well as convenient.

CHAPTER XVIII.

THE INSTINCTS.

By these we mean guiding impulses. All feelings are blind; many feelings move to action; but instincts are the only feelings which guide. The guiding impulses or instincts are clearly a distinct class of feelings. Where intelligence can not act, instinct moves the animal to blindly conform to law. Creative Wisdom has implanted in the animal marvelous energies to adapt means to ends without knowing why. Instinct is adaptative or regulative impulse; it is a blind tendency to wise ends. (*The discussion of Instinct [see Chapter II, p. 15] seems to be as full as is desirable in an elementary work. A careful examination of the chapter on Instinct will aid the student to master the following chapters.*)

CHAPTER XIX.

THE PHYSICAL FEELINGS—THE APPETITES.

By the physical feelings we mean our capabilities to feel organic affections of the body. The feelings occasioned by external excitants affecting the sensorium are called special sensations; the feelings occasioned by the affections of the organs and tissues of the body are called general sensations; but the feelings occasioned by cravings for bodily needs are termed appetites. Our capabilities to feel in these ways are termed

The Physical Feelings. { The Special Sensations. The General Sensations. The Appetites.

All feeling is mental, but mental agitations and impulses originating in organic affections of the body may appropriately be termed physical feelings.

Sensation. By this is meant the conscious affection of the sensorium. Agitations occasioned by affections of the special sensor apparatuses, as in seeing, hearing, smelling, tasting, touching, are termed special sensations. Agitations occasioned by affections of the general sensor apparatuses are called general sensations; as, sensations of hunger, thirst, weariness. (*See Chapters IV, V, and VI. Sensation is there examined at length. You are recommended to review these chapters before advancing.*)

Mechanism of Sensation.—The nervous mechanism includes the end organs, the sensor-nerves, and the central organs. It is the office of the end organs to transmute the physical molecular processes into physiological processes. The molecular-commotion moves through the nerves to the central organs. The molecules of the central organs are capable of assuming to each other inconceivably varied relations in transmuting and redistributing nerve-commotion. Such is the vital mechanism of sensation. The self-conscious soul feels the excitations of this mechanism, and these feelings are called sensations. Self as sense-perception out of his sensations forms ideas called sense-percepts. "But the connections between the different cerebral areas and their functions are so complex and subtle that physiological science will need a long time to disentangle them; it may be doubted whether it will ever succeed in doing this completely."

THE APPETITES.

By these we mean the cravings for bodily wants. Our acts of cognition are more or less definite, and we are able to examine them with considerable certainty. We shall find it much more difficult to scrutinize our feelings; but patient, penetrating effort will enable us to conquer this new world.

Analysis of Acts of Appetite.—You have not taken food for twelve hours. The dead tissues have been removed during sleep. The aching void within is the cry of hunger, or the appetite for food. The soul feels the bodily cry of hunger, and also feels the desire to satisfy the appetite. These feelings occasion the impulse to seek and take food. A limited quantity of food temporarily satisfies hunger, but when the system requires more nutriment, the craving begins again. You may analyze thirst, and tell what you discover. Does the soul feel the cry of thirst?

Office of the Appetites.—Self, as appetite, feels the cries of the body for bodily wants; these cries give rise to desires for means to satisfy the wants. When our bodies need rest, we desire sleep to satisfy the cry of sleepiness. Craving for objects to gratify the organic needs of the body is the office of appetite. Each appetite has its special office. What is the office of hunger? of thirst? of restiveness? of respiration?

Characteristics of an Appetite.—How do you distinguish an appetite from other feelings? From your analysis you discover the three peculiarities of an appetite:

1. *An appetite is a craving occasioned by an organic need of the body.* Give the physiological explanation, and show that this is true of hunger, thirst, sleepiness.

2. *An appetite is intermittent.* When satisfied, the craving ceases for a time, but returns. Explain physiologically, and show that respiration, sleepiness, hunger, are intermittent.

3. *An appetite has physical limits.* The amount that can be taken of food, or of drink, or of air, or of sleep, or of exercise, is limited. Explain physiologically. All feelings having these characteristics may be safely classed as appetites.

The Appetites.—The following seem to be the only feelings that can be classed as appetites. Each of these feelings has the three characteristics of an appetite:

Appetites.—
- Hunger, the appetite for food.
- Thirst, the appetite for drink.
- Sleepiness, the appetite for sleep.
- Restiveness, the appetite for exercise or rest.
- Sexuality, the appetite for sex.
- Respiration, the appetite for air.

Appetite Defined.—It is difficult to define a feeling, though we are just as conscious of our feelings as of our knowings. We are not in doubt about what the feeling is, but we find it hard to tell.

1. *The appetites are cravings for the gratification of bodily wants.* Because the organic cries of the body give rise to mental cravings, we call these feelings physical feelings. These cravings have a physical origin and a physical object.

2. *Original definition.* You may write a definition in your own language. You must not confound desires occasioned by these cravings nor sensations accompanying the gratification of the appetite with the craving of an appetite.

3. **Various Definitions.**—1. GREGORY: Appetites are cravings having for their object the well-being of the body. 2. PEABODY: Appetites are cravings of the body designed to secure the continued life of the individual and the race. 3. McCOSH: Appetites are mental cravings for objects to gratify bodily needs. 4. STEWART: Appetites are cravings which take their rise from the body, and are designed for the preservation of the individual and the continuation of the species.

Appetency is craving for specific gratification, and is the basis of feeling. You crave pears—you say you are very fond of pears. This fondness or appetency gives rise to the craving. So with all appetites.

Natural and Modified Appetites.—Each appetite is an endowment, but an appetite may be modified by experience.

1. *Natural appetites are unperverted appetites.* The appetites for suitable food and drink, for pure air, for necessary sleep, are natural appetites.

2. *Modified appetites are called artificial appetites,*

or perverted appetites, or unnatural appetites. The appetite for opium is an acquired appetite—i. e., the natural appetite for food is so modified by experience as to create a craving for opium. The alcoholic and tobacco appetites are perverted appetites.

<small>Unnatural appetites are natural appetites perverted. They are due to diseased conditions of the organism. Their longings become agonies. They enslave and tend to destroy their victims.</small>

Guides of the Appetites.—Reflex action, instinct, and intelligence, each play a part in guiding to the lawful gratifications of the appetites.

1. *Reflex action* is involved in the organic cries of want and in the satisfied feeling which follows the gratification of the appetite. As to the gratification of the appetites, the action of our bodies is very machine-like. This is well; for, if left to reason, we should starve, or destroy our lives by overeating.

2. *Instinct* covers much of the ground, guiding each brute to the proper gratification of its appetites. How? We do not know. This knowledge is too high for us.

3. *Intelligence guides rational beings.* Man finds out the law and obeys it. In so far as animals are intelligent, intelligence as well as instinct guides them in satisfying their appetites.

Lawful Gratification of the Appetites.—Like all other energies, the appetites have their laws. A rational being learns and obeys these laws, but the brute complies instinctively.

1. Lawful gratification gives pleasure. In this the appetites are like all other endowments. The Father, everywhere, has made happiness to result from law obeyed.

2. Lawful gratification is God-approved, and works good. The divine approval is manifested in connecting pleasure with the lawful gratification of appetite. The body is the organism in connection with which the mind works. That this organism may be kept in the best possible condition, it is necessary that the appetites be lawfully gratified. Asceticism and epicureanism are fundamental errors.

Unlawful Gratification of the Appetites.—All violations of law bring misery. Violations of physical laws produce physical misery.

1. *Unlawful gratification gives pain.* Sooner or later violations of the laws of appetite bring suffering. The trembling debauchee and the wretched dyspeptic are extreme cases.

2. *Unlawful gratification is disapproved.* The wretchedness following the unlawful gratification of the appetites marks the divine disapproval.

3. *Unlawful gratification works evil.* The alcoholic appetite causes much of the crime, insanity, and pauperism that curse society. All unlawful gratification of the appetites tends to brutalize man and destroy society.

Temperance.—This means self-control. While educating children, parents and teachers train them to the habit of controlling their appetites. Thus the appetites are made faithful servants. This is fundamental in education. *Intemperance* is the want of self-control. The child, whether five or fifty years of age, gives loose rein to the appetites, and sinks the man in the animal.

SUGGESTIVE STUDY-HINTS.

Review.—Begin with sense-perception, ascend the Psychological Pyramid (p. 204) and the Psychological Tree (p. 56) to the physical feelings. Define and give office, characteristics, and products of each of the intellectual faculties. Give two distinctions between knowing and feeling. Why are the feelings called sensibilities? susceptibilities? What is feeling? Name the three classes into which all the feelings are divided. Tell what you know about instinct.

What is meant by the physical feelings? How do instincts and physical feelings differ? Name the three classes of physical feelings. Define each. Why are they called physical feelings?

Draw the optic apparatus and describe optic sensation and optic perception. Treat in the same way each of the special senses. Name the fifteen general senses.

What do you mean by the appetites? Analyze an act of thirst. What do you observe?

What is the office of the appetites? Illustrate by sleepiness. Give the three characteristics of an appetite. Illustrate by hunger.

Name the appetites and test by the three characteristics of an appetite. Is respiration an appetite?

Give the author's definition of the appetites. Give your definition. Give the definition of Gregory; of Stewart. Define appetency. Illustrate. Define inappetency. Illustrate. What do you mean by appetible? By inappetible? Illustrate each.

What do you mean by natural appetites? By modified or artificial appetites? Illustrate. Is the craving for opium a natural appetite? For tobacco? For alcohol?

What are the three guides in the gratification of an appetite? What does reflex action do? Instinct? Intelligence?

What do you mean by lawful gratification of appetites? By unlawful gratification? What follows? How are the divine approval and disapproval manifested?

Letter.—Write your friend a thoughtful letter, explaining the nature of the appetites. Show the relation between self-control and happiness.

Analysis of Chapter XIX.

I. **The Physical Feelings.**
    1. The Special Sensations.
    2. The General Sensations.
    3. The Appetites.

II. **Appetite Analyzed.**
    1. Hunger.
    2. Thirst.

III. **Office of the Appetites.**
    1. To supply bodily wants.
    2. To perpetuate the race.

IV. **Characteristics of Appetites.**
    1. Craving originating in bodily wants.
    2. Intermittent.
    3. Physical limits.

V. **The Appetites.**
    1. Hunger.
    2. Thirst.
    3. Sleepiness.
    4. Restiveness.
    5. Sexuality.
    6. Respiration.

VI. **Appetites Defined.**
    1. Author's definition.
    2. Original definition.
    3. Various definitions.

VII. **Kinds of Appetites.**
    1. Original, or natural appetites.
    2. Artificial, or modified appetites.

VIII. **Guides to the Appetites.**
    1. Reflex action.
    2. Instinct.
    3. Intelligence.

IX. **Gratification of the Appetites.**
    1. Lawful.
    2. Unlawful.

X. **Temperance, or Self-control.**
    1. Appetites made servants.
    2. Habits of self-control.
    3. Intemperance—the animal dominates the man.

CHAPTER XX.

THE EMOTIONS—EGOISTIC EMOTIONS.

We mean by the emotions our capabilities to feel in view of ideas. Emotions are strung on ideas as pearls on threads of gold. Good news awakens joy, but bad news occasions sorrow. All our higher feelings arise in view of ideas, and are termed emotions.

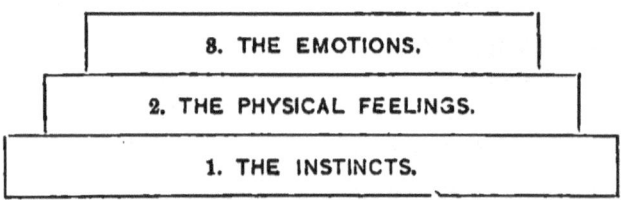

Sometimes we speak of emotions as intellectual feelings, because they are occasioned by knowing. Often we call the emotions our heart-powers, because we have learned to use the term heart so as to include all our higher feelings.

Names.—
{ The Emotions.
  The Intellectual Feelings.
  The Heart Powers.
  The Higher Feelings. }

An emotion is used to designate both a power to feel and an act of feeling. A capability for an emotion distinct in kind is called an emotional power; and the feeling is the exertion of the power. I love my mother; the capability to love is an emotional power, but loving is exerting this power. The term *emotion* applies equally to the capability and the exercise of the capability; as, I am endowed with the capability to feel the emotion of joy and I rejoice, or feel the emotion of joy.

Classes of Emotions.—
- Egoistic or Self-Emotions.
- Altruistic Emotions or Sympathies.
- Cosmic Emotions.
  - Truth Emotions.
  - Beauty Emotions.
  - Duty Emotions.

Some emotions refer to self, and are called egoistic emotions; some refer to others, and are called altruistic emotions; some are unlimited, but arise in view of the true, the beautiful, and the good, and are called cosmic emotions. Emotions limited to self are self-emotions; emotions limited to others are altruistic emotions; but unlimited emotions are cosmic emotions.

THE EGOISTIC EMOTIONS OR THE SELF-EMOTIONS.

These are the feelings which minister to self. You desire pleasure, long for wealth, and hope for fame; these feelings look to self, and we apply to them the following

Names.—
- Egoistic Emotions.
- Self-Emotions.
- Personal Emotions.

As egoistic emotions minister to self, they are termed self-emotions. Since they terminate in one's own person, they are called personal emotions.

Acts of Egoistic Emotion Analyzed.—Your teacher pronounces your essay excellent; you feel satisfaction, joy, pride. You fail to solve the problem; you are dissatisfied, chagrined, humiliated. You feel exultant in view of self succeeding; you feel mortified in view of self failing. As these are self-emotions, we call them egoistic emotions. Ideas pertaining to self occasion personal emotions.

From a careful examination of many of your self-emotions, you can infer the

Office of the Egoistic Emotions.—These feelings look to the well-being of self. The instinct of self-preservation is deeply implanted in all animals. We shrink from danger and welcome good. The office of the egoistic emotions is self-preservation and self-exaltation. You have also discovered from your analysis the

Characteristics of Egoistic Emotions.—It is not difficult to distinguish personal emotions from other mental acts.

1. *Egoistic emotions are feelings occasioned by ideas referring to self.* Some one calls you a coward; you feel indignant. Some friend leaves you a fortune; you rejoice. All emotions that terminate in self are self-emotions.

2. *Egoistic emotions look to self-betterment.* The personal emotions are not always selfish, but they all look to self; hence they are called egoistic. All emotions which look to self-betterment are self-emotions. These emotions may sink into selfishness and egotism.

Egoistic Emotions Defined.—Personal emotions, directly and indirectly, minister to self. They are the soul-energies which move us to act for our own preservation and exaltation.

1. *Self-emotions are the feelings which minister to self.*

2. *Original.* Make a definition of your own. Illustrate.

3. Various Definitions.—BROOKS: The egoistic emotions are those that center in self. SULLY: The egoistic emotions are such as imply personal reference. McCOSH: Egoistic emotions are the feelings called forth in view of good and evil as bearing on self.

Classes of Self-Emotions.—By examining several concrete cases, you will be able to classify egoistic emotions chronologically. Take emulation. You wish to excel in a spelling-match. Before the contest, you exult in anticipated triumph; the exultation is a *prospective* emotion. During the contest your soul throbs with interest and courage; these feelings are *immediate* emotions. After the contest, you feel chagrin and disappointment in view of your failure; chagrin is a *retrospective* emotion.

You prepared an essay and read it before your class. What prospective emotions did you feel? What immediate emotions did you feel while writing and reading the essay? What emotions do you now feel when you remember the cheers and the criticisms?

Prospective Emotions.—
- Hope or Fear; Expectation or Despair; Assurance or Dread.
- Courage or Cowardice; Modesty or Impudence.
- Egoistic Desires—Desire for Knowledge, Desire for Esteem. Etc., etc.

Immediate Emotions.—
- Joy or Sorrow; Gladness or Depression; Rapture or Melancholy.
- Content or Discontent; Good Humor or Bad; Sweet Disposition or Sour.
- Pride or Humility; Patience or Impatience; Vanity or Meekness. Etc., etc.

Retrospective Emotions.—
- Satisfaction or Regret; Complacency or Displacency.
- Self-Gratulation or Reproach; Self-Approbation or Disapprobation.
- Emotions of Pleasant Memories or Unpleasant. Etc., etc.

Prospective Self-Emotions.—The egoistic emotions occasioned by contemplating the future with reference to self are called prospective emotions. Carefully study your list of prospective emotions, and state cases involving each. The egoistic desires are longings for self-betterment.

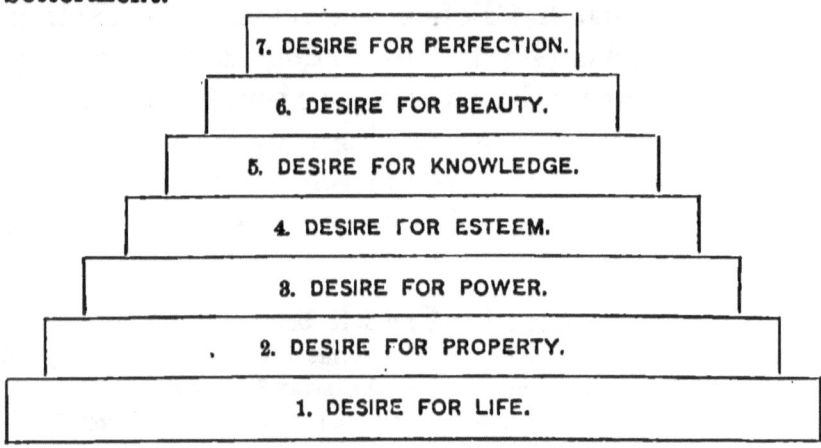

Our longings for self-betterment, as given above, are termed the seven primitive egoistic desires. As a study of the egoistic desires, you may reconstruct the pyramid, placing at the base the desire *you* think deepest, and the others in the order of their hold on human nature.

HAPPINESS is not a desire, but a result of lawfully gratified desires. Not happiness, but food, is the desire of a hungry man. Not happiness, but knowledge, is the desire of the earnest student. We are so constituted that the lawful gratification of our desires gives us pleasure. President Porter says:

"There is in man no separate desire of happiness. No man ever desired happiness in the general or the abstract. No one can ever catch himself or his neighbor thinking of happiness in the abstract, or desiring it. The satisfaction which comes from lawfully-gratified desires is generalized as happiness."

Immediate Self-Emotions.—I am conscious of present good and evil. The self-emotions occasioned by contemplating the present with reference to self are called immediate egoistic emotions. You may extend at your leisure the list of these emotions, and explain and illustrate each.

Retrospective Self-Emotions.—Memory brings back the past—the good we enjoyed and the evil we suffered. The emotions occasioned by contemplating the past with reference to self are called retrospective egoistic emotions. Notice that the self-emotions occur in pairs. Explain and illustrate each of the retrospective self-emotions in the preceding diagram.

Education of the Egoistic Emotions.*—These feelings dominate in childhood, but later are dominated by altruistic and cosmic emotions. We find it necessary to appeal to self-emotions in the government of children. Some of the egoistic emotions can not be too earnestly cultivated; among these we class cheerfulness, hope, desire for knowledge, and the desire to make the most of one's self. Great care, however, is needed to avoid the danger of self-emotion degenerating into selfishness, and egoistic emotion into egotism.

Comparative Psychology.—Brutes gain impressions something lower than ideas, and recall these impressions. The low forms of egoistic emotions, of which brutes are capable, are occasioned by impressions, immediate or revived. These brute emotions differ widely from rational egoistic emotions. Superficial investigators are in danger of being misled by deceptive appearances. Many of these brute feelings are instinctive; many

---

* See "Education of Self-Emotions," "Applied Psychology."

arise from sensuous impressions; but the higher egoistic emotions are wanting in brute life.

SUGGESTIVE STUDY-HINTS.

Review.—What do you mean by feelings? Is feeling physical or mental? Why do you call some feelings physical feelings? How do knowing and feeling differ? What do you mean by feeling being blind?

What do you mean by emotions? Illustrate. Show that we must know before we can have emotions. Why are the emotions called intellectual feelings? Why are they called heart-powers?

What do you mean by egoistic emotions? By altruistic? By cosmic? Give an example of each.

Why are egoistic emotions called self-emotions? Personal emotions? Give the distinction between egoistic and egotistic.

Give your analysis of regret; of rejoicing; of hope. What difference is there between a power to feel and a feeling? Does the feeling always imply the power to feel?

What is the office of the egoistic emotions? Why is self-preservation called the first law of nature? How do these feelings tend to exalt self? Illustrate.

Name the first characteristic of the egoistic emotions; the second. Illustrate each from your own experience.

State the author's definition of the egoistic emotions; your definition; McCosh's definition.

What is meant by chronological? By logical? By pyschological? What are retrospective egoistic emotions? Immediate? Prospective? Give three examples of each.

Write eight retrospective egoistic emotions; eight immediate emotions; eight prospective emotions. Why do you write the emotions in pairs?

What do you mean by the desires? By the desire for life? For property? For power? For beauty? For esteem? For perfection? For knowledge? What is happiness? Is it one of the primitive desires? Give President Porter's views.

When do the egoistic emotions predominate? In the government of children, must these feelings be addressed? Give some egoistic emotions which should be stimulated. Give some that should be repressed. Tell what you know about educating the self-emotions.

Letter and Diagram.—You may construct a diagram of the egoistic emotions which you may include in your letter to your friend.

CHAPTER XXI.

THE ALTRUISTIC EMOTIONS.

These are feelings ministering to others. Good and evil as bearing on self call forth egoistic emotions; but good and evil as bearing on others call forth altruistic emotions. These feelings are known by these and similar

Names.— { Altruistic Emotions.
Sympathies and Antipathies.
Affections and Disaffections.
Benevolent Emotions and Malevolent Emotions.
Loves and Hates.

These expressions apply equally to our capabilities to feel these emotions and to the feelings. I have the power to love and I love my friend. I feel the emotion of pity; I am endowed with the capability to feel pity.

The feelings occasioned by the realization of our relations to other beings are called altruistic emotions. Because we feel for and with others, these emotions are called sympathies. Because we incline to others, these feelings are called affections. Because we wish well to others, these feelings are called benevolent emotions. But we feel antipathies as well as sympathies; we hate as well as love. Altruistic emotion best expresses the meaning, including feeling against and from others, as well as feeling for and with others; but the other names mentioned are expressive, and are fixed in our literature.

Analysis of Altruistic Emotions.—We notice a young man struggling against poverty and misfortune to educate himself. We feel for and with him, we sympathize with him. We wish him success. We rejoice when he succeeds. The good Samaritan looked upon the unfortunate traveler, robbed and wounded, and ready to die. He pitied him, and this pity moved him to administer to his wants. By analyzing mother-love, friendship, emulation, and similar feelings, you discover the

Office of the Altruistic Emotions.—Self, as love, thinks no evil, suffers long, is kind. A neighbor is sick and needy. Your sympathies move you to cool his aching brow and minister to his needs. *To work good to others* is the office of the altruistic emotions.

Characteristics of the Altruistic Emotions.—These feelings are occasioned by ideas pertaining to others, and grow out of our relations to other beings.

1. *Altruistic emotions look to others.* When benevolent, they prompt the good of others; but when perverted, they become malevolent, and work ill to our neighbors.

2. *Altruistic emotions are feelings for and with others.* My friend is fortunate; I rejoice with her. She is unfortunate; I pity and aid her. The opposite is also true; I may feel against and away from another, as when I envy my successful neighbor, or hate and seek to injure a rival.

3. *Altruistic emotions are two-sided.* This is true of all emotions, but eminently so of these. Ingratitude is almost as common as gratitude. Hate too often dominates love. Antipathies are almost as wide as sympathies.

Altruistic Emotions Defined.—We feel for or against others. Man is a social being endowed with capabilities to feel emotions that prompt the good of others. The mental agitations and impulses occasioned by a knowledge of our relations to others are called altruistic emotions.

1. *Altruistic emotions are capabilities to love or hate others.* They are the powers to feel for and with others, or feel from and against others. They are the emotions that minister to others.

2. *Original.* Work out a good definition. Illustrate.

3. **Various Definitions.**—1. SULLY: Altruistic emotion, in its perfect form, is feeling for and with others. 2. McCOSH: Altruistic emotions are capabilities to feel an interest in others. 3. BROOKS: Altruistic emotions are feelings which go out to another with a wish of good or evil. 4. WHITE: The powers to feel good or evil toward others are termed altruistic emotions.

Classes of Altruistic Emotions.—The terms expressive of these emotions are marvelously numerous. Charity has more than fifty English synonyms. The few groups of altruistic emotions inserted here will suggest to you the indefinite extension of the list. Clearly, some of these terms are synonyms; but, for the most part, each expresses a distinct shade of feeling. You will find it profitable to linger over these terms, defining and illustrating each from your own experience.

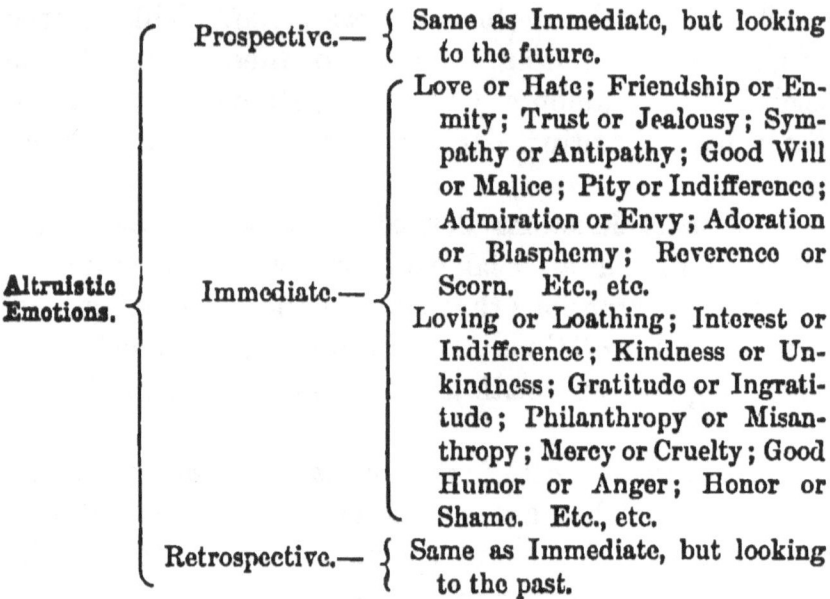

Love.—The soul-energy that draws hearts together is called love. The lovely awakens love. We love the lovely. We can not love the hateful.

1. *Supreme love.* God is love and He is altogether lovely. Infinite loveliness awakens our souls to their deepest depths. I love the loving Father with all my heart. Veneration, reverence, worship, grow out of supreme love. Love tends to union. What attraction is to the physical universe, love is to the spiritual universe. The one unitizes the world of matter; the other the world of mind.

2. *Parental love.* This is one of the purest and noblest of feelings. It unitizes the family, and works the highest good to offspring. Mother-love is the salt of the earth.

3. *Conjugal love.* An absorbing reciprocal affection makes of two lives one. Each family, united by love, becomes a paradise. Happiness comes from a union of hearts and a union of lives.

4. *Filial love.* Loving and loved, children cheerfully yield to parental authority and counsel, and grow into lovely and loving men and women.

5. *Fraternal love.* The offspring of the same parents are bound together by strong ties. As the race is one great family, the realiza-

tion of the brotherhood of man and fatherhood of God leads to a higher exercise of filial and parental love.

6. *Love of friends.* He is the friend indeed who sticketh closer than a brother. The love between David and Jonathan, and between Damon and Pythias, surpassed the love between men and women. Friendship is an ennobling emotion. A man who is true to his friends, though a robber, is capable of great things. True friendship never dies.

7. *Love of country.* Love is the tie that binds together rational beings. We degrade this noble emotion when we call the instinctive affection of brutes, love; and much more when we term the brutal lusts of men love. But patriotism may well be called the love of country.

Sympathies.—Fellow-feelings, or feelings for and with our fellow-beings, are called sympathies. Sympathies bind social beings together. Our impulses to do good to others spring from our sympathies.

1. *Growth of sympathies.* Capabilities to feel, like capabilities to know, are endowments. Man is endowed with altruistic emotions, called fellow-feelings or sympathies. Very early the child laughs with those who laugh, and weeps with those who weep. Children respond to the emotions of their companions. Later, the youth represents to himself the joys and sorrows of others and sympathizes with them. When we can enter into another's inmost heart and feel for and with him, our sympathies are fully active.

2. *Analysis of acts of sympathy.* Jesus at the grave of Lazarus is a perfect example. Study the details. In this, as in all acts of sympathy, the mental process seems to be as follows: (1) Observation is the first step. We must know the joys and sorrows of others. We must note the facial and vocal expression of emotion. (2) Interpretation of the signs of emotion is the second step. We recall our emotional experience. I have lost a parent. I can sympathize with my bereaved friend. (3) Imagination is the third step. I make real the peculiar disposition and circumstances of my friend and put myself in his place, and thus enable myself to fully share his joys or sorrows. This is sympathy. Next to love, sympathy best expresses benevolent altruistic emotion.

3. *Suffering and Sympathy*—It is only through our personal ex-

periences that we gain the power of sympathizing with others. We should never be able to feel another's pain, if we had never felt a pain of our own. So it is in all the trials of our fellows; before we can enter into the feelings of one who is tempted, or who is disappointed, or who is humiliated, or who is bereaved, we must ourselves suffer—being tempted, or being disappointed, or being humiliated, or being bereaved. It is hard to have these trials for ourselves; but it is good for others that we have and exercise sympathy with those who are called to such trials for themselves. And, as we can never gain this power except through these trials, let us find a comfort in the thought that every trial sent to us is a call to added fitness in the all-important ministry of loving sympathy.

Hates, Antipathies, Malevolent Emotions.—We may abhor sin and hate every evil way; but when our hearts become bitter, and we would work the injury of others, our emotions are malevolent. These ugly emotions take many forms. Now anger, now spite, now malice, now revenge, now jealousy, but always hate. These hateful emotions drive social beings apart and fill the cup of misery. The less we have to do with them the better. While hating sin with a perfect hatred, we may love sinners and seek to save them. Malevolence in all its forms is perverted and misdirected emotion. Malevolent emotions are perverted feelings; they are not endowments but perversions. "God made man upright." "The emotions are all good in themselves, and are not to be eradicated but guided."

Play of the Emotions.—More wonderful than the combinations in music are the play and interplay of the emotions. The heart is truly an instrument of a thousand strings. The key-board embraces many octaves. When attuned to harmony, its music is sweeter than the music of the spheres. Love fills the soul with bliss and inspires every noble endeavor.

Egoistic and Altruistic Emotions, incident to Success or Failure.—The thoughtful student will linger long over the following diagram, given by Dr. Bascom. You may here get a clearer insight into the emotion world than by reading volumes of theory. Look into the mirror of consciousness and see yourself in each emotion. With the diagram before you, rehearse your greatest success as well as your greatest failure. Tell the emo-

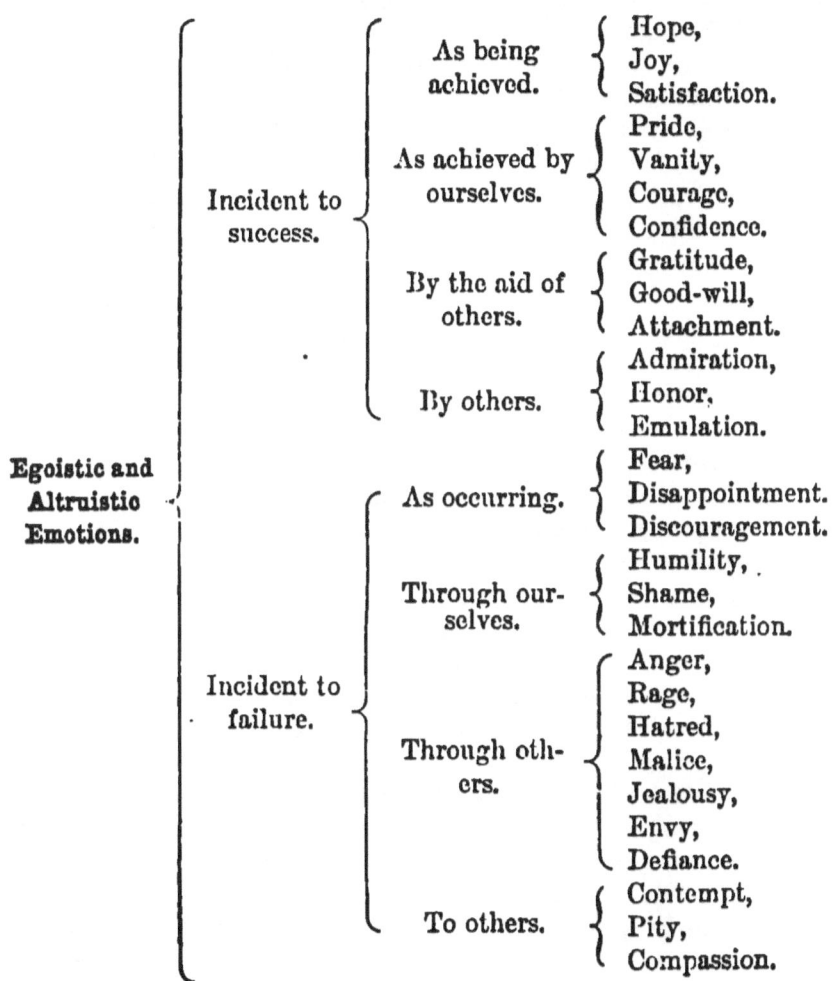

tions you felt in each case. Now take Washington at the close of the Revolution, and Napoleon in his last imprisonment. Tell the emotions you imagine that each felt.

SUGGESTIVE STUDY-HINTS.

Review.—Define consciousness. State its office; its characteristics. What is a conscious-percept? Name five. Give the distinction between physical feelings and instincts; between the physical feelings and the emotions. Give the definition, office, and characteristics of the egoistic emotions. Define and illustrate retrospective, immediate, and prospective emotions.

What do you mean by altruistic emotion? Give the etymology of the word. Why are these feelings called sympathies? affections? benevolent emotions? love? Why are they also called antipathies? disaffections? malevolent emotions? hates? Give examples of each from your own experience.

What is the office of the altruistic emotions? Give the three characteristics of these emotions. Illustrate.

State the author's definition of the altruistic emotions; your definition; the definition of Dr. Brooks.

Give ten groups of altruistic emotions. Illustrate. Give ten synonyms of charity.

Explain the seven kinds of love mentioned. Explain the meaning of sympathy. Illustrate by Jesus at the grave of Lazarus.

What do you mean by malevolent emotions? Give some of these. Are these original endowments or perversions?

Tell about the play and interplay of the emotions. When is there harmony? when discord?

Give some egoistic emotions incident to success. Incident to failure. Give some altruistic emotions incident to success. Incident to failure.

When is a feeling called a *passion?* What is meant by the passion for strong drink? by the passion of anger? by the passion of love? by the passion of avarice? by the passion of ambition? What do you understand by the *ruling passion?*

Letter.—In a thoughtful letter you will tell about these ennobling emotions. Inclose to your friend an analysis of this chapter.

CHAPTER XXII.

COSMIC EMOTIONS—TRUTH EMOTIONS.*

By cosmic emotions we mean the feelings occasioned by ideas of the true, the beautiful, and the good. The reign of law, the beauty of earth and sky, and the all-pervading good, fill me with a boundless joy. Egoistic emotions terminate in self; altruistic emotions terminate in others; but cosmic emotions are boundless.

Names.—
- The Cosmic Emotions.
- The Rational Emotions.
- The Spiritual Emotions.
- The Higher Emotions.

Because these feelings belong peculiarly to our higher nature, they are called spiritual emotions. Because only rational beings are endowed with these capabilities, the powers to feel in view of cosmic ideas are called rational emotions. Because the soul goes out to the universe in the feelings occasioned by the true and the beautiful and the good, they are called cosmic emotions.

Cosmic Emotions—
- Truth Emotions, or Knowledge Emotions.
- Æsthetical Emotions, or Beauty Emotions.
- Ethical Emotions, or Duty Emotions.

We are a part of a universe of related things, and we are endowed with powers to perceive things and discern relations. As one by one they open to our view, great truths thrill us. The feelings awakened by.

---

* Review Chapter XV before studying this chapter.

truth are called *truth* emotions. We look without and within; beauty charms us. The feelings occasioned by beauty are called *beauty* emotions. We find out our relations to others; we feel imperative impulses to do to others as we would have them do to us. These feelings are occasioned by ideas of right, and are called *duty* emotions.

THE TRUTH EMOTIONS.

By these we mean our capabilities to feel, in view of truth discerned. These feelings are known by the following

Names.— { Truth Emotions. Knowledge Emotions. Philosophic Emotions. }

Because these emotions are occasioned by the discernment of relations, they are termed philosophic emotions; as they well up, in view of knowledge gained, they are termed knowledge emotions.

Analysis of Truth Emotions.—Archimedes had studied long and hard to find the law of specific gravity. While bathing, the happy thought struck him. He ran out without his clothes, shouting "Eureka! Eureka! I have found it! I have found it!" He discovered an important truth which occasioned ecstatic truth emotions. Give examples from your own experience.

Office of Truth Emotions.—Truth is the food of the soul. The discovery of truth occasions much of our deepest joy.

1. *Truth emotions* move us to search for truth as for hidden treasures. A thirst for knowledge is deeply impressed upon our nature.

2. *Truth emotions* reward research with abiding joy. Happy are they who hunger and thirst after truth. The office of the truth emotions is to move us to seek truth, as well as to enable us to appreciate and enjoy the true.

Characteristics of Truth Emotions.—We discern truths. In view of these truths, we feel truth emotion. The emotions of Harvey, when he discovered the circulation of the blood; of Newton, when he discovered gravitation; of Columbus, when he discovered a continent, may be feebly imagined.

1. *Truth emotions are occasioned by truths discerned.* These emotions are deepest when truths are first discerned, but, like beauty, truth is a joy forever.

2. *Truth emotions are boundless—are cosmic.*
"We mingle with the universe and feel
What we can not all express nor all conceal."

Truth Emotions Defined.—As you experience these emotions every hour, they are best defined by referring them to your own conscious experience.

1. *Truth emotions are our capabilities to feel in view of truth.* Our feelings, occasioned by the discernment of truth, are truth emotions.

2. *Original.* Construct a good definition and illustrate it.

3. **Various Definitions.**—1. BAIN: Knowledge emotions are the delights we experience when we discern truth. 2. GARVEY: Truth emotion is the radical impulse to seek and enjoy truth. 3. BASCOM: Truth emotion inspires pursuit and enjoyment of knowledge.

Nature of Truth Emotions.—"I will return to my peaceful mathematics," was the resolve of a savant weary of political turmoil. "A night with the peaceful stars is better than a thousand elsewhere." Truth emotions are usually peaceful, but when great truths burst upon the mind these emotions become torrents. Think of the emotions of Newton when he discovered the law of gravitation; of Franklin, when he discovered the identity of electricity and lightning; of Paul, when he first realized that Jesus was God. True education leads the learner to discover truth for himself, thus making student-life a perpetual joy. Though usually tranquil and peaceful, the truth emotions are an overflowing fountain.

Growth of the Truth Emotions.* —Children are full of curiosity and open-eyed wonder. New objects delight them. Their troublesome questions are interminable. We discover the buddings of truth emotion. With the years the desire to find out increases and the joys of discovery multiply. Childhood revels in objective truth. Thinking the thoughts of God after him, delights childhood and fills the soul of manhood with inexpressible joy. True teaching and right learning educate truth emotions.

SUGGESTIVE STUDY-HINTS.

Review.—What do you mean by a faculty? a power? a capability? a soul-energy? Give a distinction between a cognitive power and an emotional power. Is self active or passive when he feels? What do you understand by the soul acting as a unit?

What do you mean by cosmic emotions? Why are these feelings called rational emotions? spiritual emotions? higher emotions? cosmic emotions? Give the termination of egoistic emotions; of altruistic emotions; of cosmic emotions.

What do you mean by the truth emotions? What distinction do you make between the powers to feel in view of truth and the feelings?

---

* See "Education of the Truth Emotions," "Applied Psychology."

Tell the story of Archimedes; of Franklin's kite; of Newton's apple. What do you call the feelings thus awakened? Why?

Give the office of the truth emotions; of self emotions; of altruistic emotions. What feelings move us to search for truth? Give two characteristics of the truth emotions.

Give the author's definition of the truth emotions; give your definition; give Bain's; give Garvey's; give Bascom's.

Are truth emotions always peaceful? Why should the learner be led to discern truth for himself? Tell about the growth and education of the truth emotions.

Letter.—The treatment of the truth emotions is so brief that you need to further develop the subject. Make a good topical analysis of this chapter as a part of your letter to your friend.

CHAPTER XXIII.

ÆSTHETIC EMOTIONS.

By these we mean our powers to feel in the presence of beauty. The feelings occasioned by beauty, sublimity, or humor are called æsthetic emotions. As beauty predominates, these feelings are often called the beauty emotions.

Æsthetic Emotions—
{ Emotions of Beauty or Ugliness.
Emotions of Sublimity or Insignificance.
Emotions of the Humorous or the Prosy. }

Analysis of Beauty Emotions.—You gaze upon the night-blooming cereus; slowly the flower expands. You exclaim, "How beautiful!" Your feelings occasioned thus are called beauty emotions.

Characteristics of Beauty Emotions.—You are conscious of peculiar feelings of satisfaction and joy in the presence of beauty of form, beauty of color, beauty of sound, beauty of motion, beauty of character. These feelings are beauty emotions.

1. *Beauty emotions are occasioned by the beautiful.* We find beauty everywhere. We behold the beautiful landscape, and our souls thrill with beauty emotions.

2. *Beauty emotions are boundless—are cosmic.* As we gaze upon the beautiful sunset, we forget self, forget the world, and mingle with the universe. Like truth emotions, beauty emotions are complete in themselves. They satisfy.

Office of the Æsthetic Emotions.—We live in a universe of beauty and sublimity and humor, and we are endowed with capabilities to appreciate and enjoy beauty, sublimity, humor. The beauty emotions place the soul *en rapport* with the beauty world. Poetry and eloquence and song and the beauty of holiness and the beautiful earth and the sublimely beautiful heavens fill us with rapture. God is beauty.

Æsthetic Emotions Defined.—Self, as noumenal perception, immediately beholds beauty. In view of beauty, self, as beauty emotion, feels beauty, joy, and satisfaction, and the impulse to produce and possess the beautiful.

1. *Æsthetic emotions are the capabilities to feel in view of beauty.* The beauty emotions are the soul-energies to feel beauty. The agitations and impulses occasioned by beauty are esthetic emotions. Beauty as used here includes sublimity and humor.

2. *Original.* Give a definition expressive of your views. What is sublimity? What is wit?

Objective and Subjective Beauty.—What is beauty? All know, but no one can tell. Intuitively we perceive concrete beauty, and consciously feel its spell. But the beauty idea is a necessary notion, is ultimate, is inexplicable. You may say that beauty is a thing of proportion and harmony; you merely give two of its numerous attributes. Whatever occasions beauty emotions we call beautiful, as the lily or the rainbow.

1. *Objective beauty.* I look upon the blushing rose and feel beauty. I listen to songs of birds, and feel beauty. I read the "Lay of the Last Minstrel," and feel beauty. I ponder the life of Florence Nightingale, and feel beauty. The something external which occasions beauty emotions is called *objective beauty*. Space, time, causation, and objective beauty are external realities. Beauty is objective.

2. *Subjective beauty.* By the subjective we mean the mind itself. Self stands face to face with beauty—knows beauty intuitively. We are endowed with the intellectual power to behold beauty. Self feels beauty when in its presence. We are endowed with powers to feel beauty. The capabilities to perceive and enjoy beauty are subjective. Perceiving and feeling beauty are acts of the mind, and may be called *subjective beauty*. Beauty is subjective.

Ugliness.—The opposite of beauty is ugliness. If beauty is proportion and harmony, ugliness is the lack of these. The ugly gives rise to ugly emotions. Ugliness is not merely the absence of beauty, it is something external that occasions repellent and disagreeable emotions. The beautiful pleases, the ugly displeases; the beautiful attracts, the ugly repels; the beautiful occasions joyous emotions, the ugly occasions depressing emotions. We desire the beautiful, but have an aversion for the ugly. Make a diagram of emotions incident to beauty and ugliness.

Beauty of Character is the highest type of beauty. When integrity, efficiency, and modesty blend in proportion and harmony, we have a Joseph, a Washington, a Jesus. Perfect character is perfect beauty. However ugly the body, the beauty of holiness covers the grand man or woman with a halo of glory. All moral deformity is ugly. A base character, as a Judas or a Nero, is the extreme of ugliness.

Emotions of Sublimity.—A cascade is beautiful; Niagara is sublime. Electrical experiments are beautiful; the thunder-storm is sublime. Dress-parade is beautiful; the battle is sublime. Vastness occasions emotions of the sublime. Whatever carries the mind into the infinite occasions the idea and feeling of sublimity.

"Beauty pleases and delights; sublimity awes, yet elevates." The emotion of insignificance is the opposite of the emotion of sublimity. Both emotions are occasioned by the familiar fable, "The mountain labored and brought forth a mouse." Give other examples.

Emotions of the Humorous.—In view of the ludicrous, the witty, the humorous, the ego effervesces with pleasure. These emotions are called emotions of the ludicrous, of the witty, of the humorous. Isaac Barrow well says, "It may be demanded what the thing we speak of is, or what this facetiousness doth impart. To which question I might reply as Democritus did to him who asked the definition of a man. ''Tis that which we all see and know; any one better apprehends what it is by acquaintance than I can infer him by description. It is, indeed, a thing so versatile and multiform, appearing in so many shapes, so many postures, so many garbs, so variously apprehended by several eyes and judgments, that it seemeth no less hard to settle a clear and certain notion thereof than to make a portrait of Proteus, or to define the figure of the fleeting air. Its ways are unaccountable and inexplicable, being answerable to the numberless rovings of fancy and windings of language.'"

The emotions occasioned by the flat or the dry are the opposite of those occasioned by sparkling wit. "Humor, however strange it may seem, is very commonly associated with sympathy. It was remarked by Sir Walter Scott of Robert Burns, when he appeared in Edinburgh, that in his conversation there was a strange combination of pathos and humor. I am sure that these two, humor and sympathy, often go together. The man who never laughs, or who can not laugh heartily, I suspect is deficient in tenderness of heart, while he *may* be characterized by many virtues. Certain it is that in the writings of many of our great authors pathos and humor are found in the closest connection. "I believe that the fountains of smiles and tears lie nearer each other than most people imagine." *

Education of the Æsthetic Emotions.†—We are rapidly reaching the conclusion that æsthetic culture is as important as intellectual culture. To this end, home is made beautiful, and the modern primary school, as well as the kindergarten, is full of beauty. Environments,

---

* McCosh.
† See "Education of Beauty Emotions," "Applied Psychology."

objects, pictures, songs, plays, art-work, all tend to develop the beauty emotions. As the learner advances, he is thrilled with higher and still higher forms of beauty. What a revolution!

SUGGESTIVE STUDY-HINTS.

Review.—What do you mean by the emotions? What distinction do you make between egoistic, altruistic, and cosmic emotions? Do ideas cause emotions, or merely occasion them?

What do you mean by the altruistic emotions? Is a capability to feel beauty and a beauty feeling the same? Illustrate. Name the classes of æsthetic emotions.

Analyze three cases of beauty emotions; three of the sublime; three of the humorous.

State the office of the beauty emotions; of the emotions of sublimity; of the humorous emotions; give examples in each case.

Tell the characteristics of beauty emotions; of sublimity emotions; of humorous emotions; give examples in each case.

Repeat the author's definition of æsthetic emotions; your definition; definitions of Haven, Bain, etc.

What is beauty? Objective beauty? Subjective beauty? Give an example of objective beauty; of subjective beauty.

What do you mean by ugliness? Give examples. Explain what you mean by beauty of character. Give examples. What is an ugly character? Give examples.

Tell what you know about sublimity. How do beauty and sublimity differ? Give examples.

Tell what you know about humor. How do wit and humor differ? Illustrate.

Tell what you know about the culture of the æsthetic emotions.

Letter.—In your letter tell about the beauty emotions in poetry and art.

ANALYSIS OF CHAPTERS XXII AND XXIII.

I. **The Cosmic Emotions are:**
    The truth emotions.   The æsthetic emotions.
    The ethical emotions.

II. **Analysis of**
    1. Truth emotions.   2. Beauty emotions.
    3. Sublimity emotions.   4. Humor emotions.

III. **Office of**
    1. Truth emotions.   2. Beauty emotions.
    3. Sublimity emotions.   4. Humor emotions.

IV. **Characteristics of**
    1. The truth emotions.   2. The æsthetic emotions.

V. **Definitions of**
    The truth emotions.   The æsthetic emotions.
    Beauty.
        1. Objective.   2. Subjective.

VI. **Emotions of Sublimity.**

VII. **Emotions of Humor.**

VIII. **Education of**
    1. Truth emotions.   2. Æsthetic emotions.

CHAPTER XXIV.

CONSCIENCE, OR THE ETHICAL EMOTIONS.

By conscience is meant the power to feel ethical emotions in view of right. The ethical emotions are the feelings occasioned by perceiving and discerning right. These feelings tend to universal right, and hence are classed with the truth emotions and the beauty emotions as cosmic emotions.

Names.— {
Conscience, or the Ethical Emotions.
The Emotions of Conscience.
The Emotions of Right.
The Emotions of Good.
The Duty Emotions.
}

As these emotions look to good, to right, to duty, they are called duty emotions, emotions of the right, emotions of the good, and emotions of conscience. By common consent the capability to feel rightness is termed conscience, and the feelings incident to ideas of right and wrong are called emotions of conscience, or ethical emotions.

Analysis of Ethical Emotions.—Take Paul: "I persecuted Christians conscientiously, for I thought I ought." Because he believed Jesus to be an impostor, he felt it his duty to crush out Christianity. The feeling "I ought" moved Paul to persecute. He believed it was right, and felt that he ought. The impulses to do what we believe to be right are impulses of conscience. Take Joseph Reed. When tempted to betray his country by the offer of $50,000 and high office, Reed replied, "I am not worth purchasing; but, such as I am, the King of Great Britain is not rich enough to buy me." He believed that it was wrong to sell his country. The feeling "I ought not" moved Reed to refuse the bribe. The impulses to refuse to do what we believe to be wrong are impulses of conscience.

Office of Conscience.—Conscience is the mental power to feel rightness. Self, as conscience, always moves to the right. "Get right and keep right," are its imperatives. To feel rightness is the sole office of conscience. But ethical emotions are prospective, immediate, or retrospective; hence the three imperatives of conscience:

1. *Find out the right.* Self, as intellect, finds out right, but self, as conscience, inspires the search. "Be sure you are right, then go ahead." I wish to invest in a tempting lottery; is it right? I am offered $10,000 to lobby a bill through Congress; ought I to accept the offer? Is it right to play cards, attend theatres, dance, flirt, drink wine, or smoke? At every step these troublesome questions meet us. The impulses of self as conscience to find out the right are ethical emotions. Paul acted blindly but conscientiously. Because he refused to investigate, and went on blindly persecuting Christians, he calls himself the chief of sinners. The world is full of these sincere wretches. The sun shines, but men shut their eyes and declare there is no sun; or, if there is, they can not see it. *Find out the right* is the first imperative of conscience.

2. *Choose and do the right.* *Do right* is the deepest impulse of the heart. You have investigated to the utmost. You believe temperance is right and drinking intoxicants wrong. Appetite craves alcohol. Conscience says, "Touch not, taste not, handle not—the accursed thing." The impulse to choose temperance and live temperately is an emotion of conscience. You repress your lawless brute cravings and act in accord with your ethical emotions. You choose and act conscientiously. *Choose and do the right* is the second imperative of conscience.

3. *Get right and keep right.* Peter denied Christ. Remorse, the supreme agony, overwhelmed him. Remorse, as a reformatory energy, is conscience pleading, "Cease doing wrong and begin doing right." The mute pleadings of conscience aroused Peter, and he became the bravest of the brave. *Continuing* wrong is the unpardonable sin. The drunkard signs the pledge; his heart glows with deepest satisfaction. This is conscience moving him to keep right. The emotion of duty done is the highest joy. It sustains us amid all trials. It sustains the martyr at the stake. Paul exclaims, "I have kept the faith, and will receive the crown." When we do right, we feel the approval of the Author of right; but, when we do wrong, we feel his disapproval. The poet has beautifully expressed this idea:

"An approving conscience is the smile of God, remorse his frown."
Get right and keep right is the third imperative of conscience.

Characteristics of Conscience.—Since conscience is our only power to feel rightness, it is easy to distinguish ethical emotions from other feelings. Other marked characteristics in addition to those given may be pointed out.

1. *Ethical emotions are incident to ideas of right and wrong.* No other ideas occasion these feelings, nor do these emotions occur except in connection with ethical ideas. Brutes are incapable of gaining ethical ideas, and hence feel no ethical emotions.

2. *Ethical emotions are imperative.* Conscience is the only imperative soul-energy. *I ought, do right,* etc., are the imperatives of conscience. Moral law is supreme, as are the emotions of right. Not *may* but *must* is the ethical feeling. "I can not tell a lie"; I can not afford to do what I believe to be wrong; I can not afford to disregard my ethical impulses.

3. *Ethical emotions dominate.* Pleasure, self-interest, and even love must yield to the imperative of conscience. "Do right though the heavens fall." "I would rather be right than be President." These are good illustrations. Conscience is the supreme soul-energy. Intellect and will, as well as all the lower feelings, yield to conscience.

Definitions of Conscience.—What is conscience? It is not knowing, for self, as intellect, does all his knowing. It is not choosing, for self, as will, does all his acting, choosing, and directing. It is not a compound faculty, for a faculty is a mental element. Clearly, conscience is the power to feel rightness.

1. *Conscience is the power to feel ethical emotions in view of ethical ideas.* It is the mental energy to

feel in the presence of right and wrong. The capability to feel rightness is an ultimate endowment of the human soul. No analysis can resolve the emotion of right; no synthesis can derive these emotions from other feelings. As the impulsion to right is a mental activity, distinct in kind, we are compelled to class conscience as a mental faculty. When the rubbish is removed, and the mists are cleared away, how royally conscience stands out in the mental economy!

2. *Original definitions.* You may write out your definition of conscience. There must be no mystery. Let there be sunlight clearness. The vast range of feelings occasioned by a knowledge of right and wrong are termed ethical emotions. The capability to feel ethical emotions is called conscience. Our impulses to do what we believe to be right are acts of self as conscience.

3. **Various Definitions.**—1. Dr. I. G. John: Conscience is the moral impulsion in man. 2. Hopkins: Conscience is the impulse felt by a rational being to obey law. 3. Bascom: Conscience is the power to perceive and feel obligation.

Remarks.—Self, as conscience, feels rightness, in view of ethical ideas. But all ideas are intellectual products. Self, as will, moved by ethical emotions, chooses right. Confounding conscience with its antecedents, ethical ideas, and its consequents, ethical actions, occasions endless confusion. Ethical ideas, ethical emotions, and ethical actions are as distinct as gold, silver, and copper. Because emotions of right are central, conscience is often used to include its antecedents and consequents. But the psychologist must sharply distinguish between knowing right, feeling right, and doing right. In the light of intelligence, we feel impulses to choose and do what we believe to be right. The power to feel oughtness is conscience.

Ethical Knowledge.—How do we find out what is right? Precisely as we find out what is true in botany.

The moral universe is an objective reality. Into this world we have direct insight.

1. *Ethical percepts.* Self, as noumenal perception, immediately knows concrete right. You observe a noble woman treating kindly a starving old man, and notice his deep gratitude. You know intuitively that the act of kindness and the act of gratitude are right. We *perceive* concrete right.

2. *Ethical concepts.* We think ethical percepts into ethical concepts. We perceive many acts of kindness and of gratitude, and we know directly that each is right. We discern resemblances and think these acts into groups. This group of kind acts becomes *kindness*, and this group of grateful acts becomes *gratitude*.

3. *Ethical judgments.* We think ethical concepts into ethical judgments. We discern agreement between the notions right and gratitude, and say *gratitude is right*. We discern incongruity between the notions right and ingratitude, and say *ingratitude is wrong*.

4. *Ethical laws.* We discover laws. I investigate light. I find that in this case and this, its intensity varies inversely as the square of the distance. As nature is uniform, I find that I have discovered a law of light. So in ethics I perceive that honesty is right in this case and this. I find that honesty tends to the general good, and that men everywhere believe that they ought to be honest. Moral as well as physical forces are constant. I have discovered a moral law. Ethical knowing is purely intellectual: it is self, as intellect, investigating the moral world.

Conscience is not a Moral Guide.—Self, as intellect, finds out what is right. Self, as conscience, feels a strong impulse to do what he believes to be right. Steam impels the boat, but the pilot guides. Conscience is the moral impulsion in man, but intellect guides. To call conscience a moral judgment, or a moral sense, or a moral guide, tends to hopeless confusion.

Conscience in Literature.—A crude psychology is imbedded in literature. The distinctions between intellect, emotions, and will, are not always clearly discerned. A blind feeling is often represented as intelligent. The conception of a faculty as an ultimate and inexplicable endowment of the soul, as a simple and distinct capability, is modern. Even the etymology *con*, with, and *sciens*, knowing, embodies, as I think, a fundamental error. But the thoughtful student need not be misled. Errors wrought into human thought can be removed only by the slow processes of time and the leaven of truth. However, the common sense of the race has ever been right. Conscience to the masses is simply a feeling of rightness. "It was an error of the head (intellect) not of the heart (conscience)," gives the true idea. "My judgment was at fault but my intentions were good," is sound psychology. "Conscience doth make cowards of us all," and "The righteous are bold as a lion," give the correct meaning.

Intentions and Conscience.—Intentions are purposes. What were your intentions? Self, as consciousness, perceives his intentions. We can not be mistaken as to our intentions.

1. *Good intentions* are purposes to do what we believe to be right. When we act with good intentions we act conscientiously. Paul believed he ought to persecute the Christians. He did it "in all good conscience," for his intentions were good.

2. *Bad intentions* are purposes to do what we believe to be wrong. When we act with bad intentions we act unconscientiously. Judas knew that it was wrong to betray Christ. He acted unconscientiously, for his intentions were bad. I know always with absolute certainty whether my intentions are good or bad. It is the certainty as to good intentions that makes the right-

cous bold as a lion. One man with good intentions shall chase a thousand.

"He whose cause is just is trebly armed." It is the certainty as to bad intentions that causes the wicked to flee from shadows. "The wicked flee when no man pursueth."

Conscience is Infallible.—Every one is liable to reach false conclusions, and to consider the right wrong, or the wrong right. But conscience, as invariably as the needle points to the pole, moves us to choose and do what we deem the right. The good man is a conscientious man. A conscientious man habitually does what he believes to be right. A bad man is one who habitually chooses and does what he believes to be wrong. Conscience is not a guide; intellect guides. Conscience is the infallible impulse to do what we consider right.

Must we, then, always obey our consciences? Certainly. Conscience moves us to search for right with all our powers. Conscience never fails to move us to do what we consider right. We must obey.

Intuitive Ethical Ideas.—The moral universe is as real as the physical. Moral agents, moral phenomena, moral laws, moral obligations, and moral responsibilities, are objective realities. We are endowed with the power of direct insight into the ethical world. Moral phenomena are what is right or wrong in conduct.

Self stands face to face with ethical phenomena, and immediately perceives necessary ethical ideas. Take the actions of the Good Samaritan and the Levite as an object lesson. Here, right and wrong are acted. By direct insight, you gain the concrete ideas, right, ought, merit, and their opposites. Concrete right and wrong are ethical phenomena. I need not prove to you that the Levite did wrong, or that the Good Samaritan did right; you know it intuitively. This right and this wrong are ethical percepts. *Concrete ought and ought not are ethical intuitions.* You know at once that the Good Samaritan ought to have acted as he did, and that the Levite ought not to have acted as he did. The ideas *this ought* and *this ought not* are ethical percepts. *Concrete merit and demerit are ethical intuitions.* A big boy strikes his kind mother. Even the little child cries "Shame!" and intuitively blames the unnatural son. You know at once that the Good Samaritan merited praise while the Levite deserved blame. The ideas *this merit* and *this demerit* are ethical percepts.

Intuitive Ethical Truths.—Necessary inferences from necessary ideas may be called intuitive truths. The axioms of ethics, like the axioms of mathematics, are intuitive truths. We venture to submit the following statements:

1. *Moral law.* The uniform ways in which moral forces act are called moral laws. As physical phenomena occur uniformly, in the same way, we infer that physical law reigns in the physical world. As moral phenomena are uniform in all lands at all times, we infer the reign of moral law in the moral world.

2. *Author of law.* From the existence of right and laws of right, we infer a law-giver. After half a century of philosophic research, Herbert Spencer gives his final summary: "Amid all mysteries, there remains the one absolute certainty—*we are ever in the presence of the infinite and eternal energy,* from whom all things proceed." Mr. Spencer voices the conclusion of all thinkers. In the same way we reach moral certainty. Moral law necessitates a moral law-giver.

3. *Law and its author are beyond and superior to self.* This

inference seems to be unavoidable. We are subjects of law. Law reigns within and around us. Obedience to law works our good.

4. *Self is responsible to law and its author.* We are capable and free. Law is the rule of right, and works for our good. We are under obligations to obey law. As we are capable and free, we are responsible for our acts. Morality is thus based on the rock.

Laws of Conscience.—The mental energy which prompts the choosing and doing of what we deem right is called conscience. The uniform ways in which this energy acts may be called the laws of conscience. We submit a few examples:

1. *Conscience works in the light of intelligence.* Ethical emotions are agitations and impulses occasioned by ideas of right. In the absence of ethical knowledge, ethical emotions are impossible. As the brute has no ethical ideas, it feels no ethical impulses.

2. *Conscience invariably moves to acts believed to be right.* Intellectually, it is human to err. Mistakes of judgment are unavoidable. The Hindoo mother believes that she ought to sacrifice her child. Paul believed he ought to persecute Christians. But the action of gravity is not more constant than the impulse to do what we believe to be right.

3. *Acting conscientiously strengthens conscience.* Education by doing applies to the ethical emotions. As exercise strengthens muscle, and remembering strengthens memory, so acting conscientiously strengthens conscience. Moral theories and moral sermons may help or hinder. Only habitually doing what we believe to be right can make us strong to do right and resist wrong.

4. *Suppressing ethical emotions weakens conscience.* Doing what we believe to be wrong is disregarding or suppressing our emotions of right. As restraining the limbs weakens them, so disregarding conscience tends to weaken ethical emotions.

Growth of Conscience.—Very early, children give indications of ethical emotions. When child-experience involves right and wrong, concrete right is perceived and the impulse toward right felt. But the egoistic emotions and the physical feelings are now strong, and largely determine child action. Conscience moves to the right, but moves feebly. Year by year the ethical emotions grow stronger. Do right, the imperative of conscience, more and more influences action. Later, the ethical emotions begin to dominate all other impulses. Now the child has become a conscientious moral agent, doing the right because it is right. Growth of conscience is indicated by the wonderful changes from feeble ethical impulses felt by the child to the dominant ethical emotions felt by the conscientious man.

"The conscience," says Dr. McCosh, "grows as all living things do, but it grows from a germ. The faculties of the mind, like the properties of a body, are all of the nature of tendencies. There are intellectual tendencies in infants and savages, but they need to be called forth and ripened by light and by heat directed toward them. It is the same with the moral power; it is in all men native and necessary, but it is a germ requiring to be evolved. It grows as the oak grows. As the tree needs earth in which to root itself and air of which to breathe, so the conscience needs a seat in our mental sphere, with a stimulus to make it germinate and expand. When reared in a bare soil, it will be dwarfish. When exposed to cold and blighting, it will be stunted and gnarled. In a good soil and a healthy atmosphere, it will be upright and well-formed. In particular, it grows and spreads out with the intelligence which enables it clearly to apprehend facts and to discover the consequences."

Education of Conscience.*—Moral theories do not make moral men, nor does the possession of a conscience make any man virtuous.

1. *Right doing develops conscience.* — Habitually doing what one believes to be right develops the moral faculty. Intellectual culture does not necessarily promote conscientiousness. Indeed, great thinkers are

---

* See "Education of Conscience," "Applied Psychology."

sometimes monsters of depravity. Bacon was designated as the wisest and meanest of mankind. He knew the way, approved it, too, but still pursued the wrong. Sermons and moral lectures are good, but preachers' children and even preachers may be very immoral. Acting conscientiously alone educates conscience.

2. *Non-use or misuse weakens conscience.* One who constantly disregards the urgings of conscience will have a weak conscience. Just as a person who seldom recalls his experiences will have a weak memory. Conscience, as an impulse to right and a restraint from wrong, becomes weak, becomes seared, because unheeded. Not so conscience as remorse. Too late, apathy gives place to this dread fiend. Remorse comes to stay. The guilty soul agonizes in almost hopeless despair. "I knew my duty, but did it not," touches the deepest depths of human woe.

3. *Sowing wild oats.* In the light of history, Froude says: "Remorse may disturb the slumbers of a man who is dabbling in his first experience of wrong; and when the pleasure has once been tasted and is gone, and nothing is left of the crime but the ruin which it has wrought, then, too, the Furies take their seats upon the midnight pillow. But the meridian of evil is, for the most part, left unvexed, and when a man has chosen his road, he is left alone to follow it to the end." Would you lift the curtain and know the end? Witness the death-scene of Charles IX of France. Ponder the fate of Jean Valjean. Study Macbeth and the dream of Clarence. Ponder the miserable end of a Judas, an Arnold, a Burr. Remorse is a sure crop.

4. *As happiness results from law obeyed, so misery*

follows law violated. A beggar on good terms with his conscience is infinitely better off than the guilty millionaire or wicked king. As you sow, so shall you reap. All human experience verifies this truth. "A man's character is but the stamp upon his soul of the free choice of good or evil through life." "Sow acts, you reap habits; sow habits, you reap character; sow character, you reap destiny."

5. *Train up the child in the way it should go.* "Before knowledge place culture, and before culture place character." Keep the children's faces toward the light; keep their hearts open to the truth; keep them doing, *ever* doing, right things, and let the wrong severely alone. Wrong is never so distinctly comprehended as when purity shines upon it from the depths of a truth-loving heart. Never allow a child to think a wrong thing or form a wrong ideal, if it is possible to prevent it. Lead children to spend their precious time in doing right.

"Happy are they who hunger and thirst after righteousness." Let beatitudes take the place of curses; let the eternal *do* take the place of the everlasting "*don't.*"

SUGGESTIVE STUDY-HINTS.

Review.—You may ascend the pyramid, defining and giving the office of each mental power until you reach conscience.

What is meant by conscience? Why are our feelings in the presence of right called ethical emotions? emotions of right? emotions of good? duty emotions? conscience?

Analyze three acts of conscience. When you feel *ought* or *ought not*, is it an act of conscience? Tell the story of Reed; of Washington; etc., etc.

State the office of conscience. Name the three imperatives of conscience. Give two examples of each.

Mention the first characteristic of conscience; the second; third. Give two examples of each.

Give author's definition of conscience; your definition; definition of Dr. John, etc. Criticise definition of Bascom.

What are the antecedents of acts of conscience? Consequents? Is conscience knowing right, feeling right, or doing right?

How do you find out what is right? How do we get ethical percepts? ethical judgments? ethical laws? Give an example of each. Show that ethical knowing is purely intellectual.

Show that conscience is not a moral guide. Illustrate. What powers guide us?

Give the etymology of conscience. Does this give the correct idea? Is conscience always correctly used in literature? Has the common sense of the race been correct on this as on most subjects?

What do you mean by intention? How does conscience make cowards?

What do you mean by fallible? infallible? Is self as judgment fallible or infallible? Is conscience fallible or infallible? Illustrate by the magnetic needle. What do you mean by a good man? a bad man? Must we always obey conscience?

How do we gain concrete ethical ideas? Give five examples. What are moral phenomena? Do we have direct insight into the moral world? Illustrate by the good Samaritan. Show how we gain the concrete ideas—ought, ought not, merit, demerit, praise, blame, etc.

ANALYSIS OF CHAPTER XXIV.

I. **Names.**
    Conscience.   The ethical emotions.
    The emotions of conscience.   The emotions of right.
    The emotions of good.   The duty emotions.

II. **Acts of Conscience Analyzed.**
    A right act.   A wrong act.

III. **Office of Conscience.**
    1. Find out right.   2. Choose and do right.
    3. Get right and keep right.

IV. **Characteristics of Conscience.**
    Ethical emotions occasioned by right.
    Ethical emotions imperative.
    Ethical emotions dominant.

V. Conscience Defined.
    1. Author's definition.   2. Original definition.
    3. Various definitions.

VI. Ethical Knowledge.
    1. Ethical percepts.   2. Ethical concepts.
    3. Ethical judgments.   4. Ethical laws.

VII. Intentions.
    1. Good intentions.   2. Bad intentions.

VIII. Conscience Infallible.
    1. An infallible impulse.   2. A good man.
    3. A bad man.

IX. Intuitive Ethical Ideas.
    1. Right and wrong.   2. Ought and ought-not.
    3. Merit and demerit.   4. Responsibility and irresponsibility.

X. Intuitive Ethical Truths.
    1. The reign of moral law.   2. Author of law.
    3. Law superior to self.   4. Self responsible to law.

XI. Laws of Conscience.
    1. Conscience works in the light.
    2. Conscience always moves to duty.
    3. Conscience is strengthened by doing right.
    4. Conscience is weakened by doing wrong.

XII. Growth of Conscience.
    1. Feeble in children.   2. Gradually gains power.
    3. Dominates in youth.   4. McCosh's views.

XIII. Education of Conscience.
    1. Right doing.   2. Non-use.
    3. Sowing wild oats.   4. Happiness.
    5. Keep the face to the light.

CHAPTER XXV.

THE EMOTIONS—GENERAL VIEW.

Emotions are strung on ideas as gems on golden cords. Emotions are feelings occasioned by knowledge. The golden sunset, the song of birds, and the fragrant flowers, as they come to us in waves of light and sound and odor, thrill us with pleasure. As we explore nature and life, science, biography and literature, the entire key-board of our emotional nature responds, and moves us to act well our parts. We feel while we know, and will while we feel.

Order.— { 1. Knowledge.— { 1. Perceptive Knowledge. 2. Representative Knowledge. 3. Thought Knowledge. } 2. Emotion. 3. Will. }

The emotions are the capabilities of self to feel in view of ideas. The feelings occasioned by knowing are termed emotions. The capabilities to feel in view of knowing are by some called the *intellectual* feelings. "The heart powers" is the expression of the masses. The head with them means the intellect; and the heart, the emotions. Formerly, heart was often used in the sense of mind; now it is used to include our emotional powers, and is often restricted to our affections. The emotions—the powers to feel in view of knowing—is every way the preferable name.

Names.— { The Emotions. The Intellectual Feelings. The Heart Powers. }

Mind as emotion moves outward. Some feelings look to self, and hence are called *egoistic emotions*. Some feelings are termed *altruistic emotions*, because they look to others. But the feelings that look to the truth world, the beauty world, and the duty world, are called *cosmic emotions*. When an emotion arises from contemplating the past, it is termed a *retrospective* emotion. A present emotion is called an *immediate* emotion, but a feeling occasioned by contemplating the future is termed a *prospective* emotion. We thus reach a satisfactory and convenient classification of the emotions.

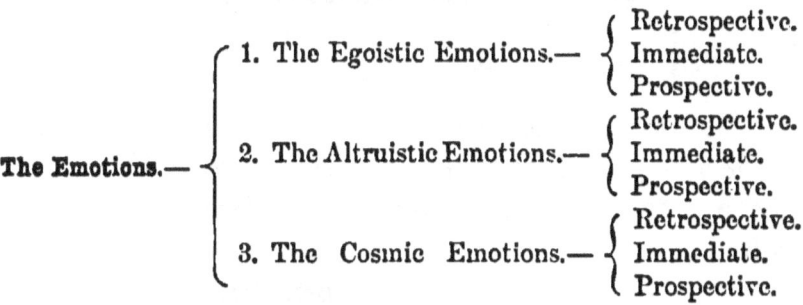

The egoistic emotions are our powers to feel in view of self. The feelings occasioned by ideas pertaining to self are called egoistic emotions. The power to feel and the feeling are as distinct as perception and perceiving. *Personal emotions* means emotions pertaining to the person. *Self emotions* and *egoistic emotions* better express the meaning. As these emotions arise from contemplating self with reference to the past, the present, or the future, they are called retrospective, immediate, and prospective emotions.

Names.— { The Egoistic Emotions. / The Self Emotions. / The Personal Emotions. } { Retrospective. / Immediate. / Prospective. }

THE EMOTIONS—GENERAL VIEW.

The altruistic emotions are powers to feel in view of others. The feelings occasioned by ideas pertaining to others are termed altruistic emotions. When we feel for and with others, these feelings are called sympathies, affections, benevolent emotions, love, etc.; but when we feel away from and against others, they are termed antipathies, disaffections, malevolent emotions, hate, etc.

Names.—
{ Altruistic Emotions.
  Sympathies and Antipathies.
  Affections and Disaffections.
  Benevolent and Malevolent Emotions.
  Love and Hate. }
{ Retrospective.
  Immediate.
  Prospective. }

The cosmic emotions are our powers to feel in view of the true, the beautiful, and the good. These feelings are termed cosmic emotions. Because they are limited to rational beings, they are named *rational emotions*. As they are occasioned primarily by noumenal percepts, they may be called *noumenal emotions*. Some name these feelings *spiritual emotions* and *higher emotions*, because of their tendency to exalt the soul. Self as cosmic emotion goes out to the universe. These feelings are as boundless as the universe and eternity. *Cosmic emotion* seems to express the exact meaning.

Names.—
{ The Cosmic Emotions.
  The Rational Emotions.
  The Spiritual Emotions.
  The Noumenal Emotions.
  The Higher Emotions. }
{ Retrospective.
  Immediate.
  Prospective. }

The cosmic emotions are occasioned by cosmic knowing. Self, as noumenal-perception, has immediate insight into the truth world, the beauty world, and the duty world. We know intuitively, in their concrete forms, the true, the beautiful, and the good. But self as reason finds out what is true, what is beautiful, what is right. In the presence of truth we feel truth emotions. In the presence of beauty we feel beauty emotions. In the presence of right we feel duty emotions.

The Cosmic Emotions.— { The Knowledge Emotions, or Truth Emotions. The Æsthetic Emotions, or Beauty Emotions. The Ethical Emotions, or Duty Emotions.

Physiology of the emotions. The soul is embodied in an organism. The interaction between mind and body is wonderful. Study that expressive face under the play of diverse emotions. How joy lights up the countenance! How grief drapes the face in gloom.

"When ideas are of objects appetible or inappetible they stir up emotion. We have a glimpse of the way in which the feelings work in the brain. The idea which evokes the feeling, and is its substratum, works in the cerebrum; and the excitement produced, like the original sensation, may be partly mental and partly bodily—the bodily excitement often rising to movements in changes of color, in paleness and redness of countenance, in blushing and in trembling, in laughter and in tears. It is the office of psychology to unfold the emotions; it is the business of physiology to trace the bodily affections from the brain downward to the nerves and fibers." *

The Human Temperaments.†—"The temperaments are formed by the proportion of those elements that enter into the bodily structure, causing the diversities in shape, form, and mental characteristics that we observe; and whether we employ the words 'lymphatic, sanguine, bilious, and nervous,' or 'vital, motive, and mental,' to denote the bodily constitution of individuals, these terms correspond

* McCosh.
† Superintendent J. M. Greenwood in "Principles of Education Practically Applied."

to those real distinctions which prompt the possessor to move or act in a certain direction. The mind is a unit; it manifests its activity in various directions. A distinct kind of mind activity is called a faculty of the mind; consequently, there are as many faculties of the mind as it has distinct kinds of activity. In like manner, the body is one organism, constructed upon temperamental conditions. The manner of their combination produces tendencies either to mental activity or to sluggishness, causing all those variations in human nature that we observe. When the intellect, sensibility, or will prevails, there is found a corresponding temperamental development which exerts a controlling influence, and shapes and colors the whole character of the possessor. He lives and acts in harmony with his nature. Teachers furnished with eyes, ears, good sense, and an inclination to study, can tell what tendencies prevail in the pupils they are called upon to teach. This is justly regarded as the key to eminent success."

SUGGESTIVE STUDY-HINTS.

Review.—Study this chapter with the tree (p. 56), and the pyramid (p. 204), and the diagrams of the egoistic, altruistic, and cosmic emotions before you.

What distinction do you make between knowing and feeling? between an intellectual power and an emotion? Illustrate. Explain the logical order of mental activity. Do we feel while we know? Do we will while we feel?

Define the emotions. Explain the names given to these capabilities. Why do you prefer the term emotion?

Explain the classification of emotions. Illustrate retrospective, immediate, and prospective emotions. Define the egoistic emotions. Explain the several names applied to these feelings. Are these names equally expressive?

Define the altruistic emotions. Explain the various names given to these feelings, and state your preference.

Define the cosmic emotions. Why do you prefer this to the other names applied to these feelings? Name the groups of cosmic emotions. Define each. What do you mean by cosmic knowledge?

Illustrate the physiology of the emotions. What is the office of psychology? of physiology?

PART VI.

THE WILL-POWERS.

CHAPTER XXVI.—Attention.

XXVII.—Action.

XXVIII.—Choice.

XXIX.—The Will-Powers.—General View.

PSYCHOLOGICAL PYRAMID.

	THE WILL.	THE WILL POWERS.	CHOICE. ACTION. ATTENTION.	
		THE EMOTIONS.	THE COSMIC EMOTIONS. THE ALTRUISTIC EMOTIONS. THE EGOISTIC EMOTIONS.	
	THE FEELINGS.	THE PHYSICAL FEELINGS.	THE SPECIAL SENSES. THE GENERAL SENSES. THE APPETITES.	
THE CAPABILITIES OF THE MIND.		THE INSTINCTS.	HUMAN INSTINCTS. COMMON INSTINCTS. STRICTLY BRUTE INSTINCTS.	
		THE THINKING POWERS.	REASON. JUDGMENT. CONCEPTION.	REASONS. JUDGMENTS. CONCEPTS.
	THE INTELLECTUAL FACULTIES.	THE REPRESENTATIVE POWERS.	IMAGINATION. PHANTASY. MEMORY.	IDEALS. PHANTASMS. MEMORIES.
		THE PERCEPTIVE POWERS.	NOUMENAL-PERCEPTION. CONSCIOUS-PERCEPTION. SENSE-PERCEPTION.	NOUMENAL-PERCEPTS. CONSCIOUS-PERCEPTS. SENSE-PERCEPTS.

PRODUCTS.

SIXTH PART.

THE WILL-POWERS.

By these we mean our capabilities to attend, determine, and act. Will is the power to make intentional efforts. Knowing, feeling, willing is the logical order of soul activity; hence we place at the summit of the psychological pyramid the will-powers.

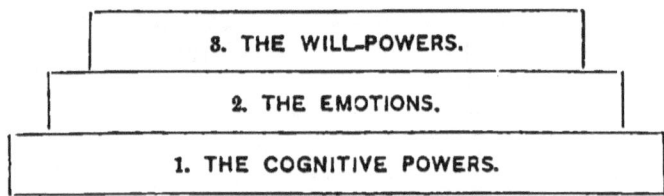

Knowing occasions emotion; emotion occasions choice and action. The telegram states that your brother is dying; you are grieved to the heart; you hasten to soothe him in his dying hour.

The Will-Powers.— { 3. Action. 2. Choice. 1. Attention. }

You concentrate your powers on the geometry lesson; self, as *attention*, concentrates his efforts. You determine to spend vacation in California; self, as *choice*, determines. You execute your plan; self, as *action*, executes his determinations. Because choice is the pre-eminent will-power, we place it as the cap-stone of the psychological pyramid.

Will, Emotion, Intellect.—Will is mind in liberty. Voluntary acts are intentional acts. We are endowed with capabilities to form and execute plans. Liberty, intention, and volition are the characteristics of will, and distinguish the will-powers from the emotions and the intellect.

CHAPTER XXVI.

ATTENTION.*

By attention is meant the power to concentrate our efforts. Self, as attention, concentrates his efforts, prolongs his efforts, and changes his efforts. Like consciousness and memory, attention in some degree enters into all distinct mental activity. What the will can do is to fix the attention.

1. *Self, as attention, concentrates effort.*—As we can, under an adequate motive, observe one point in the scene before us and neglect everything else; as we can single out one sound and be deaf to the general hum; as we can apply ourselves to the appreciation of one flavor in the midst of many, or be aware of a pressure on a particular part of the body to the neglect of the rest—so in mental attention we can fix one idea firmly in the view, while others are coming and going unheeded.

2. *Attention is characteristic of cultivated minds.*—In the uneducated and badly educated it is more or less wanting. The power of giving the whole of the mind to any subject or work, what-

---

* Re-examine Chapter I; also, see "Education of Attention," "Applied Psychology."

ever be its nature, without permitting it to wander, is not common, and where it does exist it is usually the result of severe discipline. The mind, while it is the most active agent with which we are acquainted, is also one of the laziest. Not lazy through idleness, but because it shirks. It loves to remember, for remembering is not work. It loves to form phantasms, for phantasy is sport, day-dreaming is pleasant. It loves reverie. It does not love to think, for thinking is work. Whoever has taught children and observed their ways closely has a thousand proofs of this. Place a spelling-book in the hand of a little boy and watch him. Nine times out of ten he will try to learn his task by going over it a great many times. The mind is shirking, for the *mind* does not work that way. It is his mental effort to get the lesson *without* fixing his whole attention. He is trying to substitute a great deal of mechanical repetition for a little hearty mental labor. The whole power of his mind is never absorbed in his task. When the mind is fully at work, when the whole power of attention is aroused, it always *does one thing at a time*. This is a foundation or beginning principle in education.

3. *Much novel-reading is mental shirking.* This is true as a rule. The novel-reader drifts, not thinking or even imagining; self seems to be little more than emotion and phantasy. An excessive novel-reader becomes incapable of concentrated and prolonged effort. Though a woman in years, she may be a child mentally. Only the concrete and emotional interest her. She is incapable of solid reading, or penetrating, abstract study. She is a human butterfly.

4. *Attention can be educated.* Education must accustom the learner to an exact, rapid, and many-sided attention, so that at the first contact with an object he may grasp it sufficiently and truly, and that it shall not be necessary for him always to be changing his impressions concerning it. (*The treatment of Attention in Chapter I is considered sufficiently extended for an elementary work.*

CHAPTER XXVII.

ACTION, OR EXECUTIVE VOLITION.

Self does things—acts. Action engages full half our mental energies. Self, as action, executes his determinations, and thus makes ideals actuals. The capability to carry impulse or determination into action is called executive volition, or action. In general, action includes all efforts of body and soul; but the term is here used in the sense of executive volition. *Action is the power of self to execute his determinations.*

Names.— { Action.
Executive Volition.
Executive Power.
Volition. }

Acts of Executive Volition analyzed.—Charles, on his way to school, met Robert, who begged for his company for a hunt. Charles desired to enjoy the sport, and his impulse was to go; but he deliberated, weighing the pleasures of the hunt against the benefits of the school, and the painful consequences of playing truant. After a few moments he decided to go on to school. Without a moment's delay, he acted—executed his choice—and proceeded on his way to school.

I know that my neighbor is in need. Shall I administer to his wants? I fix my mind upon the question—I attend. Indifference and avarice move me to leave the matter to others. The grudge I have against the needy one moves me to let him suffer. Conscience strongly moves me to go to his relief. In view of these conflicting urgings, I make up my mind to help my neighbor—I choose. I now direct my efforts to devising ways and means to execute my determination and form a plan. Next I execute my plan, administering to my neighbor's wants—I act. You readily perceive in these simple acts the distinctive work of each of the three will-powers.

Office of Executive Volition.—We are endowed with the capability to do things intentionally. Brutes execute their impulses; men execute their determinations. In the mental economy the office of executive volition is to carry choice into action; as when you spend the evening with your sick friend instead of going to the theatre.

Impulsive Action.—Only deliberative acts are rational. When impulse is carried directly into action it is called impulsive action. A large proportion of human as well as brute acts are of this kind. But action, as here used, applies to intentional, purposed, deliberative acts.

Characteristics of Action.—We do things intentionally, purposely, deliberatively. I intentionally pruned the pear-tree. I purposely took a walk. I deliberately signed the contract. When we act with a purpose, the act is executive volition.

1. *Self, as action, carries choice into execution.* A being without this power might form plans, but could not carry them out. The engineer might plan a bridge, but could not actualize his ideal.

2. *Self, as action, does intentionally and freely what he does.* After careful deliberation you determined to become a student; now you intentionally and freely devote yourself to student work.

Action Defined.—You are conscious of power to carry out your plans. The capability to execute plans is termed action. Volition is self acting.

1. *Action is the power of self to execute his determinations.* We can do what we determine to do. Volition is will in action.

2. *Original definition.* What do you mean by

action? Write a clear definition and give two illustrations.

3. **Various Definitions.**—1. HAZARD: Action is the power to make effort. 2. BROOKS: Executive volition is the power to carry choice into action. 3. PORTER: Action is the power to execute purposes. 4. HAVEN: Executive volition is the capability to put choice into action. 5. BAIN: Executive volition is the power for purposed action; the tendency to put forth effort is inherent in our constitution.

Kinds of Action.—An act may be mechanical, impulsive, or deliberative.

1. *Reflex action.* Such acts as breathing, winking, walking, ordinarily are reflex actions, and are strictly physical. The acts of the lower orders of animals and of young infants are almost wholly reflex.

2. *Impulsive action.* The infant is attracted by the glittering toy and tries to reach it; there is no deliberation, no choice, but simply impulse and action. The brute feels, and carries impulse directly into action. There is no deliberation, no rational choice. When we act from impulse and without purpose, our acts are impulsive acts. Instinctive action is impulsive action.

Simple and Complex Impulses.—When a single impulse moves to action, the action is termed an act from a simple impulse; but when two or more conflicting impulses move to action, the action is termed an act from complex impulses. In all cases the act itself is simple.

1. *Acts from simple impulses.* The dog wants the meat, and immediately seizes it. The child desires the flower, and immediately plucks it. These are simple impulsive acts.

2. *Acts from conflicting impulses.* The dog has been punished for his acts. Now dread of punishment contends with a craving for the meat. Mother has told the child not to pluck certain flowers. Now the little one wavers between the desire for the

flowers and the dread of its mother's disapproval. The acts resulting are from conflicting impulses, but the acts themselves are simple acts.

3. *Deliberative or rational action.* Rational beings deliberate before acting. Impulse is subordinated to reason. Self, as reason, weighs the considerations. In view of all the reasons, we choose and act; such action is rational action. This is the meaning of action as here used.

SENSORIUM AND MOTORIUM.

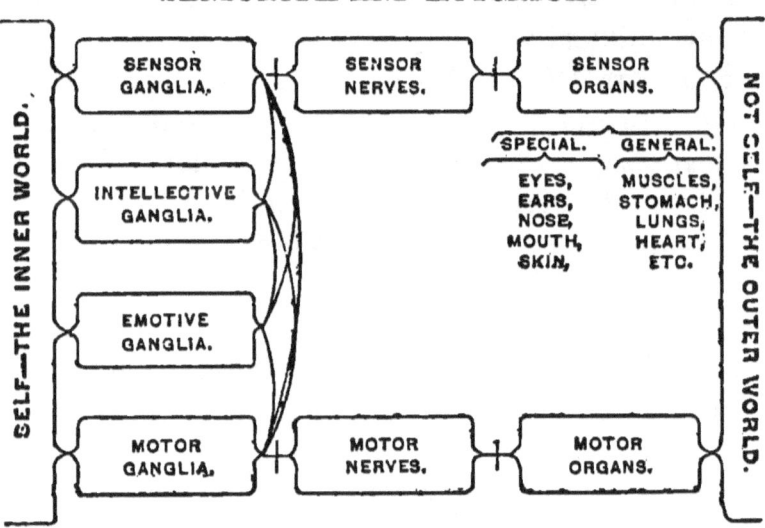

Action and Motion.*—We again stand face to face with the profound mystery of interaction between mind and matter. We know that self as sense-perception is affected by matter, and that self as will affects matter. Self as volition excites the motor ganglia. The motor excitation passes in molecular waves through the motor nerves to the muscles. In response to motor excitation, the muscles contract and relax, thus producing motion.

* See pages 45 and 52.

How self excites the motor ganglia is to us an insoluble mystery; but, like all similar mysteries, the solution could not profit us now. We can afford to wait.

"To move any part of the body *voluntarily* requires the following particulars: (1) The possession of an educated reflex-motor mechanism, under the control of those higher cerebral centers which are most immediately connected with the phenomena of consciousness; (2) certain *motifs* in the form of conscious feelings that have a tone of pleasure or pain, and so impel the mind to secure such bodily conditions as will continue or increase the one and discontinue or diminish the other; (3) ideas of motions and positions of the bodily members, which previous experience has taught us answer more or less perfectly to the *motifs* of conscious feeling; (4) a conscious *fiat* of will, settling the question, as it were, which of these ideas shall be realized in the motions achieved and positions attained by these members; (5) a central nervous mechanism, which serves as the organ of relation between this act of will and the discharge of the requisite motor impulses along their nerve-tracts to the groups of muscles peripherally situated. As to the definite nature of the physical basis which underlies the connection of ideas of motion, fiat of will adopting one idea, and the starting outward of the right motor impulses, our ignorance is almost complete. Self, as will, can issue his fiat, but can do nothing more. Science, at the present, can only conjecture what then takes place." *

Language and Action.—In its *broadest* sense, language includes all communications from the inner to the outer world. Motion is the means used. Take away motion and the universe becomes silent and dumb.

1. *Language is the intentional expression of cognitions, feelings, and purposes, by means of motion.* Self, as action, utters ideas, emotions, and determinations by signs, by sounds, and by symbols.

2. *Reflex action supplements volition.* You intentionally speak to your friend; what proportion of the

---

* G. T. Ladd, "Physiological Psychology."

movements are reflex? You intentionally write a letter; how much of the action is reflex? You play and sing; how largely are the movements reflex? You carve a Madonna; what proportion of the movements are reflex? Some estimate that fully nine tenths of the movements in these acts are strictly reflex. How infinitely wonderful are speech and song and art!

3. *Music, the language of the emotions, is a thing of motion.* Destroy movement, and dead silence reigns. The grand strains that lift us up and inspire us are produced by means of motion.

Habit and Action.—Effort of body or mind is called action. By habit we mean acting without effort. In bodily activity, the first steps are always taken with consciousness, which is often painful in its intensity; but by repetition the same acts are performed with little or no consciousness. Walking, to a baby, is a solemn act, requiring its whole attention; walking, to us, is automatic. The tyro in music or in the crafts is awkward, constrained, and intense in his attention to the movements of his work; the master is intent on the end, the movements being made with the minimum of consciousness. Indeed, so long as a part of the attention is necessarily directed to the manner of doing, the work will be imperfect.

In mental processes the same truth holds. Thinking, in any new direction, is usually slow and laborious, but with practice it moves with ever-increasing freedom. The child, in adding, pauses, hesitates, and thinks at each step; the accountant grasps results with mechanic-like precision. The housewife performs her cookery while chatting with a neighbor upon topics foreign to the occupation, the work going on semi-automatically.*

Growth of Action.—Movement, in some form, is certainly the earliest animal activity. At first the movements are purely reflex. Very early the infant begins to try to do things. Slowly it gains a mastery over the body. The helpless babe becomes the active, graceful

* James Johonnot.

child. Action gives pleasure. *"Education by doing"* is based on the intense activity of this faculty during childhood and youth.

Education of Action.* —Intentional effort tends to develop executive volition. The child is full of impulses to action, but these efforts need to be directed. Well guided action is an important feature of child education.

SUGGESTIVE STUDY-HINTS.

Review.—Carefully ascend the pyramid. Define each group of faculties and state the office of each faculty in the group. Define each faculty and give its characteristics.

What do we mean by the will-powers? Distinguish between intellect, emotion, and will. Illustrate.

What is meant by attention? Give its office and its characteristics. Illustrate the importance of educating attention.

What do we mean by action? Why is this power called executive volition? Analyze a voluntary act.

Give the office of action. Illustrate the distinction between impulsive acts and determined acts.

State the characteristics of action. What do you mean by intentional action? Illustrate.

Give author's definition of action; your definition; Hazard's; Bain's.

Explain and illustrate reflex action; impulsive action; rational action. In what sense is action here used?

Show that the soul as will originates motion. Trace motion from the inner to the outer world. Explain the motorium (see p. 45).

What is language? How do we express our thoughts? our emotions? our resolves? What proportion of our movements is reflex action?

Explain habit and action. Describe the growth of action. How are motives related to rational action?

Letter.—You will take time to prepare a well-digested letter to your friend.

---

* See "Education of Action," "Applied Psychology."

Analysis of Chapter XXVII.

I. Names.
    Action.   Executive volition.
    Executive power.   Volition.

II. Acts of Volition Analyzed.
    Rational acts.   Impulsive acts.

III. Office of Action.
    Self executes choices.   Self carries impulse into action.

IV. Characteristics of Action.
    1. Is voluntary.   2. Is intentional.

V. Definitions of Action.
    Author's.   Original.   Various definitions.

VI. Kinds of Action.
    1. Reflex action.   2. Impulsive action.
    3. Rational action.

VII. Impulsive Acts.
    From a simple motive.   From conflicting motives.

VIII. Action and Motion.
    Mind a *causa sui*.   The motorium.

IX. Development of Action.
    1. Growth.   2. Education.

CHAPTER XXVIII.

CHOICE.

By this is meant the power of preference. Shall I spend my vacation in Europe or in the Yellowstone Park? After long deliberation I finally make up my mind to go to Europe. I prefer visiting the Old

World. I choose in view of motives. I determine to spend my vacation in a foreign land.

Names.— { Power of Choice.
Power of Preference.
Power of Self-Determination.
Will. }

I am rational, benevolent, free; I am a person. I am endowed with the power of self-determination; I am a sovereign. I can prefer one thing to another; I am free to choose. I determine for myself; I am independent. I originate activity; I am a creative first cause. Because I am endowed with the capability to choose, I am a man and not a brute. Because I can at will originate motion, I can understand the universe.

Acts of Choice Analyzed.—What is choosing? You carefully scrutinize some of your own acts of choice. What mental processes precede choice? What follow choice? What do you do when you choose? Now take this example: Moses chose to suffer with his people rather than be king. Ambition and pleasure contended with duty, but Moses did not hesitate. With him right outweighed kingdoms. He made up his mind to cast in his lot with his enslaved people. He preferred duty to pleasure. He chose to suffer for the right rather than rule in the wrong. You find that his choice was occasioned by motives or reasons for choosing. You find that his determination to stand by his people was his choice. You also find that his choice was followed by action—a life devoted to the good of his people. You will be profited by analyzing the choice of Solomon, of Naomi, etc.

Office of Choice.—In the mental economy, self, as

choice, decides. The power of self-determination is the master faculty of the soul. You make up your mind, you determine, you choose.

1. *Self, as choice, determines.* Washington made up his mind to propose to Mrs. Custis, and she made up her mind to accept him. Making up your mind, deciding, determining, and choosing, are expressions for the same mental act.

2. *Self, as choice, originates activity.* You determine to take a walk. Your choice starts nerve-currents which incite muscular action. Napoleon chose to stake his fate upon a single battle, and many thousand soldiers fought at Waterloo.

3. *Self, as choice, prefers.* Clay preferred being right to being President. You prefer education to riches. The patriot exclaims, "Give me liberty, or give me death." Choice is the power of preference.

Characteristics of Choice.—We find nothing in the material world with which to compare this activity. Matter is passive; only mind is endowed with spontaneity. Choice stands alone, and man is the only terrestrial being that can say "I will."

1. *Choice is uncaused cause.* The choice is made in view of motives, but the motive is the reason for choosing, and not the cause of the choice. I determine to build a house; the choice is the cause of the building, but the determination to build is occasioned and not caused. The power to originate movement is called choice or will. Take away this power, and a man ceases to be a person and becomes a mere machine.

2. *Avoidability characterizes choice.* The thief takes my horse, but he could have done differently.

Whatever choice I make, I am conscious that I could have chosen otherwise. Avoidability characterizes choice. I am responsible.

3. *Self is free to choose.* Choice is mind in liberty. It is the power to determine as one pleases. Liberty is a necessary idea. I know intuitively that I am free. Self, as choice, is unrestrained.

Choice Defined.—"Choice is the power of self to decide what he will do." "Choice is the capability to initiate acts." "Choice is the power of preference in view of motives." "Choice is the power of spontaneous determination." "Choice is mind in liberty." "Choice is personal cause." "Choice is the capability to elect one of two or more alternatives." Here we find substantial agreement. Whatever their theories, thinkers agree as to the office of choice, and view with awe this marvelous power. All men know what it means, yet here we meet the profoundest of mysteries: man is a creative first cause.

1. *Choice is the power to determine in view of motives.*

2. *Original.* Construct a definition of your own.

3. **Various Definitions.**—1. HARRIS: Choice is the power of self-determination. 2. BAIN: Choice is the capability to decide. 3. BASCOM: Choice is the power to close deliberation and initiate action. 4. HAZARD: Choice is the mental energy that originates motion.

Motives occasion Choice.—Motives are incentives to choice. Ambition incited Macbeth to murder. Motives are mere considerations, and may be intensified or weakened at will. A strong motive is simply a powerful incentive to choice. A weak motive is merely a slight incentive to choice. The soul, as choice, is sovereign; motives incite, but are subject to the pleasure of the sovereign. Motives are reasons for choosing, but choice is rational self-determination made in view of motives. I make up my mind to take a trip to Europe. My motives are to get rest and to behold the wonders of the Old World.

1. *Low motives* are incentives to gratify the appetites and passions, regardless of law. Appetite moves the inebriate to drink to intoxication. The debauchee is a creature who is a willing slave to his appetites. In him the low motives prevail.

2. *High motives* are incentives to right and noble choices. Conscience ever incites us to choose what we consider right. Right is the highest of all motives.

Choice—its Antecedents and Consequents.—As we have advanced, it has become more and more apparent that the soul is a unit, and that a faculty is merely one of its capabilities. Rational choice involves each capability of the soul; we feel while we know, and will while we feel.

1. *Antecedents of choice.* Rational beings work in the light. We choose in view of motives. (1) Self, as intellect, evolves and weighs motives. A motive is simply a reason for choosing. Before deciding upon a plan of work of great moment, you tax all your intellectual faculties to the utmost. (2) Self, as emotion, in view of ideas, feels impulses to choose. Our higher emotions move us to choose the true, the beautiful, and the good. Our appetites and passions clamor for gratification regardless of law.

2. *Choice.* Self, as choice, decides or chooses, and thus ends the strife of contending emotions. Without

intelligence, rational choice is impossible. Without emotion, we should never choose. The antecedents of choice are knowing and feeling. We know, we feel, we choose. This law of mental succession is as invariable as the laws of gravity. Ideas occasion emotions; ideas and emotions occasion choice.

3. *Consequents of choice.* As ideas and emotions lead on to choice, so choice leads on to action. We execute our determinations—we act. Rational choice necessarily precedes rational action. Rational acts are consequents of rational choice. Cognition, choice, action: this is the logical as well as the chronological order of soul-activity.

Choice and Motion.—The correlation of energies leads us back and back to a primary energy—back and back to *the* primary energy. Reason can not stop short of the infinite First Cause. Self, as will, is a primary energy.

1. *Self, as choice, initiates motion.* Matter is necessarily passive; only mind is self-acting. I determine to place my hand on my head; this act is purely mental. The determination, as I suppose, in some unknown way causes molecular motion in the motor ganglia; the vibrations continue through the motor nerves; the excitation affects the muscles, causing them to contract and relax; my hand moves as I determined it should. I originate motion. Mind controls matter. That self as choice originates motion, seems certain; but *how mind acts on matter* is the unsolved mystery.

2. *Self, as choice, dominates the body.* So universal consciousness testifies. I walk, I sit, I speak, I write; at will I act in these ways. Why do you sing? "Because I choose to." Why do you read? "Because I

choose to." This is the language of the human race, and it is sound psychology. Our spirits dominate the house of clay in which we sojourn.

3. *The infinite will moves the universe.* I am conscious that my finite will moves my material body, and am thus enabled to apprehend the stupendous truth that the infinite will moves the universe and is the original cause of all movement. As I move my body, Jehovah moves the universe. As my body is subject to my will, so the universe is subject to "the infinite and eternal energy from whom all things proceed."

Choice and Law.—Law is choice. Human determination becomes human law. Divine determination becomes divine law.

1. *Laws of nature.* The infinite determinations impressed upon mind and matter are called the laws of nature.

The laws of attraction are the divine will impressed upon material things. Mental laws are the infinite will impressed upon mind.

2. *Expressed laws* are expressed determinations. Expressions of human determinations become human laws. Determinations of the parent become laws to the child. Legislative determinations become laws to the people. Endowed with finite will and the capability to make finite laws, we can apprehend the infinite will and infinite laws.

Fatalism—*Choice is caused.*—The fatalist intrenches himself behind the following chain of argument:

1. Self, as intellect, perceives and elaborates, but does not originate. Sensations cause perceptions, and perceptions cause thought.

2. Self, as emotion, feels, but knowing causes feeling.

3. Self, as will, chooses, but knowing and feeling cause him to choose.

4. We can not avoid choosing as we do, for motives cause choice.

5. Liberty, merit, responsibility, are misnomers, for man is a mere automaton.

6. There is no God, for there is no uncaused cause. Man is a hopeless atheist.

Classing mind as a material force, and viewing choice from the stand-point of the conservation of force, the fatalist weaves around himself his fatal web.

Liberty—*Choice is uncaused cause.*—Choice is mind in liberty. We are free to choose. Motives occasion but do not cause choice. The following facts are summoned as witnesses:

1. *Universal consciousness attests* the freedom of self as choice. You and all rational beings are conscious of liberty in choosing. You know that you are a self-determining being. Choice is mind in liberty.

2. *Literature represents man as free and responsible.* This characterizes the literature of all ages and peoples. Only theorists are fatalists. Common sense, in all the ages, has built upon the rock of personal liberty.

3. *Law is based on the freedom of choice.* Because he knows that he could have chosen and acted otherwise, the criminal considers his punishment just.

4. *Liberty of choice is a necessary truth.* Whatever choices we have made, we know that we could have chosen otherwise. Self, as noumenal perception,

stands face to face with his acts of choice. We know intuitively that we are free to choose. Being free, we are responsible, and merit and demerit characterize our choices.

5. *Choice is uncaused cause.* You decide to sing "Hail, Columbia." Your determination originates motion. The self-activity that originates motion is a first cause. Self, as choice, is a creative first cause. Realizing in ourselves creative free-will, we apprehend the infinite free-will. Man is a hopeful theist.

"The question whether man is so far an automaton that his will is stimulated to action through the agency of feelings produced by knowledge over which he has no control, is as old as philosophy. And perhaps no man lives who has distinctly raised the question in its application to himself, and who has not decided it in the negative. We are conscious of our own freedom."

Growth of Choice.—Will includes all active operations of mind. The motor ganglia, the motor nerves, and the muscles are the active organs or implements of will. Determinations to act initiate movements.

1. *Reflex action.* In early infancy, all movements are reflex. The infant strikes and kicks and crows automatically. Reflex action seems to prepare the organism for voluntary action.

2. *Voluntary action.* When a child or brute *tries* to act in a certain way, the act is called voluntary. All intentional acts are voluntary. The infant begins to turn the head to keep the light in view. This is still reflex action. But, when the babe tries to grasp the light, we call the effort the beginning of voluntary action. At first, impulse leads directly to action. There is no deliberation, no choice.

3. *Determined action.* After two or three years of effort, the child gets command of itself. It walks, it runs, it talks. Its acts are now voluntary. But action still follows, for the most part, from impulse. Now the child begins to consider before yielding to impulse. Mollie hesitates to go with Willie, because ma will not like it, and at last she chooses not to go. From these almost imperceptible beginnings, the power to determine in view of motives and to adhere to plans, steadily grows. Growth makes the difference between the impulsive and pliant child and the man of iron will.

Education of Choice.*—" What you achieve is simply a question of will." The men and women of great will-power move and rule the world. The soft and pliant Damocles, the wishy-washy thing, and the vacillating creature with no mind of his own, are the ciphers of society. Decision of character is the basis of a grand manhood. The superior man chooses for himself, forms his own plans, and changes not, except for sufficient reason. Development of choice calls into activity all the faculties, gives decision of character, and tends to a grand manhood.

Comparative Psychology.—Instinct and perceptive intelligence guide brute action. Brutes do not deliberate. Impulse becomes action. Brutes are not endowed with the power of rational choice, and hence are not moral beings. As brutes are destitute of the power of choice, they are not responsible. Brute impulse dominates brute action; hence, merit and demerit do not apply to brute actions.

* See " Education of Choice," " Applied Psychology."

SUGGESTIVE STUDY-HINTS.

Review.—You may now ascend the psychological pyramid to the summit. Show that each faculty is merely a distinct capability of self. Show that the soul is a unit in action. What is meant by a mental power? What do you mean by the will-powers? Explain the other names.

What do you mean by the power of choice? Give the names designating this power, and tell why each is used.

Analyze one of your acts of choice. What precedes rational choice? what follows? What do you do when you choose?

Give the first characteristic of choice; second; third. Illustrate each.

What is the office of choice? Give the first example; the second; the third.

Give the author's definition of choice; give your definition; give the definitions of several authors.

What do you mean by a motive? a high motive? a low motive? Explain the difference between causing choice and occasioning choice. Illustrate.

What are the antecedents of rational choice? consequents? Illustrate.

Show that self, as choice, originates motion; dominates the body. Why are we able to apprehend infinite will?

What is law? a law of nature? a human law? How are choice and law related?

Is the brute endowed with rational choice? Are brutes moral beings? Why?

What is fatalism? Give the line of argument. Give the conclusion.

What is liberty? Give the line of argument. Give the conclusion. What is an atheist? a theist? an agnostic?

Tell about the growth of choice. About what age is purposed action first clearly indicated? How early does the child deliberate? At what age does choice become intentional action?

How is choice developed? What do you mean by decision of character?

Letter.—You have a grand theme for your last psychological letter. Lead your friend to grasp fully the idea that he is endowed with the power of self-determination, that he is free and responsible.

Topical Analysis of Chapter XXVIII.

I. **Position.**
   1. Intellect.   2. Emotion.   3. Choice.

II. **Names.**
   Power of choice.   Power of preference.
   Power of self-determination.

III. **Acts of Choice.**
   Choice of Moses.   Choice of Solomon.
   Your choice.

IV. **Office of Choice.**
   Self-determination.   Preference.
   Origination of motion.

V. **Characteristics of Choice.**
   Uncaused cause.   Avoidability.
   Mind in liberty.

VI. **Definitions of Choice.**
   Author's.   Original.   Various definitions.

VII. **Motives.**
   Definitions.   Low motives.   High motives.

VIII. **Acts of Choice.**
   Antecedents.   Choosing.   Consequents.

IX. **Choice and Motion.**
   Choice initiates motion.   Choice dominates the body.
   Infinite choice moves the universe.

X. **Choice and Law.**
   Law is choice.   Laws of nature.
   Human laws.   Moral laws.

XI. **Choice and Sin.**
   Sin, intentional violation of law.
   Only rational beings can sin.

XII. **Fatalism—Choice is caused.**
   1. Sensations cause perception. 2. Emotions cause choosing.
   3. We can not avoid choosing. 4. Man is an automaton.
   5. There is no God.

XIII. **Liberty—Choice is causa sui.**
    1. Consciousness attests liberty. 2. Literature attests liberty.
    3. Law is based on liberty.   4. Liberty a necessary idea.
    5. Choice, uncaused cause.   6. There is a God.

XIV. **Growth of Choice.**
    Reflex action and volition.   Impulsive action.
    Determined action.

XV. **Education of Choice.**
    Importance.   Time.   Method.

CHAPTER XXIX.

THE WILL-POWERS—GENERAL VIEW.

Will is Self-Willing.—Our will-powers are our capabilities of self-direction, self-determination, and self-action. Because will is mind in liberty, these are called the voluntary powers; because determination leads on to action, these are called the active powers.

Names.— { The Will-Powers.
The Voluntary Powers.
The Powers of Self-Control.
The Active Powers.
The Will. }

Intellect, Emotion, Will.—Step by step we have ascended the psychological pyramid. At its summit we find the will-powers. Choice is the cap-stone. Our voluntary powers, we discover, are simple, as compared with our cognitive powers or our emotions. Of our mental energies, we find our emotions by far the most numerous, complex, and varied. Our intellectual faculties are relatively few, yet exceedingly subtile in their interdependence and action. Our voluntary powers are yet more simple, and offer their chief difficulty in the problem of liberty.

As possessed of intellect alone, we have represented man by one line; as possessed of intellect and sensibility, we have represented him by two lines; and we now represent him as possessed of intellect, sensibility, and will by three lines, united thus:

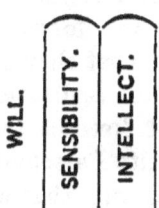

Without intellect, there are no ideas, and therefore no emotions; without emotion, there is no motive; without motive, there is no choice; without choice, there is no rational action.*

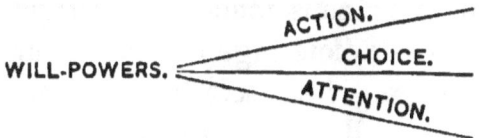

Attention is the self-directing power of the mind; volition is the self-acting power of the mind; choice is the self-determining power of the mind. As attention, self concentrates his efforts; as choice, self decides; as action, self executes his decisions.

Will is Self.—" We have now finished our study of the various factors of the self. It is now necessary very briefly to notice their relation to each other. The unity of the self is the will. The will

* Dr. Mark Hopkins.

is the man, psychologically speaking. Knowledge we have seen to be in its essence a process of the realization of the universal self-consciousness; feeling to be the accompaniment of self-realization; and its specific quality to be dependent upon the definite form of self-realization accomplished. Will we have just seen to be the self realizing itself. This is involved throughout in physical and prudential control, and it is explicitly developed when we study moral control. Here the will is seen to be self-determination. The will, in short, constitutes the meaning of knowledge and of feeling; and moral will constitutes the meaning of will.

"Moral will is the conscious realization by man that the real and the ideal *ought* to be one, and the resulting attempt to make them one in specific acts and in the formation of character. Religious will is conscious realization that they are one because man is a self-determining power. It is the realization that a perfect will is reality. It is the realization of freedom through the realization of the union of finite and the infinite Personality. It is only when we recognize this latter activity of will that we are able really to comprehend the previous forms of activity." *

Will, the Court of Final Appeal.—Ideas fight. Emotions wage war. Appetites and passions clamor for gratification; egoistic emotions contend for self; love pleads for others; conscience imperatively battles for right. Fiercer conflicts rage in the human soul than on fields of carnage. But self, as choice, is sovereign. Reason examines all the arguments and weighs all the motives. In view of all the considerations, self, as choice, decides. Happy he who chooses wisely!

* John Dewey, in "Psychology."

INDEX.

ABSTRACTION, 156.
Action, chapter xxvii, 266.
Acts of action analyzed, 266.
   of æsthetical emotions analyzed, 234.
   of altruistic emotion analyzed, 223, 226.
   of appetite analyzed, 208, 209.
   of attention analyzed, 4.
   of choice analyzed, 274.
   of conception analyzed, 155.
   of conscience analyzed, 240.
   of consciousness analyzed, 72.
   of egoistic emotions analyzed, 216.
   of imagination analyzed, 134.
   of judgment analyzed, 171.
   of knowledge emotion, 231.
   of memory analyzed, 103.
   of noumenal-perception analyzed, 87.
   of phantasy analyzed, 125.
   of reason analyzed, 180.
   of sense-perception analyzed, 60.
Æsthetic emotions, 234.
Affections, 222.
Agnosticism, 96.
Altruistic emotions, chapter xxi, 222, 256.
Analogy, 118.
Analytic observation, 156.
Antecedents of choice, 277.
Antipathies, 227.
Appetites, chapter xix, 208.
Applied psychology, xv.
Arguments, 184.
Attention, chapters i and xxvi, 4, 264.
Attention and consciousness, 77, 113.
Attention and memory, 113.

Author of law, 248.
Author's preface, xvii.
Avoidability, 275.
Axioms, 156.

Bad intentions, 246.
Beauty-emotions, 234.
Beauty, objective, 236.
Belief and reason, 191.
Benevolent emotions, 222.
Body and soul, 52.
Brain, 39.

Capabilities, 56, 57, 262.
Cause, 28, 95, 181.
Cerebration, 44.
Cerebrum, 42, 43.
Certainty, 189, 190.
Character, 237.
Characteristics of action, 267.
   of æsthetic emotions, 234.
   of altruistic emotions, 223.
   of an appetite, 209.
   of attention, 6.
   of choice, 275.
   of conception, 158.
   of conscience, 243.
   of egoistic emotions, 217.
   of imagination, 136.
   of instinct, 16.
   of judgment, 173.
   of memory, 110.
   of noumenal-perception, 88.
   of phantasy, 126.
   of reason, 183.
   of sense-perception, 61.
   of truth-emotions, 232.
Choice, chapter xxvii, 273.
Choice and law, 279.
Classes of æsthetic emotions, 234.

INDEX.

Classes of altruistic emotions, 224.
  of cosmic emotions, 230.
  of emotions, 216, 256.
  of feelings, 206.
  of self-emotions, 218.
  of percepts, 103.
Classification, 157, 163.
Comparative psychology, 50, 68, 79, 121, 132, 143, 167, 177, 192, 220, 282.
Comparison, 156.
Comprehension, 162.
Conception, chapter xiv, 155, 164, 166.
Concepts, 159, 199.
Conclusions, 185.
Conscience, chapter xxiv, 240.
Consciousness, chapter vii, 71.
Conscious-percepts, 76.
Contiguity, 118.
Contrast, 117.
Correlation, 118.
Cosmic emotions, 230, 257.
Culture and attention, 264.

Deduction, 188.
Definition, 163.
Definition of action, 267.
  of appetite, 210.
  of altruistic emotion, 224.
  of æsthetic emotion, 235.
  of choice, 270.
  of conception, 158, 198.
  of conscience, 243.
  of consciousness, 102, 96.
  of egoistic emotions, 217.
  of imagination, 137, 148.
  of instinct, 17, 106.
  of judgment, 94, 193.
  of memory, 111, 144.
  of noumenal-perception, 102, 93.
  of phantasy, 127, 144.
  of reason, 183, 196.
  of sensation, 60.
  of sense-perception, 101, 62.
  of truth, 232.
Denomination, 159.
Desires, egoistic, 219.
Determined action, 282.
Disbelief, 189.
Divine energies, 28.
Doubt, 189.
Dreams, 129.
Duty emotions, 241.

Editor's preface, vii.
Education of æsthetic emotions, 238.

Education of attention, 265, 10.
  of altruistic emotions, 226.
  of conception, 167.
  of conscience, 250.
  of conscious-perception, 78.
  of cosmic emotions, 250.
  of imagination, 142.
  of judgment, 177.
  of memory, 120.
  of noumenal-perception, 97.
  of phantasy, 132.
  of reason, 192.
  of sense-perception, 66.
  of senses, 51.
  of self-emotions, 220.
  of truth-emotions, 233.
Egoistic emotions, chapter xx, 215, 256.
Elementary psychology, xiv.
Elements of memory, 109.
  of conception, 156.
  of faith, 191.
  of judgment, 174.
Emotion, intellect, will, 264.
Emotional imagination, 140.
Emotions, general view, 255.
  classed, 256, 216.
  defined, 255.
Energies defined, 28.
Enthymeme, 186.
Ethical emotions, 240.
  imagination, 140.
  knowledge, 244, 248.
Executive volition, 266.
Experience and memories, 112.

Faculties of the soul, 56, 57, 162.
Failure—emotions, 229.
Faith, 190.
Fatalism, 279.
Feelings, 57, 206, 255.
Forgetting, 119.
Forms of thinking, 200.

Ganglia, 36, 47.
Generalization, 157.
Genus, 162.
Good intentions, 246.
Gratification of appetites, 211.
Growth of attention, 8.
  of conception, 167.
  of conscience, 249.
  of conscious-perception, 77.
  of imagination, 142.
  of judgment, 177.
  of memory, 119.
  of noumenal-perception, 97.

INDEX. 291

Growth of phantasy, 132.
  of reason, 191.
  of self-emotions, 220.
  of sense-perception, 66.
  of sympathy, 226.
  of truth-emotion, 233.
Guides to appetite, 211.

Habit, 271.
Happiness, 211, 219, 251.
Happy dreams, 132.
Hates, 227.
Heart, 215, 246.
Higher emotions, 230.
Humor, 237.

Ideals, 138, 150.
Imagination, chapter xii, 133.
  defined, 137, 148.
  and memory, 139.
  and phantasy, 142.
Immediate self-emotions, 220.
Imperatives of conscience, 242, 243.
Important terms, 25.
Impulsive action, 267.
Individual, 161.
Induction, 187.
Infallible, conscience, 247.
Infinity, 95, 279.
Insanity, 131.
Instinct, chapter ii, 15, 206.
Intellectual faculties, 57, 195, 196.
Intellect and instinct, 19.
  emotion, will, 57, 264.
Intemperance, 212.
Intentions, 246.
Introductory lessons, 4–44.
Intuition, 100, 104, 247.
Intuitive ethical ideas, 247.

Judgment, chapter xv, 171, 177.
Judgments, 176, 200.

Kinds of action, 268, 281.
  of imagination, 140.
Knowledge emotions, 231.

Language, 270.
Lawful gratification, 211.
Law and choice, 279.
Laws, 30.
  of conscience, 249.
  of memory, 114.
Liberty, 280.
Limits of imagination, 136.
Literature, conscience, 245.

Love, 225.
Low motives, 277.

Malevolent emotions, 222.
Matter, 27, 94.
Memory, chapter x, 108.
  and phantasy, 128.
Memory-knowledge, 111.
Mental phenomena, 26.
  laws, mental energies, 29, 30.
Mesmerism, 131.
Mind, 27, 33, 94.
Misery, 212.
Moral guide, 245.
  law, 248.
Motion and action, 45, 269.
  and choice, 278.
Motives, 276, 277.
Motorium, 45, 269.

Natural appetites, 210.
Necessary ideas, 86, 91.
  judgment, 177.
  realities, 90.
Nerve-cells, 35.
Nerve-currents, 38.
Nerves, 36.
Noumena, 26, 86.
Noumenal-perception, chapter vii, 85.
Noumenal percepts, 89.

Office of action, 267.
  of æsthetic emotion, 235.
  of altruistic emotion, 217.
  of appetite, 209.
  of attention, 264, 265.
  of choice, 274.
  of conception, 157.
  of conscience, 241.
  of consciousness, 73.
  of egoistic emotion, 217.
  of imagination, 134.
  of instinct, 15.
  of judgment, 72.
  of memory, 110.
  of noumenal-perception, 88.
  of phantasy, 125.
  of sense-perception, 61.
  of truth-emotions, 231.
Origin of instincts, 21.

Perceptive faculties, 100.
  knowing, 100.
  products, 103.
Personal emotions, 216.
Perverted appetites, 211.

INDEX.

Phantasy, chapter xi, 124.
   and imagination, 141.
   in dreams, 129.
Phenomena, 26.
Philosophical imagination, 141.
Philosophic emotions, 231.
Physical feelings, 44, 60, 207.
   forces, 28, 30.
Physiological psychology, 51, 201.
Physiology of the emotions, 258.
Play of emotions, 227.
Pleasure, 211.
Powers of the mind, 56, 57, 262.
Premises, 185.
Private students, xix.
Products of conception, 159, 199.
   of conscious-perception, 103, 76.
   of imagination, 138, 150.
   of judgment, 175, 200.
   of memory, 111, 147.
   of noumenal-perception, 89, 103.
   of phantasy, 149.
   of reason, 184, 200.
   of sense-perception, 103. 63.
Properties of concepts, 159.
   of judgments, 175.
Prospective self-emotions, 219.
Psychology defined, 32.
Psychological pyramid, 106, 152, 204, 252.
   tree, 56.
Pyramid of energies, 28.

Rational action, 269.
   emotions, 230.
Reason, chapter xvi, 180.
Reasoning processes, 183, 187.
Reasons, 183, 184, 200.
Reflex action an instinct, 19.
   sensor-action, 45, 268, 281.
Remorse, 242, 251.
Representative powers, 107, 108–146.
Resemblance, 117.
Retrospective emotions, 220, 225.
Right, 93.

Science, 31.
Self-betterment, 219.
Self-consciousness, chapter vii, 71.
Self-control, 212.
Self-determination, 274.
Self-emotions, 216.
Sensation, chapter v, 44, 60, 207.
Sense-perception, chapter vi, 59, 101.
Sense-percepts, 63, 103.
Sensibilities, 206.
Sensorium, 35, 45, 207, 269.

Sensor-lines, 48, 50.
Sensor-organs, 38, 39.
Somnambulism, 130.
Soul-energies, 28.
   energies, outline, 56, 57, 262.
Space, 27, 86, 92.
Species, 161.
Spiritual emotions, 230.
Sub-consciousness, 80.
Subject-lessons, xiii.
Sublimity, 237.
Success-emotions, 228.
Suggestion, laws of, 116.
Suggestive Study-Hints:
   Action, 272.
   Æsthetic emotions, 238.
   Altruistic emotions, 229.
   Appetites, 213.
   Attention, 12.
   Choice, 283.
   Conception, 168.
   Consciousness, 83.
   Ethical emotions, 258.
   Imagination, 144.
   Instinct, 23.
   Judgment, 178.
   Memory, 121.
   Noumenal-perception, 98.
   Phantasy, 133.
   Reason, 193.
   Self-emotions, 221.
   Sensation, 53, 207.
   Sense-perception, 68.
   Terms, 33.
   Truth-emotions, 233.
Syllogisms, 184.
Sympathies, 226.

Teaching psychology, xx.
Temperance, 212.
Terms of a judgment, 175.
Tests of necessary ideas, 88.
The instincts, 20.
Thinking, 153, 196, 201.
Thought powers, 155–195.
   pyramid, 163.
Time, 87, 92.
Topical analyses, 14, 24, 34, 54, 70, 84, 99, 123, 133, 144, 150, 170, 179, 194, 214, 240, 253, 273, 284.
Training, 252.
Tree of necessary ideas, 91.
Truth-emotions, chapter xxii, 230.

Ugliness, 236.
Unbelief, 189.
Uncaused cause, 281.

Unconscious cerebration, 81.
Unlawful gratification, 212.

Verification, 189.
Vision, 131.
Volition, 264.
Voluntary action, 281.

Ways of studying mind, 2.
Wild oats, 251.
Will defined, 253, 285.
Will, emotion, intellect, 264.
Will-powers, 57, 263, 285.
Wit, 237.

THE END.

www.ingramcontent.com/pod-product-compliance
Lightning Source LLC
Chambersburg PA
CBHW030812230426
43667CB00008B/1186